Unmaking the Global Sweatshop

UNMAKING THE GLOBAL SWEATSHOP

Health and Safety of
the World's Garment Workers

EDITED BY
Rebecca Prentice and Geert De Neve

PENN

UNIVERSITY OF PENNSYLVANIA PRESS

PHILADELPHIA

Copyright © 2017 University of Pennsylvania Press

Published by
University of Pennsylvania Press
Philadelphia, Pennsylvania 19104-4112
www.upenn.edu/pennpress

Printed in the United States of America on acid-free paper
10 9 8 7 6 5 4 3 2 1

Cataloging-in-Publication Data is available from the Library of Congress.

ISBN 978-0-8122-4939-2

CONTENTS

ABBREVIATIONS

Accord	Bangladesh Accord on Fire and Building Safety in Bangladesh
Alliance	Alliance for Bangladesh Worker Safety
BDT	Bangladesh Taka
BGMEA	Bangladesh Garment Manufacturers and Exporters Association
BKMEA	Bangladesh Knitwear Manufacturers and Exporters Association
BLA	Bangladesh Labour Act
BOI	Board of Investment (Sri Lanka)
CCC	Clean Clothes Campaign
CSR	Corporate social responsibility
EPD	UNIDO's Export Promotions Division
EPZ	Export processing zone
ETI	Ethical Trading Initiative
FTZ	Free trade zone
GPN	Global production network
HR	Human resources
ILO	International Labour Organization
IndustriALL	IndustriALL Global Union
ITGLWF	International Textile, Garment, and Leather Workers' Federation
MoLE	Ministry of Labour and Employment (Bangladesh)
MSI	Multi-stakeholder initiative
MFA	Multi-Fibre Arrangement
NAP	National Tripartite Plan of Action on Fire Safety and Structural Integrity (Bangladesh)
NCR	National Capital Region (India)
NGO	Nongovernmental organization
NTUI	New Trade Union Initiative (India)

OECD	Organisation for Economic Cooperation and Development
PIL	Public Interest Litigation
RMG	Ready-made garment
SEZ	Special economic zone
SEWA	Self Employed Women's Association
TNC	Transnational corporation
UNIDO	United Nations Industrial Development Organization
WRC	Worker Rights Consortium
WTO	World Trade Organization

Introduction: Rethinking Garment Workers' Health and Safety

Geert De Neve and Rebecca Prentice

Academic writing, media representations, and consumer activist discussions of labor conditions in the global South almost always center on pay and the living wage, overtime and working hours, freedom of association, unfree labor, and, above all, child labor, with Western consumers being particularly concerned about buying products tainted with the blood and sweat of children. The health and safety of workers employed in export-oriented garment industries usually receives scant attention. The International Labour Organization (ILO) does not even consider the right not to be injured at work a "core" labor right (Spieler 2006). When catastrophic industrial disasters occur, such as the 2013 collapse of the Rana Plaza building in Bangladesh, public outcry sometimes leads to greater scrutiny of the structural safety of buildings, equipment, and workplaces, but the everyday health and well-being of garment workers continues to be neglected. This volume, by contrast, seeks to rethink this perspective by giving visibility to the health concerns of garment workers across the globe and by placing the whole spectrum of work-related health and well-being issues at the center of analysis.[1]

Health—while sometimes mentioned indirectly as part of assessments of working conditions and production pressures—has rarely been studied as a direct entry into garment workers' lives. And, yet, most of the issues around working conditions listed above have an immediate effect on workers' health and on their well-being more generally. Overtime pressures and the lack of a living wage, for example, are largely experienced through bodily and embodied processes. They often translate directly into poor physical health or manifest themselves as mental health issues experienced through anxiety, fear, intimidation, stigma, or exhaustion (Lynch 2007; Prentice 2015, chapter 6; Ashraf this volume; Hewamanne this volume).

The absence of a public debate on workers' health is all the more remarkable given the widespread adoption of corporate codes of conduct in supplier factories, including codes dealing explicitly with health and safety. Designed to make labor practices more transparent across complex global supply chains, such codes, however, tend to focus rather narrowly on safe and hygienic working environments (including sanitation and food storage), occupational health issues, and the prevention of accidents and injuries at work (see, for example, ETI Base Code 2014; CCC Code of Labour Practices 1998; Barrientos and Smith 2007; Ruwanpura 2013, 2014), ignoring the ways in which garment work affects workers' health and well-being more broadly. Workers' overall well-being can be unsettled by a range of health concerns caused by long hours, physically taxing work, poor equipment, an intense pace of work, harassment under disciplinary regimes, and a lack of labor voice. Many of these health impacts, moreover, are not just technical or bureaucratic shortcomings of work organization, but systemic outcomes of the ways in which garment production regimes operate globally (Bair et al. this volume; Neveling this volume).

The main features of this global regime are the complex networks through which garments are now produced and sold across continents. Big brands like H&M and Gap do not own their factories but instead subcontract production to suppliers in low-wage countries. These countries depend on the garment trade for export earnings and employment. As consumers have grown accustomed to cheap clothing and endless variety, suppliers have been forced to contend with rising expectations of quality and speed at ever lower prices (Barrientos 2012; Plank et al. 2014; Taplin 2014). The pressures of global competition in a quickly changing market are exerted upon workers in the form of insecure employment, unpredictable working hours, quickened production rhythms, and excessive overtime.

This volume seeks to place garment workers' health and safety at the very heart of a critical exploration of their lives and well-being. The long neglect of health and safety has manifested itself in at least two alarming ways, each of which is equally disturbing: major one-off disasters causing injuries and deaths on the one hand, and routine violations of workers' everyday health rights and needs on the other. A string of disasters in Bangladesh and throughout Asia, including factory fires and building collapses, are a telling outcome of the persistent neglect of worker safety. The shocking frequency with which such disasters are occurring reveals how even the basic safety of garment workers has not yet been secured.

The collapse of the Spectrum sweater factory in Bangladesh in 2005, caused by substandard building construction, led to 64 deaths and 80 people injured (Miller 2012). The Tazreen Fashions factory fire of 2012 resulted in the deaths of more than 112 workers with more than 200 injured, with the Bangladeshi factory owner being charged in December 2013 with culpable homicide or death by negligence (Bajaj 2012; Sumon et al. this volume). A textile factory fire in Karachi, Pakistan, in 2012, allegedly caused by a short circuit, similarly led to the deaths of more than 250 workers who failed to escape due to blocked doors and windows (Hobson 2013). And finally, one of the most devastating industrial disasters to reach the global media was the April 2013 collapse of Rana Plaza, an eight-story commercial building housing five garment factories in Dhaka. This incident resulted in the deaths of at least 1,134 workers and grave injuries to hundreds more (Ahamad 2014). While investigations and court cases are still ongoing to establish the exact causes and responsibilities, the fact that worker safety is being widely compromised in the pursuit of profit by both Northern retailers and Southern manufacturers is no longer beyond dispute.

But far more pervasive—and invisible—is the violation of workers' health on a day-to-day basis. As local manufacturers attempt to meet ever tighter production deadlines, workers are routinely asked to work long hours, sometimes with little forewarning and often for days on end. Workers' health is usually what suffers first and most. A recent evaluation of Better Factories Cambodia, for example, concluded that "loss of buying power, combined with pervasive excessive working hours and poor health and safety conditions, have contributed to a wave of incidents of mass fainting among Cambodian factory workers—allegedly caused, at least in part, by exhaustion, overheating, and malnutrition" (International Human Rights and Conflict Resolution Clinic et al. 2013, iv). With extremely low wages, workers are routinely unable to sustain a nutritious diet, indicating that the costs of maintaining their own health are greater than the remuneration their labor fetches in the market (Attanapola 2005; Labour Behind the Label 2013). Monotonous, routine work and static bodily positions manifest themselves in the bodies of workers as musculoskeletal pain, eyestrain, physical exhaustion, and stress. Such recurrent assaults on garment workers' health not only escape public notice, but also undermine workers' long-term physical and mental well-being as well as the very sustainability of their employment.

This book, therefore, seeks to make a contribution to our understanding of garment workers' health, the reasons why it has been neglected and ignored, the ways in which it is implicated in—and shaped by—global regimes of outsourcing and subcontracting, and the interventions that are being negotiated to curb the most harmful effects of garment work. In doing so, we consider the political economy of global garment production in order to critique depoliticized approaches to health and safety that reduce complex issues of power and inequality to mere matters of technical or bureaucratic intervention. Indeed, we believe that a critical focus on workers' health can shed light on two related issues. First, it can illuminate the meanings and experiences of employment in global garment factories by revealing how everyday garment work is experienced through particular work pressures, managerial regimes, and disciplinary processes that are lived and made sense of through the body. Health, we argue, provides a lens "down" onto the very labor processes that require working bodies while adversely affecting them. Second, health also offers a unique lens "up" onto the global dynamics of outsourcing and subcontracting that produce particular labor regimes at local sites of production. These regimes are typically marked by tight production schedules, high work pressures, unpredictable work rhythms, and low wages for workers. We thus consider health as a "site" or "field" where the impacts, contradictions, and negotiations over labor regimes are played out and where global capital-labor conflicts take concrete material and symbolic forms. As Kanchana Ruwanpura's contribution to this volume illustrates, access to something as straightforward as a factory clinic ends up becoming an ongoing issue of contention and negotiation on the shop floor, through which management's and workers' relative power is simultaneously enforced and challenged.

The contributors to this book reconsider the health and safety of garment workers in three key ways, thereby making a number of contributions. *First*, a health focus allows us to critically reflect on the kinds of regulatory regimes that have emerged in tandem with the industry's globalization. Like the garment industry itself, these regulations display an emphasis on the voluntarism and corporate self-regulation of neoliberal governance, yet for the most part have failed to protect workers in meaningful and enduring ways. A health focus enables us to fundamentally question the code-based and voluntary regulatory interventions through which corporate actors have sought to remedy the worst impacts of global outsourcing. *Second*, we explore the many actors and institutions involved in the garment industry, ranging from fashion company owners and employers to workers, nongovernmental organizations (NGOs), trade unionists, and state actors. We show that poor labor standards cannot be understood except in relation to the global production networks through which garment work is generated, and that solutions cannot be grasped outside of the complex and multilayered networks of actors that strive for improvements. A *third* contribution of this volume lies in its focus on everyday health and its place in shaping the well-being and happiness of garment workers. Taking an ethnographic approach to garment workers' own health-related concerns broadens our very conception of what health and safety are all about, and how they are being experienced and addressed on a day-to-day basis. Such an approach also calls into question some of the boundaries—like those between work and home—that have often been used to delimit health and safety as concerns solely of the workplace. Sandya Hewamanne's chapter, for example, opens up the concept of health and shows how health and safety are first and foremost social experiences, while Alessandra Mezzadri's contribution reminds us that health and its care travel with workers well beyond the factory gates and into workers' homes and family lives.

Highly localized disasters, like the collapse of Rana Plaza, in many ways reveal the global in miniature, and a focus on health, we believe, can shed new light on the complexity of these global dynamics, the dangers and harms they engender, and the forces that seek to counteract them. The chapters of this volume are organized in three sections that we introduce in what follows. The first three chapters trace some of the history and geography of the contemporary garment industry, showing how debates over the regulation of labor standards offer a useful window onto how the industry is organized and governed. The next three chapters further unpack the political economy of the industry, exploring the actors and structures that shape both the global relations of production and the struggles over "responsibility" and "accountability" for labor standards. The last three chapters present ethnographies of health—inside and outside of factories—to argue for an expansive understanding of health and safety that embraces the well-being and labor rights of workers.

The Rise and Fall of Labor Standards

As the garment industry has become increasingly "global," so too have questions about how labor standards in the industry should be regulated. Neoliberal policies that have shaped the development of the global market—privatization, deregulation, and free trade—have also served as an ideological charter for the governance of labor standards. With weak state regulations and the absence of a transnational regulatory system, labor standards in the garment industry have been predominantly governed by an array of private initiatives (Esbenshade 2004; Locke 2013; O'Rourke 2003). Under pressure from labor rights activists and consumer groups, corporations have adopted self-regulatory measures such as corporate codes of conduct and third-party monitoring. In many ways, these initiatives reflect a neoliberal embrace of market-based solutions to labor standards and write off state regulation as both inadequate and impractical in a transnational industry.

Jennifer Bair, Mark Anner, and Jeremy Blasi take us into the historical context of regulation, showing the structural similarities between the organization of production in New York City's early twentieth-century garment industry and the kinds of global production networks we see today. In both cases, the widespread use of outsourcing, ruthless competition for contracts among suppliers, and buyers driving down costs resulted in low wages and sweatshop conditions. Then as now, subcontracting arrangements prevented direct relationships between garment workers and the retailers who sold the finished goods, making questions of liability and responsibility for labor conditions hard to disentangle.

Bair and colleagues describe the important reforms brought about after the 1911 Triangle Shirtwaist factory fire in New York City which killed 146 workers, mostly young immigrant women. The fire, which was witnessed by hundreds of New Yorkers and was widely reported in the media, stirred public sympathy for garment workers who had already begun agitating for labor rights over the previous years. The reforms that followed the Triangle fire included the establishment of a city-wide Bureau of Fire Prevention, a Factory Investigating Commission, and a Citizens' Committee for Public Safety to press public officials for statutory regulations. But the most meaningful and enduring reforms came from the efforts of the garment workers' union in the form of "jobbers' agreements": three-way collective bargaining agreements among suppliers, buyers (known as "jobbers"; today we call them brands or retailers), and trade unions.

Jobbers' agreements combated poor labor standards by changing the terms of competition between suppliers. Binding contracts mandated the use of unionized suppliers, and these contractual relationships between buyers and suppliers could only be cancelled for specified reasons—not simply because another supplier was willing to work more cheaply. Jobbers' agreements obligated buyers to ensure labor standards, and succeeded not only in improving working conditions but also increasing wages in the industry. By addressing the root causes of poor labor standards (intense competition between suppliers, which drove down prices and hence wages and working conditions), jobbers' agreements created conditions of stability and predictability in the sector. Jobbers' agreements were prevalent throughout the American garment industry until they disappeared in the 1990s, by which time trade unions were severely weakened, brands were oriented toward global sourcing strategies, and the phase-out of the international quota system known as the Multi-Fibre Arrangement (MFA) put American producers in competition with lower wage countries. With the disappearance of jobbers' agreements, a crucial question remains about whether their guiding principle—that contracts between buyers, suppliers, and organized labor can create predictability, stability, and higher labor standards—might be applied to today's global production system.

Turning to contemporary Bangladesh, Bair and colleagues contemplate whether the collapse of Rana Plaza will serve the same stimulating role of the Triangle fire in bringing material improvements to the garment industry. The most notable development so far is the Accord on Fire and Building Safety in Bangladesh (the Accord, 2013). Created by two international trade unions, global fashion brands, and civil society organizations, with the participation of the International Labour Organization (ILO), the Bangladesh Accord seeks to improve working conditions in Bangladesh's export-oriented garment industry through a rigorous program of factory inspections, upgrades, and closures, within a legally binding framework that holds multinational corporations responsible for the fitness of the buildings in which their apparel is manufactured. With more than 200 signatory brands—mostly based in Europe—the Bangladesh Accord also attempts to stabilize the ready-made garment industry by committing signatories to source from the country for at least five years.

Bair and colleagues point out that like the jobbers' agreements, the Bangladesh Accord creates a contractual relationship between the fashion brands and organized labor to uphold labor standards in supplier factories. But unlike the jobbers' agreements, the Bangladesh Accord is narrowly focused on building safety, leaving aside a host of labor issues including wages, working hours, and health. The capacity of organized labor to represent the diverse needs of migrant and women workers is also a question. The Bangladesh Accord has only a limited role for the state, and engages more with global trade unions based in Europe than with the many diverse Bangladesh-based trade unions and labor rights organizations (cf. Ashraf this volume).

Because jobbers' agreements in the United States operated in a national context buffered from global competition by protectionist policies, it remains a question whether such agreements could serve as a template for labor reform in today's transnational production context governed by voluntary corporate regulation. Florence Palpacuer's chapter gives insight into the rise of corporate self-regulation, which has characterized the global garment industry over the past thirty years. Presenting her research with the Clean Clothes Campaign (CCC)—a Netherlands-based international network of nongovernmental organizations and labor unions—Palpacuer describes how the European anti-sweatshop movement contributed to the development of private initiatives that epitomize the neoliberal, market-based, and voluntary model of regulation widespread in the industry today.

Palpacuer shows how in the 1990s, the CCC made a strategic decision to work in partnership *with* corporations rather than adopting the more combative stance of the American anti-sweatshop movement.[2] Instead of pursuing boycotts or protectionist policies, the CCC has worked with businesses to develop corporate codes of conduct based on the core labor standards established in the 1990s by the ILO. Voluntary labor standards and the codes-and-monitoring approach have become the cornerstone of labor governance in the garment sector with the aim of creating transparency in global supply chains. As the academic and activist literature documents, codes have been widely adopted as part of the ethical sourcing policies of fashion brands. But codes are limited in the kinds of labor issues they address, have poor enforcement mechanisms, and can be manipulated by companies concerned more with safeguarding their reputation than improving labor standards (Barrientos and Smith 2007; De Neve 2009; Mezzadri 2012; Pearson and Seyfang 2001; Ruwanpura 2012). For some members of the anti-sweatshop movement, the embracing of codes has been a capitulation to corporate interests; others see it as an important stepping-stone for new legislation by first creating a voluntary framework of social compliance.

By targeting corporations to develop private initiatives—rather than states to create and enforce new regulations—the anti-sweatshop movement has contributed to the reconceptualization of "labor rights as human rights" (Palpacuer this volume; cf. Seidman 2007). Such an approach promotes universal human rights, such as those enshrined in ILO's core labor standards, and encourages campaigns based on their most egregious violation in the form of child or forced labor. Working within a transnational arena, NGOs appeal to multinational corporations to safeguard universal, individual human rights rather than to pressure states to secure the labor rights of their citizens as a collective (cf. Hilgert 2013). As Palpacuer notes, workers themselves, and the grassroots labor organizations that represent them, are often sidelined by such a human rights approach, raising questions about what capacities workers have at the lowest levels to pursue rights, however they might be framed.

Drawing on Shareen Hertel's (2010) concept of the "paradox of partnership," Palpacuer discusses how private forms of regulation can lead to an enhancement rather than a disruption of corporate power. As Hertel writes, when NGOs partner with business "they are engaged in a struggle against what could be considered a natural product of contemporary capitalism— namely the 'race to the bottom' in labor standards as capital seeks out cheaper labor in a highly internationalized global marketplace" (Hertel 2010, 174; cf. Dolan and Rajak 2011). As the failure of codes—including those on health and safety—has become undeniable, particularly in the face of disasters like the Rana Plaza collapse, the anti-sweatshop movement has shifted course from advocating market-based solutions to pushing more strongly for greater intergovernmental regulations. One example is the United Nations' "Ruggie Framework," which formalizes the obligations of states and corporations with regard to labor laws (Bair 2015). Similarly, the Accord on Fire and Building Safety in Bangladesh (2013) combines both voluntary and binding forms of regulation, whereby corporations accede to provisions that hold them legally accountable for labor standards in their supply chains. Such "hybrid" forms of regulation combine the neoliberal insistence on voluntary self-regulation with an increasing role for states and international bodies in enforcing the liability of multinational corporations.

But beyond states, global civil society actors, and international organizations, brands too have been working on the problem of substandard labor conditions. Fashion brands now routinely share information on their websites about the company's efforts in pursuit of "social responsibility" and "ethical compliance," and a growing market in "ethical" products invites consumers to express a personal commitment to social justice, labor rights, or environmental issues with their purchasing choices (Carrier and Luetchford 2012; Richey and Ponte 2011). Caitrin Lynch and Ingrid Hagen-Keith's chapter tells the story of School House, an "ethical" collegiate clothing brand developed by a Duke University graduate in the late 2000s. Telling the story of one woman's failed attempt to create an ethical and economically sustainable clothing company, it reveals the structural conditions that make such an enterprise difficult to achieve. As Lynch and Hagen-Keith indicate, it also raises broader questions about the extent to which ethics can be pursued within the capitalist market system.

School House LLC was founded by Rachel Weeks in 2008. Having studied industry efforts to produce ethical garments in Sri Lanka as a Fulbright scholar in 2007, she returned to North Carolina to launch her own line of collegiate clothing. The garments were sourced entirely from Sri Lanka, with the mission of paying workers a living wage. Weeks made extensive use of marketing and social media to promote an image of the brand as fun, trendy, and principled: "doing good while looking good" (Lynch and Hagen-Keith this volume). At its peak of popularity, School House garments were sold at more than 100 colleges in the United States. Nonetheless, School House remained a tiny player in the industry, and Weeks found suppliers "bumping" her orders because they prioritized larger, more lucrative ones. Struggling with too many shipment delays, in May 2011 School House began sourcing instead from North Carolina. Attempting to maintain the company's "ethical" bona fides, the brand was now marketed as rejuvenating American craftsmanship and battling local unemployment under the slogan "Made in America." Unfortunately, American suppliers were expensive and at times unwilling to meet School House's changing production demands. The company's new ethical branding also found little appeal among its customers, and the business was suspended.

Lynch and Hagen-Keith's account provides a window onto the structural conditions of the garment industry: big players crowding out smaller players who have little influence over busy suppliers; suppliers finding it hard to meet retailers' and consumers' demand for fast fashion; and consumer fickleness raising questions about the sustainability of ethical production ventures. Central to the problems faced by School House was its attempt to appease two constituencies simultaneously: suppliers and consumers. As a small company, School House failed to gain influence over its suppliers in Sri Lanka, both in terms of getting orders delivered and in terms of implementing its ethical agenda. Weeks managed to get her Sri Lankan suppliers to agree to pay garment workers a living wage, but did not have sufficient leverage to insist upon adherence to her own code of conduct. At the same time, while busy negotiating with suppliers (and devoting time to raising funds from investors), Weeks was also preoccupied with advertising and social media to convince her consumer niches of her changing ethical branding. As soon as she failed to sell her message to them and lost consumer support, the company was unable to survive.

In light of the failure of School House, it is worth considering the more encouraging picture for smaller brands presented in Niklas Egels-Zandén's (2015) recent study of a small Swedish company's ongoing attempt to pay a living wage at its Indian supplier. While recognizing that smaller brands might be limited in their resources and bargaining power, Egels-Zandén also points to specific features that might enable smaller companies to make a difference: they are less exposed to the public eye than larger companies, have stronger ethical motives, are less bound by formal systems, can develop trusting relationships with suppliers, and take a more flexible and adaptable ethical approach (ibid., 6–9). What perhaps distinguished the success of the Swedish retailer's living wage project compared to the experience of School House was the former's already firm position in the consumer market and their established trusted relationship with their main Indian supplier. School House, by contrast, was a novel start-up company attempting to advance a strong ethical agenda while still struggling to gain a foothold in the market, and as a result failed to materialize both its commercial and ethical ambitions.

The chapters by Palpacuer and Lynch and Hagen-Keith show the difficulties of establishing "ethical" production norms within a deregulated global market. The garment industry has seen a consolidation of market share into a shrinking number of giant corporations (Gereffi and Frederick 2010; Staritz 2011), which is why activist groups like the Clean Clothes Campaign expend such effort to influence leading fashion companies. As Lynch and Hagen-Keith show, it can be hard for a small player to enact change in an industry shaped by the power of big brands and retailers. The example of School House also casts doubt on the reliability of consumers to prioritize ethical values when shopping for clothing. Taken together, these accounts show the structural conditions of the contemporary garment industry and the limitations of market-based solutions.

If we want to rethink how to protect the health and safety of garment workers, we need to move beyond the voluntarism of codes and monitoring. Palpacuer points toward some of the inherent differences between legally binding and voluntary approaches to labor standards: the first is anchored in the state's ability to make and enforce laws, and the second appeals to the morality of corporations or consumers as arbitrated by the market. The success of the jobbers' agreements in improving labor standards in the twentieth-century American garment industry was due to the important roles played by state regulation and organized labor. The Bangladesh Accord, which combines both voluntary and binding forms of regulation, is one initiative that may be indicating a shift away from corporate self-regulation towards a more "hybrid" model. But the question about the extent to which labor conditions can be improved without upending the structure of global production networks altogether endures, and is explored in the next section.

From Structures to Actors, and Back

In the aftermath of catastrophic industrial disasters, public shock usually leads to immediate calls for tighter regulation of labor standards and for more stringent implementation of codes of conduct, which are normally not vigorously enforced. At such heightened moments, narrowly conceptualized understandings of labor standards find their expression in kneejerk attempts to "raise the minimum wage" or "intensify factory inspections," and are more often than not reduced to pragmatic matters of structural building safety or machine injury avoidance. As the chapters in this volume make clear, however, such reactions remain highly depoliticized, with poor labor standards, ill health, and worker exploitation remaining divorced from their structural roots: the global dynamics of outsourcing and the transnational purchasing practices that typify buyer-driven global production networks (Barrientos 2012). As has been well established by now, those purchasing practices are marked by unpredictable order flows, excruciatingly competitive rate negotiations, perennial shifts in sourcing patterns, and—if orders materialize at all—tight deadlines, quality rejections, price renegotiations, and mid-production cancellations. Put differently, the issues at stake are all too often understood in a purely technocratic fashion for which technical solutions are to be designed, rather than being recognized as the upshot of the highly unequal power relations that—at every level—shape the global organization of garment production and drive pressures, risks, costs, and responsibilities down the chain (De Neve 2009).

While informed by an approach to worker health and safety that takes a "relations *in* production" perspective, by focusing on actors and interactions on the shop floor (Ruwanpura this volume; Ashraf this volume), this volume pays equal amounts of attention to the multilayered "relations *of* production" through which conditions of labor and relations of exploitation are reproduced at the sites of manufacturing (Burawoy 1983; Neveling this volume).

What such a perspective reveals is that highly wanting labor standards are not in any way an exception or aberration, and that a linear progression of economic upgrading leading to social upgrading is little more than wishful thinking (Ruwanpura 2015; Rossi 2013). Rather, disturbing labor conditions appear as the systemic outcome of labor value capture and appropriation by actors higher up the chain. Jamie Cross (2010), with reference to special export zones, has argued that such spaces of production are remarkably *un*exceptional in that there is an overwhelming continuity between the labor regimes found within and outside of such zones: everywhere they are marked by high levels of informality, insecurity, and precariousness of work (cf. Neveling 2006, 2015).

By contrast, Patrick Neveling's chapter offers us a unique historical perspective on the systemic forces at work in the creation of what he characterizes as a global garment production regime (see also Neveling 2015). By tracing the development of export processing zones (EPZs) around the world—from Puerto Rico to Ireland, China, and India—Neveling reveals how it was the shared interests of nation-states and capital that drove the global spread of EPZs. Later, an emerging neoliberal policy environment enabled the EPZ model to establish itself in very different environments, yet with strikingly uniform outcomes. One such outcome is the superexploitation that such zones generate, in which wage levels typically stand below what is needed for the reproduction of labor power itself. A first casualty of this wage exploitation is workers' health and safety, as working bodies are routinely drained, depleted, and exhausted in order to sustain individuals and households in the short term. Neveling's global genealogy of EPZs indicates how deficient labor conditions are a structural feature of the global garment regime, not an unintended side effect. The degradation of labor is what the globalization of the industry is all about, as profits are sought from forcing down wages and maximizing labor output (Collins 2003; Miller 2012).

Another outcome of the global EPZ regime is the "striking imbalance between an interest in the safety of capital and securing profit margins for investors on the one hand and the safety of workers on the other" (Neveling this volume). In early reports and evaluations of EPZs reviewed by Neveling, safety was first and foremost understood as the safety of *investors* against financial risks or failure, rather than being about averting *worker* injuries and fatalities on the shop floor. If health or safety appeared in policy documents at all, it was as a cost or expense to be covered and recouped rather than as an inherent value to be pursued. Local states and industry organizations—United Nations

Industrial Development Organization (UNIDO) being a leading one among them—acted to promote industry interests and to limit investor risks, rather than safeguard worker health and safety, despite high levels of fatal accidents in the early years of EPZs. Intervention was left to the self-regulated corporate sector, but it was not until well into the 1990s that codes of conduct and voluntary labor standards began to be formulated in response to the abuses and exploitation of this dominant production regime (Nadvi and Waltring 2004).

Moreover, such corporate voluntary interventions were themselves prompted by the growing anti-sweatshop movement, particularly from the 1990s. This movement sought to pressure brands to improve working conditions in their supply chains and consumers to shop ethically. States, however, were largely let off the hook. In the global South, producer country states were assumed to be weak, hopelessly compromised in their interests, and siding with capitalists to expand the garment sector and step up much needed export earnings at the expense of labor rights. In the global North, states were thought to be too removed from the sites of production, uninterested in regulation, and hesitant to go against the interests of their own multinational corporations. The result was a neoliberal model of voluntary self-regulation that skillfully navigated different local regulatory regimes and steered well away from state regulation or any binding agreements. Against the rising power of multinational corporations, it was not only states that became marginalized but also the courts whose role in arbitrating standards or enforcing regulation became heavily compromised.

Given the overwhelming failure to ensure garment workers' safety, a novel response emerged in the wake of heavy losses to life and earnings over the last decade or so. Following several major disasters at production sites across South Asia, demands have been formulated for financial compensation to support the families of victims. Since the collapse of the Spectrum sweater factory in Savar District, Bangladesh, in 2005, amounts of cash assistance paid to victims have been extended and compensation rules have become more formalized. Doug Miller has pointed to the key role of Bangladeshi and international civil society actors—trade unions, NGOs, labor rights organizations—in the battle for compensation following the Spectrum collapse (Miller 2012, chapters 4–6). The main demands raised by all workers' organizations were: "punishment for the factory owners, increased compensation for the victims of the collapse, a major overhaul of health and safety in the RMG sector, and jobs for those workers unemployed by the disaster" (ibid., 54). What came out of the ensuing struggle, however, was an overwhelming emphasis on obtaining relief and compensation, which ultimately led to the establishment of several major voluntary schemes for the families of Spectrum victims, involving contributions from the local employer and various sourcing companies. An equally significant outcome, however, was progress made toward the formulation of more standardized, rights-based compensation procedures and a formula for compensation to be used in case of future disasters in countries that lack relevant insurance and liability instruments (ibid., 74).

Despite the "catalytic moment" of the Spectrum collapse (ibid., 55), compensation remains a partially developed, incomplete, and at times messy response that involves extensive negotiations with a range of stakeholders. It is against this background that the chapter by Mahmudul Sumon, Nazneen Shifa, and Saydia Gulrukh invites us to reconsider another possible response: appealing to the courts, including criminal law, to hold to account the factory owners whose buildings are so unsafe that they injure and even kill workers. Sumon and colleagues describe their experiences as members of a Bangladeshi activist group, Activist Anthropologist, which has been pursuing justice for workers after the Tazreen Fashions factory fire of November 2012.

Sumon and colleagues are critical of what they call the "regime of compensation" that has emerged over the last decade. This regime is dominated by extensive debates about the size and nature of relief and compensation, which in turn have come to preclude other forms of justice such as the recognition of factory owners' criminal negligence that led to the deaths and injuries in the first place. While not disputing the importance of compensation per se, Sumon and colleagues deplore two issues. First, they are critical of the ways in which compensation continues to be a largely ad hoc enterprise in which a range of NGOs and other private actors design multiple schemes and interventions, largely in competition with one another. A market of compensation schemes has emerged, which Sumon and colleagues call an "economy of compensation," in which everyone competes for maximum sums of cash assistance. Second, these authors are concerned about the ways in which compensation takes attention away from prevention, from legal protection, and from addressing structural causal processes—precisely the sorts of issues raised by Neveling in his contribution. By focusing on immediate relief and assistance, compensation may well facilitate employers' and factory owners' attempts to absolve themselves of responsibility, to avert criminal prosecution in court, and above all to continue "business as usual."

Sumon and colleagues' analysis raises a number of broader issues that speak to the themes of this volume. First of all, it draws our attention to the complex *local* politics of garment production and raises questions about the nature of the linkages between local and global actors. The garment industry involves different actors at different levels, and any intervention is bound to require varied amounts of collaboration, negotiation, and joint action. While at one level this can be immensely powerful and enabling—as we have seen in the wake of the Spectrum and Rana Plaza disasters—at another level it can also be inhibiting, especially when tensions arise between Northern and more local actors.

One such tension revealed in Sumon and colleagues' chapter is that between, on the one hand, Northern-based NGOs and activists who seek to "internationalize" a Rana Plaza–type incident in order to make brands and retailers take responsibility for their supply chains and, on the other hand, local activists and campaigners who are keen to hold *local* manufacturers accountable for their actions and who want to ensure that the state legal system works to protect citizens and their rights. Sumon and colleagues' chapter also reveals that while some interventions may be complementary and reinforce each other, different agendas may also clash, such as when a hegemonic discourse of compensation ends up normalizing negligence and sidestepping legal avenues in the pursuit of justice. Finally, the chapter reveals some of the differences between "reactive" versus "preventive" interventions. While an approach that focuses on compensation is primarily reactive, seeking to deal with the outcomes of disasters and curb the effects on victims, an approach that uses criminal liability is preventive in that it aims to act as a deterrent against employer neglect of labor rights and to prevent the continuation of "business as usual."

The last contribution in this section is Alessandra Mezzadri's chapter on the externalization of social responsibility for health and safety in the north Indian garment sector. In line with Neveling, Mezzadri urges us to consider how the garment industry is structured as a system of labor exploitation in order to understand the recurrent strains placed on workers' health as well as the ways in which ill health is dealt with. Mezzadri's chapter looks at garment production in India's National Capital Region (NCR) and in one of its satellite embroidery centers, Bareilly in Uttar Pradesh. She reminds us that not all garment workers work in factories. Just as global brands and retailers cut costs by sourcing garments from overseas suppliers, so too do supplier factories locally outsource production to smaller workshops and home-based workers.

Drawing on an analysis informed by political economy and feminism, Mezzadri's chapter makes the important point that when the labor process becomes informalized, the costs and risks of health and safety are externalized onto workers themselves. She first shows how persistent health and safety issues are routine rather than exceptional because of systemic pressures to meet deadlines, suppress wages, and make profits. Exhaustion due to the intensity of work rhythms was reported by 41 percent of factory workers as one of the main occupational health problems in Mezzadri's study. Mezzadri then goes on to explain how employers externalize the costs of social reproduction of the labor force. Rather than taking responsibility for the health of their workers, employers in both factory and nonfactory settings systematically externalize the costs and concerns of health and safety from factories and workshops to workers and households. The result is that workers and their relatives are left to deal with the direct impacts of work on their health as well as the broader effects of ill health on their livelihoods. Costs and risks of ill health are externalized to workers' own time, space, and social networks.

Mezzadri's contribution is a stark reminder not only of the fact that poor health and safety outcomes have to be related to the nature of the garment labor regime, but also that any policy intervention to improve health outcomes will need to systematically address the broader labor conditions and work pressures of the sector. Even though the academic literature reports some improvements to health and safety standards with the use of codes of conduct (Barrientos and Smith 2007; Miller et al. 2007), Mezzadri reminds us that codes by and large focus on materially visible and quantifiable improvements to the built environment (see also Ashraf this volume), and usually overlook the many spaces of informal production such as workshops and homes. Also, by failing to address long-term exhaustion, depletion of bodily strength, or persistent mental strains, codes contribute to the systemic neglect of health in the industry. More generally, Mezzadri forces us to think about the ways in which responsibility for health and safety, and for the social reproduction of the labor force more generally, is externalized away from employers and toward workers' own homes and families. The chapters of the next section continue this line of questioning and provide further ethnographic evidence of how health is affected and dealt with on the garment shop floor.

Rethinking Health as Well-Being at Work and Home

Ethnographic research generates a grounded understanding of what health means in the everyday—how health is conceptualized, and how injury or ill health are managed. It also reveals that concerns over health and safety in the workplace can become a site in which conflicting interests between workers and employers are fought over. Kanchana Ruwanpura's chapter looks at factory-based health provision in the Sri Lankan garment industry. With its impressive health indicators and high standards of literacy—attributable in part to the state's commitment to social development and "slow" growth—Sri Lanka is often considered to have some of the best garment labor conditions in the developing world. Since 2006, Sri Lankan apparel manufacturers have sought to capitalize on this reputation with the introduction of a "Garments Without Guilt" (GWG) program to certify the labor standards of member factories (cf. Lynch and Hagen-Keith this volume). Even some factories that are not part of the GWG program may offer on-site health facilities such as a factory clinic staffed by nurses with scheduled visits from a doctor.

Ruwanpura's ethnography of two large Sri Lankan factories shows that providing health services inside the factory does not mean that workers will be able to access them. She describes the fraught choices made by shop floor supervisors and zone managers, whose job it is to assess workers' health complaints, weighing up the short-term costs of excusing a worker from the line against the potentially greater disruption caused by a long-term absence for a serious but preventable ailment. Because illness is the only legitimate reason to have time off work, supervisors must also judge whether a worker is genuinely unwell or faking ill health in order to be able to go home early. But workers are not devoid of agency either. Given these barriers to accessing the clinic, workers often wait until their illness has become so severe that their supervisor will allow them to see the doctor. Others stay home from work but are forced to escalate the seriousness of their condition by checking into a hospital in order to obtain the paperwork necessary to legitimize their absence.

These struggles over health in the workplace reveal a central paradox in the labor process: employers require healthy bodies, yet they pressure ailing workers not to take time off because of disruptions to production. Ruwanpura shows "health" therefore to be a useful entryway into understanding the everyday politics of labor on the shop floor, or "relations *in* production." A worker's ability to access treatment in the factory clinic relies upon her success in negotiating with gatekeepers against whom she is hierarchically positioned and socially disadvantaged. Given the structural conditions that workers must navigate, Ruwanpura (this volume) argues, "the politics of labor regimes suggest that we need to be attentive to wider structures that make and unmake healthy working bodies."

Sandya Hewamanne's chapter also focuses on Sri Lanka and broadens our understanding of "health" by including well-being and the social effects of the stigma that follows workers from the factories to their home villages. She explains that despite Sri Lanka's position in the market as a source of high-quality apparel and good labor standards, rural women who travel to the export processing zones (EPZs) near the capital face stigma both at work and when they return home after completing a period of employment. Hewamanne reminds us that corporations profit from the devaluation of women's labor, which happens not only through their low rates of pay, but also through wider cultural discourses that depict women as disposable, often with the use of sexualized imagery. For women EPZ workers in Sri Lanka, this devaluation takes the form of stigma and compromises their future status as a wife and daughter-in-law.

Corporate codes of conduct are inadequate to mitigate the effects of the devaluation of women's labor and the stigma of having been a "garment girl" because they do not confront the fundamental contradiction of the valuing of low-wage workers in the global economy highlighted by Melissa Wright (2001, 369): "the value of [a worker's] labor, paradoxically, lies in the power of the discourse of her valuelessness." Hewamanne suggests therefore that a "living wage" could go some way to improving workers' situation by recalibrating the value of their labor (cf. Lynch and Hagen-Keith this volume).

What Hewamanne shows is that an understanding of worker health has to look beyond the shop floor, both spatially and temporally. Assaults on workers' well-being and social status travel home with them to their villages; the stigma of having been a "garment girl" can follow a worker through time, requiring intensive efforts to rehabilitate her good name across the life span, particularly as a bride and daughter-in-law back in her village. Hewamanne's chapter reveals that factory-based initiatives to improve labor conditions do not capture these complex social implications of work for the women involved, which often manifest themselves outside the workplace and long after employment has ended. Corporate social responsibility policies are not simply weak or ineffective; they are fundamentally flawed because they do not confront the political issues of labor devaluation at the heart of the garment industry. These themes are also picked up in Hasan Ashraf's chapter on health and safety in the Bangladesh ready-made garment sector.

Unlike the Sri Lankan garment industry, which promotes a reputation for quality and labor standards, Bangladesh's comparative advantage is its low labor costs for producing basic apparel. With weak state enforcement of existing labor laws, the governance of labor standards is mostly via voluntary self-regulation, with buyers insisting on corporate codes of conduct—often while simultaneously driving down prices (Muhammad 2015). Ashraf conducted research on the Bangladesh garment industry both before and after the Rana Plaza collapse, with fourteen months of ethnographic fieldwork between 2010 and 2012, and a return visit in 2014. He shows how the intense international focus on building safety in the wake of Rana Plaza has left unaddressed the more diffuse, embodied, and politically sensitive concerns about workers' health voiced from the shop floor.

Ashraf describes six months of ethnographic fieldwork at a knitwear factory he calls Asha Garments, where he worked as a machine helper and quality checker. He describes health threats from dust and smoke inhalation, noise, lack of ventilation, and exposure to lights, electric wires, and chemical adhesives. Workers perceive a trade-off between their ability to make a living and their own health, which "depreciates" (Ashraf this volume; cf. Mezzadri this volume) every day they work. Ashraf emphasizes that health problems are as much caused by "the social processes of laboring," which range from coercive supervisory tactics and incessant work rhythms to the indignity of being subject to degrading and sexualized insults on the shop floor. Global market fluctuations affect both the physical and mental health of workers, who are pressured to do overtime work with little warning. With fine ethnographic detail, Ashraf explains the anxiety of workers who do not know if or when overtime will be needed, and shows how shop floor supervisors manipulate this anxiety to keep up the work pace.

Writing about the Accord on Fire and Building Safety in Bangladesh (2013)—the "paradigm changing" multi-stakeholder initiative described by Bair and colleagues (this volume)—Ashraf tells us how the Accord and a similar but smaller inspection program known as the Alliance for Bangladesh Worker Safety (the Alliance) have developed a narrow understanding of worker safety focused on the structural integrity of the built environment. Largely created by brands, trade unions, and other stakeholders based in Europe and North America, these inspection regimes not only feel imposed from "above," but are also narrowly technocratic, ignoring the global political economy of labor that this volume seeks to unpack.

Examining the impact of the Accord and the Alliance on a return fieldwork trip in 2014, Ashraf discovered workers contending with new forms of anxiety—this time about their very futures—due to mass layoffs in the garment industry. Because the remediation of buildings is the central purpose of the inspection regimes, workers were laid off from factories requiring urgent physical upgrading. Although there are provisions in both the Accord and the Alliance to reemploy or provide continuing income for furloughed workers, Ashraf explains that financial support was not forthcoming, and workers made redundant by factory inspections faced the stress of joblessness.

Ashraf insists upon a broad conceptualization of "health" and "safety" that goes beyond building safety and beyond a narrow understanding of physical health to include workers' mental and social well-being, and their rights as persons and citizens. The concept of well-being encompasses wages and labor conditions as well as social status, dignity, living conditions, and a sense of security (of employment, health, livelihood, and future). Both Ashraf and Hewamanne's chapters emphasize aspects of well-being that are inherently *social* in nature, and that cannot be reduced to material or technical matters on the shop floor. Taking seriously the well-being of workers—and not simply their protection from unsafe buildings or equipment—means attending to their physical, mental, and social health, and exploring how health is experienced through a range of embodied practices and vulnerabilities. Such a perspective can then render visible the everyday health processes and outcomes produced by global production networks, and enable us to think of novel and creative ways to address both the health *and* safety of garment workers worldwide.

Taken together, these accounts identify severe deficiencies in the global garment production regime—deficiencies that can be observed at global, national, local, and personal scales—and critically assess the solutions on offer. Corporate self-regulation of global supply chains has clearly failed. The responsibility to respect workers' rights cannot be left to the market, contingent upon consumers choosing to buy "ethically." In the wake of the Rana Plaza collapse, we see renewed use of legal measures and regulations, ranging from binding pacts between organized labor and multinational corporations to improve the safety of buildings, to the use of the courts to hold companies accountable for occupational injuries and deaths. The ultimate aim is to uphold workers' rights as both universal human rights and localized labor rights. But what the chapters in this book also show is that labor standards are a political issue, not just a technical one. An ethnographic perspective reminds us that top-down solutions will always be inadequate, and that workers themselves need a collective voice to advocate for improvements to their own circumstances. Without rights to self-determination, freedom of association, and collective bargaining—all considered "core" labor rights by the ILO—it is hard to imagine sustainable improvements in health and safety, not to mention the future well-being of workers.

Notes

1. Ellen Rosen's 2002 book, *Making Sweatshops: The Globalization of the U.S. Apparel Industry*, explained the emergence of the global outsourcing regime that has generated poor labor conditions for garment workers around the world. Our book builds upon Rosen's work to examine the actors, institutions, and movements that seek to remedy those conditions, particularly with regard to health and safety.

2. For a comparison of European and American anti-sweatshop activism, see Bair and Palpacuer (2012). Like the European anti-sweatshop movement, American activists put pressure on brands rather than states to regulate standards and enforce labor rights (O'Rourke 2006; Seidman 2007).

Bibliography

Ahamad, Rashad. 2014. "Joyless Eid Awaits Rana Plaza Victims." *Daily Star*, July 25. Online: http://www.thedailystar.net/joyless-eid-awaits-rana-plaza-victims-34937. Accessed: August 5, 2014.

Attanapola, Chamila T. 2005. "Experiences of Globalization and Health in the Narratives of Women Industrial Workers in Sri Lanka." *Gender, Technology and Development* 9(1): 81–102.

Bair, Jennifer. 2015. "Corporations at the United Nations: Echoes of the New International Economic Order?" *Humanity: An International Journal of Human Rights, Humanitarianism, and Development* 6(1): 159–171.

Bair, Jennifer, and Florence Palpacuer. 2012. "From Varieties of Capitalism to Varieties of Activism: The Antisweatshop Movement in Comparative Perspective." *Social Problems* 59(4): 522–43.

Bajaj, Vikas. 2012. "Fatal Fire in Bangladesh Highlights the Dangers Facing Garment Workers." *New York Times*. November 25. Online: http://www.nytimes.com/2012/11/26/world/asia/bangladesh-fire-kills-more-than-100-and-injures-many.html?_r=1. Accessed: April 28, 2015.

Barrientos, Stephanie. 2012. "Corporate Purchasing Practices in Global Production Networks: A Socially Contested Terrain." *Geoforum* 44(1): 44–51.

Barrientos, Stephanie, and Sally Smith. 2007. "Do Workers Benefit from Ethical Trade? Assessing Codes of Labour Practice in Global Production Systems." *Third World Quarterly* 28(4): 713–28.

Burawoy, Michael. 1983. "Between the Labor Process and the State: The Changing Face of Factory Regimes Under Advanced Capitalism." *American Sociological Review* 48(5): 587–605.

Carrier, James G., and Peter G. Luetchford, eds. 2012. *Ethical Consumption: Social Value and Economic Practice*. New York: Berghahn.

CCC Code of Labour Practices. 1998. *Code of Labour Practices for the Apparel Industry Including Sportswear*. Amsterdam: Clean Clothes Campaign.

Collins, Jane L. 2003. *Threads: Gender, Labor and Power in the Global Apparel Industry*. Chicago: University of Chicago Press.

Cross, Jamie. 2010. "Neoliberalism as Unexceptional: Economic Zones and the Everyday Precariousness of Working Life in South India." *Critique of Anthropology* 30(4): 355–73.

De Neve, Geert. 2009. "Power, Inequality and Corporate Social Responsibility: The Politics of Ethical Compliance in the South Indian Garment Industry." *Economic & Political Weekly* 44(22): 63–71.

Dolan, Catherine, and Dinah Rajak. 2011. "Introduction: Ethnographies of Corporate Ethicizing." *Focaal: Journal of Global and Historical Anthropology* 60: 3–8.

Egels-Zandén, Niklas. 2015. "The Role of SMEs in Global Production Networks: A Swedish SME's Payment of Living Wages at Its Indian Supplier." *Business and Society* 56(1): 92–129.

Esbenshade, Jill. 2004. *Monitoring Sweatshops: Workers, Consumers and the Global Apparel Industry*. Philadelphia: Temple University Press.

ETI Base Code. 2014. *The ETI Base Code*. London: Ethical Trading Initiative.

Gereffi, Gary, and Stacey Frederick. 2010. "The Global Apparel Value Chain, Trade and the Crisis: Challenges and Opportunities for Developing Countries." Policy Research Working Paper 5281, World Bank Development Research Group, Trade and Integration Team. Washington, DC: World Bank.

Hertel, Shareen. 2010. "The Paradox of Partnership: Assessing New Forms of NGO Advocacy on Labor Rights." *Ethics & International Affairs* 24(2): 171–89.

Hilgert, Jeffrey. 2013. *Hazard or Hardship: Crafting Global Norms on the Right to Refuse Unsafe Work*. Ithaca, NY: Cornell University/ILR Press.

Hobson, John. 2013. "To Die For?: The Health and Safety of Fast Fashion." *Occupational Medicine* 63(5): 317–19.

International Human Rights and Conflict Resolution Clinic, Mills Legal Clinic, Stanford Law School, and Worker Rights Consortium. 2013. *Monitoring in the Dark: An Evaluation of the International Labour Organization's Better Factories Cambodia Monitoring and Reporting Program*. Stanford, CA: International Human Rights and Conflict Resolution Clinic, Mills Legal Clinic, Stanford Law School, and Worker Rights Consortium.

Labour Behind the Label. 2013. "Shop 'Til They Drop: Fainting and Malnutrition in Garment Workers in Cambodia." Joint Report by Labour Behind the Label (LBL) and Community Legal Education Centre (CLEC). Bristol, UK and Phnom Penh, Cambodia: LBL and CLEC.

Locke, Richard. 2013. *The Promise and Limits of Private Power: Promoting Labor Standards in a Global Economy*. Cambridge, UK: Cambridge University Press.

Lynch, Caitrin. 2007. *Juki Girls, Good Girls: Gender and Cultural Politics in Sri Lanka's Global Garment Industry*. Ithaca, NY: Cornell University Press.

Mezzadri, Alessandra. 2012. "Reflections on Globalisation and Labour Standards in the Indian Garment Industry: Codes of Conduct Versus 'Codes of Practice' Imposed by the Firm." *Global Labour Journal* 3(1): 40–62.

Miller, Doug. 2012. *Last Nightshift in Savar: The Story of the Spectrum Sweater Factory Collapse*. Alnwick, UK: McNidder and Grace.

Miller, Doug, Veasna Nuon, Charlene Aprill, and Ramon Certeza. 2007. "Governing the Supply Chain in Clothing Post MFA Phase Out. The Case of Cambodia." Global Union Research Network Discussion Paper 6. Geneva: International Labour Organization (ILO).

Muhammad, Anu. 2015. "Workers' Lives, Walmart's Pocket: Garments' Global Chain, from Savar to New York." *Economic & Political Weekly* 50(25): 143–50.

Nadvi, Khalid, and F. Waltring. 2004. "Making Sense of Global Standards." Pp. 53–95 in *Local Enterprises in the Global Economy: Issues of Governance and Upgrading*, ed. by Hubert Schmitz. Cheltenham, UK: Edward Elgar.

Neveling, Patrick. 2006. "Spirits of Capitalism and the De-alienation of Workers: A Historical Perspective on the Mauritian Garment Industry." Society and Culture in Motion Working Paper No. 2. Halle and Wittenberg, Germany: Martin Luther University of Halle-Wittenberg.

———. 2015. "Export Processing Zones, Special Economic Zones and the Long March of Capitalist Development Policies during the Cold War." Pp. 63–84 in *Negotiating Independence: New Directions in the Histories of the Cold War and Decolonisation*, ed. by Leslie James and Elisabeth Leake. London: Bloomsbury.

O'Rourke, Dara. 2003. "Outsourcing Regulation: Analyzing Nongovernmental Systems of Labor Standards and Monitoring." *Policy Studies Journal* 31(1): 1–29.

———. 2006. "Multi-Stakeholder Regulation: Privatizing or Socializing Global Labor Standards?" *World Development* 34(5): 899–918.

Pearson, Ruth, and Gill Seyfang. 2001. "New Hope or False Dawn?: Voluntary Codes of Conduct, Labour Regulation and Social Policy in a Globalizing World." *Global Social Policy* 1(1): 49–78.

Plank, Leonhard, Arianna Rossi, and Cornelia Staritz. 2014. "What Does 'Fast Fashion' Mean for Workers?: Apparel Production in Morocco and Romania." Pp. 127–47 in *Towards Better Work: Understanding Labour in Apparel Global Value Chains*, ed. by Arianna Rossi, Amy Luinstra, and John Pickles. New York: Palgrave Macmillan and International Labour Organization.

Prentice, Rebecca. 2015. *Thiefing a Chance: Factory Work, Illicit Labor, and Neoliberal Subjectivities in Trinidad*. Boulder: University Press of Colorado.

Richey, Lisa Ann, and Stefano Ponte. 2011. *Brand Aid: Shopping Well to Save the World*. Minneapolis: University of Minnesota Press.

Rosen, Ellen Israel. 2002. *Making Sweatshops: The Globalization of the U.S. Apparel Industry*. Berkeley: University of California Press.

Rossi, Arianna. 2013. "Does Economic Upgrading Lead to Social Upgrading in Global Production Networks?: Evidence from Morocco." *World Development* 46: 223–33.

Ruwanpura, Kanchana N. 2012. *Ethical Codes: Reality and Rhetoric—A Study of Sri Lanka's Apparel Sector* (report). Southampton, UK: University of Southampton.

———. 2013. "Scripted Performances? Local Readings of 'Global' Health and Safety Standards (the Apparel Sector in Sri Lanka)." *Global Labour Journal* 4(2): 88–108.

———. 2014. "Metal Free Factories: Straddling Worker Rights and Consumer Safety?" *Geoforum* 51(1): 224–32.

———. 2015. "Garments Without Guilt? Uneven Labour Geographies and Ethical Trading—Sri Lankan Labour Perspectives." *Journal of Economic Geography* 1–24.

Seidman, Gay W. 2007. *Beyond the Boycott: Labor Rights, Human Rights, and Transnational Activism*. New York: Russell Sage Foundation.

Spieler, Emily A. 2006. "Risks and Rights: The Case for Occupational Safety and Health as a Core Worker Right." Pp. 78–117 in *Workers' Rights as Human Rights*, ed. by James A. Gross. Ithaca, NY: Cornell University/ILR Press.

Staritz, Cornelia. 2011. *Making the Cut?: Low-Income Countries and the Global Clothing Value Chain in a Post-Quota and Post-Crisis World*. Washington, DC: World Bank.

Taplin, Ian M. 2014. "Who Is to Blame?: A Re-examination of Fast Fashion after the 2013 Factory Disaster in Bangladesh." *Critical Perspectives on International Business* 10(1–2): 72–83.

Wright, Melissa W. 2001. "Desire and the Prosthetics of Supervision: A Case of Maquiladora Flexibility." *Cultural Anthropology* 16(3): 354–73.

PART I

The Rise and Fall of Labor Standards

CHAPTER 1

Sweatshops and the Search for Solutions, Yesterday and Today

Jennifer Bair, Mark Anner, and Jeremy Blasi

Many observers of the contemporary apparel industry have noted the historical parallels between the deadly workplace disasters occurring in Bangladesh and the Triangle Shirtwaist Factory fire that killed 146 garment workers in New York City more than a century ago. Such comparisons are easy to draw, since some of the same factors contributed to the carnage in both cases: inadequate regulation, ineffective inspections, and structurally stressed buildings that had not been designed to accommodate large-scale manufacturing operations.

In this chapter, we look more deeply at the historical parallels between the apparel industry in contemporary Bangladesh and the garment district of early twentieth-century New York. We not only emphasize similarities in the causes of fatal factory incidents, but we also consider whether, post–Rana Plaza, Bangladesh is poised to replicate the enormous improvements in worker safety and worker well-being that were accomplished in New York in the decades after the Triangle fire. We identify two key factors that were critical in the fight against sweatshop conditions in New York. First, the government responded to the 1911 fire with far-reaching efforts to strengthen worker protection laws. This outcome had much to do with the sustained and widespread mobilization of workers and their allies, who together channeled the public's outrage at the fire into support for meaningful reform. Second, the apparel industry union succeeded in securing binding agreements (known as jobbers' agreements) with the lead firms that ultimately set the terms and conditions for the workers employed in New York's sewing shops. Jobbers' agreements evidenced a clear understanding of the economic factors driving substandard conditions in the garment district—namely, a competitive dynamic in which contractors were pitted against one another in a deadly race to the bottom, as they sought to secure orders from the lead firms that then, as now, orchestrated the supply chain.

There are important parallels, and also differences, relative to this history in the aftermath thus far of the Rana disaster. On the one hand, the government of Bangladesh responded to the crisis by developing a National Action Plan (NAP), which called for reforms to both the content and administration of the country's labor laws. These measures do not go far enough, however, as they leave crucial issues—particularly concerning the right to organize—unaddressed, and their implementation thus far has been unsatisfactory. Nonetheless, if the implementation and enforcement of these reforms are strengthened, and if they are followed by further changes to law and practice, they will serve to enhance worker safety and strengthen workers' rights more broadly, including core labor rights that are routinely ignored in Bangladesh.

More promisingly, there have been important labor-business efforts in the private sector involving the lead firms that sit atop global supply chains. Since Rana Plaza, more than 200 companies sourcing from Bangladesh have signed an agreement with global and Bangladeshi unions called the Accord on Fire and Building Safety in Bangladesh (2013) (hereafter "Accord"). The Accord partially replicates the jobbers' agreement model of holding brands and retailers (today's jobbers) accountable for conditions in their contractors' factories. Specifically, it requires brands to source only from supplier factories in Bangladesh that are inspected by independent experts, to disclose the results of inspections, and to ensure that safety hazards are remediated.

Because it commits brands to ensuring that their suppliers address factory-level problems, the Accord represents a major challenge to the footloose "cut and run" sourcing model typical of today's global garment industry. Ultimately, however, the long-term success of the Accord and of the post–Rana Plaza reforms more broadly will depend on the degree to which these and succeeding efforts strengthen the position of workers, and the organizations that represent them, within the political economy of Bangladesh.

Turn of the Twentieth Century Sweatshops: New York's Garment District and the Triangle Fire

The relationship between supply chain dynamics and sweatshops dates back to the origins of industrial apparel production in the United States, which began in earnest after the 1860s due to the increased affordability of sewing machines. The pace of growth quickened during the closing decades of the nineteenth century, as new ranks of garment workers were recruited among the immigrants arriving at what quickly became the epicenter of the American needle trades: New York City. By 1890, New York was home to well over half of the workers employed in the manufacture of women's clothing in the United States.

Relatively few of these workers were employed by the better-established manufacturers that designed and marketed clothing. Rather, the majority worked in modest sewing shops or informal workshops in private homes for small contractors who received orders from manufacturers. This system, in which manufacturers contracted with independent shops to produce some of the garments they designed and/or marketed, became known as the "outside model" of production. Over time, the outside system became so pervasive that a new term, *jobber*, was coined to refer to individuals and firms that designed or sold apparel, but relied entirely on contractors, meaning that they owned no factories and employed no workers, except perhaps for a handful of sample makers.

Already in 1893, a New York State Bureau of Labor inspector reported that while "there were probably one hundred wholesale cloak houses" in the garment district, "not over half a dozen provide their own factories and workshops" (Levine 1924, 17); the rest were jobbers contracting with independent sewing shops. The outside system was preferred not only because it enabled jobbers to better manage volatility and fluctuating demand, but also because it stimulated price competition among the contractors vying for their orders. This competition, in turn, was carried out on the basis of the single factor of production that the contractor controlled: the cost of labor. The term *sweater*, from which *sweatshop* was derived, was used to refer to the middlemen in this contracting system, whose business strategy consisted in extracting the maximum amount of labor at the lowest possible price. Low barriers to entry made it easy to launch a contracting operation; all that needed was a few sewing machines, some workers, and a single order from a jobber (Bair 2012).

The primary way that contractors tried to compete on price was by keeping wages low. Although between 1880 and 1890 the total value of the industry's output more than doubled from $32 million to $68 million, average garment worker wages declined from $15 a week in 1883 to between $6 and $7 in 1885 (Levine 1924; Tyler 1995). By decade's end, wages had not yet recovered; male cloak workers, among the better paid in the industry, were earning $12 a week, while women garment workers earned about half that amount. Contractors also tried to push production costs on to the workers, the vast majority of whom were new immigrants willing to work on any terms. Writing in 1924, Levine described how the contractor attempted to shift upon the worker "as much industrial responsibility as possible. He made the workers buy or rent their own machines, supply their own thread and needles, pay for the privilege of getting into the shop. . . . As the number of contractors increased, the manufacturer took advantage of the competition among them to play them off against one another. The contractor of those days was described as coming to the manufacturer in search of work 'hat in hand like a beggar'" (Levine 1924, 16).

In short, contracting was the core organizing principle of the apparel industry; squeezing labor was both the key competitive strategy and the root cause of sweatshop conditions. Contractors, while complicit in the sweating system, had limited power to change it, since the terms and conditions they could offer their workers were largely set by those they received from their clients. As John R. Commons pointed out in 1900, this modern putting-out system enabled all parties to evade responsibility for sweatshops: when garment workers protested their wages and asked to be paid a better price for their labor, "the contractor tells them, 'I have nothing to do with the price. The price is made for me by the manufacturer. I have very little to say about price.' That is, he cuts himself completely loose from any responsibility to his employees as to how much they are to get for their labor. The help do not know the manufacturer. They cannot register their complaint with the man who made the price for their labor. The contractor, who did not make the price for their labor, claims that it is of no use to complain to him. So that however much the price for labor goes down there is no one responsible for it" (quoted in Stein 1977, 44–46).

Yet workers did complain, and with increasing frequency. Numerous garment workers' organizations and unions were founded in New York and elsewhere in the northeast between 1880 and 1900, but none were able to survive. When a new union, the International Ladies Garment Workers

Union (ILGWU), was formed in June 1900, its long-term future looked equally uncertain. What reversed the fortunes of the ILGWU was a period of extraordinary labor militancy that erupted among the garment district's mostly young, mostly immigrant workforce in the fall of 1909. Known as the "uprising of the 20,000" for the number of garment workers that became involved, the conflict began with a dispute over the contracting system at one of New York's biggest sewing factories, the Triangle Shirtwaist Company. The Triangle Company was not a jobber that used the outside system of production, but rather a manufacturer with in-house production. Triangle organized this production, however, via a system of *inside* contracting:

> Triangle would hire a good machine operator and allocate to him half a dozen machines out of the 240 on the ninth floor. In turn, this operator, in reality a contractor for the firm, would hire the young girls, immigrants and women from his home town across the sea, as learners. He would teach them how to make the separate parts of the garment which he, as master craftsman, would join together. Mary Leventhal [a Triangle employee] kept the record of cut work distributed and the finished waists returned by the leader. Only he knew the value of the work done by his team because only he had bargained with the company for the rate on each style. (Stein 1962, 161)[1]

This system had two consequences. First, it avoided any direct employment relationship between the company and the majority of the garment workers, who were hired and paid by the contractor: "The company dealt only with its contractors. It felt no responsibility for the girls. Its payroll listed only the contractors. It never knew the exact total of its workers" (Stein 1962, 161). But inside contracting had a second, unintended consequence as well: by bringing together under one roof sets of workers who were technically employed by different contractors, and co-locating them not only with the contractor but with the manufacturer, this system allowed workers to "see the real employer beyond the contractor whom they dealt with" (ibid.).

For the contractor, the system worked as long as the amount he was paid by the manufacturer exceeded the amount of wages he paid to his workers. When that was not the case, the interests of the contractor and his workers might align, as happened at the Triangle factory about a year prior to the strike wave that became known as the uprising of the 20,000; two inside contractors at Triangle approached the manager to explain that the rates they were being paid were insufficient because, after paying their workers, there was little left for themselves. The manager dismissed their appeal, and the manager's deputies retaliated against one of the contractors by breaking the threads on his spool, setting in motion a scuffle that resulted in the contractors being dragged from the factory. Several workers walked off the shop floor in response and went directly to the local office of the ILGWU, hoping for the union's support. The union had little help to offer, however; with virtually no resources and about 400 members, it was barely staying afloat. Consequently, the Triangle workers had little alternative but to return to work.

This incident convinced the owners of Triangle to create a company union, which, they hoped, could assuage future conflicts. As a management strategy, the plan backfired, however, as relations between management and the workers deteriorated even further in the coming months. Finally, in September 1909 the conflict came to a head and Triangle locked out workers who had been protesting the company's practices. At this point, ILGWU Local 25 declared a strike against Triangle.

The Triangle strike attracted significant support, including from wealthy and well-connected members of the Women's Trade Union League (WTUL). The presence of "society" ladies on the picket lines alongside young immigrant women, mostly of Jewish and Italian descent, generated widespread publicity, and the treatment of the striking workers by police and other public officials created additional sympathy for their cause. With unrest spreading throughout the garment district, a general strike was declared on November 22. The strike, which involved more than 15,000 workers, lasted into the next year. By the time it ended on February 15, 1910, the ILGWU had signed contracts with 354 sewing shops.[2]

From a membership of less than 500 just a few years before, ILGWU Local 25 would claim 10,000 members the year after the general strike. And for workers in the hundreds of shops that were now covered by union contracts, the gains were significant. They included a 52-hour workweek, wage increases of 12–15 percent, and the end of inside contracting. The uprising of 20,000 also generated some public discussion of health and safety issues in the industry, but for the most part, these concerns centered on potential harms to the *consumer* caused by insanitary conditions in the garment shops. Manufacturers, looking to assure shoppers that their products were safe, agreed to participate in a joint management-labor body called the New York Joint Board of Sanitary Control. The board, which included representatives of the union, the manufacturers' association, and the buying public, was charged with the task of setting sanitation standards for the industry. Yet because the board did not have any legal authority to inspect factories or order repairs, it had to persuade owners to improve conditions in substandard shops voluntarily, though clear violations of the law were reported to the state Labor Department and the city Health Department.

Such substandard conditions were rampant. The Joint Board of Sanitary Control found that 99 percent of the 1,243 factories it visited were deficient in terms of safety; problems included an insufficient number of staircases, blocked aisles and obstructed exit pathways, and inadequate or absent fire escapes. In 94 percent of the factories inspected, the doors opened inward instead of outward, which, though recognized as a safety hazard by the Joint Sanitary Board, was not a violation of the building code, which stated only that doors should open out "wherever practical."

When a factory fire in Newark, New Jersey on November 25, 1910 killed twenty-five workers, the chief of New York's fire department observed that "this city may have a fire as deadly as the one in Newark at any time" (Stein 1962, 27). The dangers of such a fire were exacerbated by the geography of New York's garment industry, as many sewing shops were located on the upper floors of densely populated tenement buildings. In a 1910 report, the Women's Trade Union League pointed out that of the more than 612,000 garment workers employed in the city, a full half worked in loft factories or on high floors in tall buildings, effectively beyond the reach of firefighting equipment.

On Saturday, March 25, 1911, a fire started on the eighth floor of the Asch building at Greene St. and Washington Place in Manhattan. The Triangle Shirtwaist factory occupied the top three floors of a ten-story building, where 500 mostly young, immigrant women worked. Although the fire was brought under control in less than twenty minutes, 146 people died; many were killed upon impact after jumping or falling from windows that could not be reached by fire ladders. Some died when the inadequate fire escape collapsed under their weight. Most of the victims worked in the main sewing shop on the ninth floor where, according to survivors, the door had been locked (von Drehle 2003).

The owners of Triangle were eventually indicted and tried for manslaughter in the first degree. During the trial it was revealed that as recently as October 1910, the factory had passed a routine inspection by the fire department. The architect testified that the building, when completed a decade earlier, had been in "strict compliance with the law"; he also acknowledged that when the building was designed, there was no expectation that it would eventually house multiple factories (Stein 1962). After a trial of a little more than three weeks, the owners of Triangle were acquitted on December 27, 1911.

The fire at Triangle, which occurred in the heart of Manhattan on a Saturday afternoon, was witnessed firsthand by hundreds of people and widely covered in the media. Coming as it did less than two years after the uprising of 20,000—a mobilization that brought to light the plight of New York's garment workers in general and those at the Triangle Shirtwaist Company in particular—the fire provoked a massive response. More than a quarter million people attended a public funeral for unidentified victims on April 5.

The day after the fire, the Women's Trade Union League (WTUL) hosted a meeting of twenty civic, religious, and labor groups at its headquarters. One concrete outcome of the meeting was the decision to immediately conduct a survey of conditions in local factories by asking garment workers themselves to report on hazards, such as locked doors and blocked exits. The WTUL went on to create a Citizens' Committee for Public Safety, comprised of twenty-five prominent New Yorkers who, together with the union and a plethora of other community organizations, kept the pressure on public officials to deliver meaningful reform. In October 1911, the New York City Board of Aldermen created the Bureau of Fire Prevention, which, for the first time, centralized responsibility for the implementation and enforcement of building codes, thus eradicating the long-standing problem of unclear and divided authority for fire safety. Over the next few years, the bureau made significant changes to the city's building code, mandating fire alarms, fire extinguishers, and fireproof exits.

The most far-reaching reforms to be implemented in the wake of the Triangle fire resulted from the work of the Factory Investigating Commission, a nine-member body that was appointed by the New York State Legislature on June 30, 2011. Alongside two reformers who would become powerful future political leaders, Robert F. Wagner Sr. and Alfred E. Smith, the commission included AFL president Samuel Gompers and Mary Drier, the president of the WTUL. The commission held a series of public hearings in New York and other cities throughout the state, hearing from 222 witnesses and examining more than 3,400 pages of testimony. Within a year, the commission submitted to the legislature a three-volume report. Eight of the recommendations made in the report were introduced into law. Among these were a series of fire prevention measures including installation of automatic sprinklers and mandatory fire drills. Following this inaugural report, the committee's mandate was renewed and expanded. It would go on to produce a total of thirteen reports. The New York State legislature adopted twenty-five of the new laws it recommended in 1913 (seven of which had been proposed and defeated the previous year), and another three during its 1914 legislative session. With a remit that extended well beyond fire safety, the commission's work resulted in changes to the content and administration of the state's labor code, and strengthened the state Department of Labor.

The Triangle fire is regarded as a catalytic event in the history of American labor. As a catastrophe that played out in plain sight in the center of the country's largest city, it shocked a public that had been sensitized to the struggles of garment workers (von Drehle 2003; Greenwald 2005). Workers' allies, like the members of the WTUL, played an important role in channeling this outrage into legislative action and institutional reform. The deficiencies of the status quo with regard to worker health and safety were already evident to many, but the Triangle fire proved to be a precipitating event that shifted the balance in favor of meaningful change. These reforms helped eliminate some of the worst workplace dangers, and increased the capacities of city and state government officials charged with ensuring compliance with building and labor codes.

However, sustaining these achievements was a constant struggle, and the resources allocated to workplace safety fluctuated in accordance with political winds and economic conditions. In the years after the fire, the Joint Sanitary Board continued to document persistent hazards, particularly in older buildings. Board members expressed concern about "the growing complacency and the false sense of security, which was assumed by the public because of the passage of the fire laws" (ILR 2011).

In the decades after the fire, workplace safety was only one, albeit a particularly important, issue confronting garment workers, who were finding it difficult to hold on to the gains secured during the five-year period of labor organizing and reforms that stretched from 1909, when the uprising of the 20,000 began, to the conclusion of the Factory Investigating Commission's work in 1914. In spite of the improvements produced by the post-Triangle reforms, the underlying cause of sweatshop conditions—the price pressures that drove competing contractors to cut production costs wherever possible—had not been addressed. In contrast to the statutory approach taken to the issue of factory inspection and workplace safety in the years after the fire, the problem of industry organization and its deleterious impact on garment workers would be addressed by a novel model of collective bargaining designed by the ILGWU.

The Struggle for Joint Liability and the Success of Jobbers' Agreements in Combating Sweatshops

Membership in the ILGWU increased its upward swing following the uprising of the 20,000; by 1913, the union had more than a quarter of a million members, making it the largest union in New York (Dubofsky 1968).[3] Yet its success in organizing workers was undermined by the flexibility of the contracting system; jobbers simply shifted their orders from unionized factories to an ever proliferating number of nonunion contractors. Aware of the intractable nature of this problem, the ILGWU argued as early as 1923 that jobbers and contractors were part of an "integrated process of production" (Quan 2008). As such, they should be jointly liable for wages and working conditions in contracting shops. The challenge confronting the union was how to institutionalize this principle of joint liability.

In 1924, with the prospect of a general strike looming, Alfred Smith (the governor of New York and former member of the Factory Investigating Commission created after the Triangle fire) tried to intervene in a heated dispute between the union and the employers. He appointed a special advisory commission to investigate conditions in the industry and make recommendations. The commission's final report acknowledged that many of the problems in the industry were rooted in the outside system of production and the competition that it generated among sewing shops. The report's authors concluded that the formal independence of the contractor and the jobber was belied by the former's reliance on the latter: "By whatever name he may call himself, the jobber controls working conditions; he controls employment, and that element of control imposes upon him the responsibility that he shall so conduct his business that proper working standards may be upheld instead of undermined" (Stein 1977, 280).

The commission's recommendations included a series of changes to the structure of contracting relations as would "tend to regularize the flow of work into sub-manufacturing shops . . . cause closer relations between jobbers and manufacturers, and stabilize working conditions in the shop" (Stein 1977, 281). However, these proposals were opposed by the jobbers "because they did not in any way want to be limited in their number of contractors or to take responsibility for them" (Tyler 1995, 162). The resulting impasse culminated in a general strike in 1926, which lasted 28 weeks, generated minimal gains for workers, and left the ILGWU with a deficit of $2 million to its treasury.

As the union limped into the 1930s, it continued to put the issue of jobber-contractor relations at the center of its proposals to the employers. During contract negotiations in 1932, the union proposed a system of contractor limitation that would bring much needed stability to the industry by requiring jobbers and manufacturers to "designate for a fixed period only as many contract shops as their volume required, distributing the volume equally among" them (Danish 1957, 72). During the specified period, designated contractors could only be dropped for cause (not because the client found a contractor willing to do the work for less). The union's proposal also called for holding jobbers responsible for wages and working conditions in their contractors' shops. "In brief, the union's demand amounted to the abolition of the auction block system" prevailing in the industry (ibid.). These demands were rejected as impractical by the employers' association representing the jobbers. By early 1933, the union was financially weak and mostly unable to stem the tide of "runaway" shops springing up in less expensive nearby locales that employers hoped would be beyond the reach of the union.

This status quo was reversed later that year by the passage of the National Industrial Recovery Act (NIRA) of 1933, a piece of New Deal legislation that introduced industry-specific "Codes of Fair Competition." Both of the codes regulating the garment business—one covering cloaks and suits, and the other covering dresses and shirts—recognized the principle of jobber liability and specified that the prices paid by jobbers should be "sufficient to enable the contractor . . . to pay the employees the wage and earnings provided for in this Code, together with an allowance for the contractor's overhead" (Schlesinger 1951, 37). A number of the same principles that the union had attempted to secure in the failed negotiations of 1926 were now contained in the codes.

Of equal importance to the content of the codes was the broader environment in which they were implemented. Organized labor's position was buttressed during the 1930s by other New Deal–era legislation, including the National Labor Relations (Wagner) Act of 1935 and the Fair Labor Standards Act of 1938. By 1934, the union's membership had reached 200,000, despite hovering at just 40,000 two years before. And although the U.S. Supreme Court ruled the NIRA unconstitutional in 1935, its short lifetime had given the ILGWU breathing room to establish itself as a formidable force. Buoyed by a political-economic context far more hospitable to organizing than the one it had faced just a few years earlier, the ILGWU grew strong enough to secure collective bargaining agreements that included some of the key provisions of the now-invalidated codes.

Thus, the New Deal marked a turning point in the ILGWU's battle against sweatshops. Within a decade, jobbers' agreements had become the linchpin of an industrial relations model described as triangular bargaining—so named because the goal was to regulate, via a set of paired contactors' and jobbers' agreements, relations between the three sides of the production triangle: the workers as represented by the union, and the jobbers and contractors, each represented by their own association.

For the unionized garment workers that were covered by them, jobbers' agreements brought major gains in the area of wages and benefits. A cover story in an August 1938 issue of *Life* magazine provides some of the flavor of these improvements: "thirty years ago the industry stank of the sweatshop and the cruelest kind of exploitation. Workers toiled 16 hours a day for $2 to $8 a week. Today, they get $15 to $35 for working 35 hours a week, only a few hours more than they once worked in two days" (*Life* 1938, 43–44). In fact, during the heyday of the jobbers' agreements, garment workers' earnings kept pace with general manufacturing wages and were the highest in the nondurable segment of that sector.[4] Achievements were perhaps even more striking in the area of benefits. As Joel Seidman (1968, 62) has emphasized, the union "used its bargaining power to achieve a comprehensive system of welfare programs, including retirement pay, severance pay, weekly supplementary benefits, and hospital, disability, and medical benefits—all of them entirely financed by employer contributions."

The jobbers' agreements secured these benefits by eliminating the ability of contractors to compete by sweating labor. Although the owners of the sewing shops were the direct employers of its members, the union directed its efforts toward the top of the supply chain, negotiating the cost of labor directly with jobbers. For example, the agreements outlined (1) jobbers' obligations for wages and working conditions in contracting shops, including minimum wages by occupational category (sewer, cutter, presser, etc.), both for "week workers" (cutters, sample makers, etc.) and "piece rate workers" (primarily, sewing machine operators); (2) a process for setting piece rates sufficient to yield the minimum wage, and a process for resolving any disputes that might arise in the negotiation of these rates; and (3) hours of work, including provisions regarding maximum permissible overtime and the compensation rules for overtime work. The agreements also covered benefits such as workers' pensions, health care, and accrued vacation, which were funded by the jobber but administered by the union. This design made benefits portable—a desirable trait in an industry with high turnover among contractors and workers;

it also ensured that workers received accrued benefits even if the contractors employing them went out of business.

The linchpin of this system was the "designated contractor" principle. Jobbers were required to designate, at the outset of an agreement, all contractors that they intended to use during the course of the (typically three-year) agreement, and to register designated contractors with an Administrative Board comprised of representatives from the union and the jobbers' associations. Only unionized contractors could be designated, and jobbers could only designate the number required by their production volume. New contractors could only be added when additional capacity was needed, and jobbers were prohibited from discharging a designated contractor for any reason other than poor quality and/or late delivery.

The designated contractor system created a virtuous cycle from the vantage point of the union. Whereas previously contractors feared that recognizing the union might be a competitive disadvantage, the jobbers' agreement model created a powerful incentive for individual contractors to accept unionization because, by doing so, contractors gained the opportunity to become a designated supplier of one or more jobbers, and consequently to gain access to steady orders at fair prices.[5]

In short, the jobbers' agreements regulated the nature of the contracting relationship in order to encourage stable business ties between jobbers and contractors and to prevent the latter from competing on labor cost. This model proved effective as long as the industry was organized on both sides; it required relatively high union density and relatively universal membership of both jobbers and contractors into employers' associations, which helped prevent free riding and ensured that all parties played by the rules. To be sure, jobbers still tried to evade union contracts in New York City and in other unionized manufacturing centers by placing orders with nonunion contractors. While this resulted in some dispersion of manufacturing, the union responded by "following the work"—that is, launching organizing drives in these locations. In this way, the ILGWU expanded its reach into new areas, including states in the mid-Atlantic, the Midwest, and even Puerto Rico.

However, over the course of the 1970s and 1980s the challenge posed by runaway shops took on unprecedented scale and scope, as new trade regimes encouraged U.S. manufacturers to open factories in Mexico and the Caribbean Basin. In addition to the challenges posed by cross-border organizing, the union was also weakened by the decline of traditional jobbers and the rise of "private label" (store-brand) lines by retailers and brands. Unlike the jobbers of old, which had belonged to the industry associations that negotiated and signed the jobbers' agreements, and thus had long-standing relations with the union, retailers and brands bypassed domestic production altogether in favor of a global sourcing model. By purchasing apparel from overseas contractors, today's jobbers avoid paying for the kinds of labor standards that the ILGWU had, to a large degree, succeeded in imposing on the domestic industry.

The growth in global sourcing had predictable consequences for garment workers in the United States. For the most part, wages and conditions held steady during the 1970s, even as import penetration of the U.S. clothing market increased. But by 1980, the real wages of garment workers began to slide, and within a decade they fell below 1965 levels. Apparel employment plummeted, and by the end of the 1990s, the ILGWU gave up on trying to negotiate jobbers' agreements with the dwindling set of firms that maintained production in New York—thus bringing to an end the system of joint liability that had regulated much of the domestic apparel industry for more than five decades.

The demise of this system does not mean that the underlying problem it was developed to address has been eradicated, however. The downward pressure on wages and working conditions caused by price competition continues; what has changed is the scope of this competition, which now plays out along far-flung global supply chains connecting modern jobbers in the United States and Europe to their suppliers in the global South. The geography is different, but the fundamental dynamics at play have changed little.

Revisiting the Roots of the Sweatshop Problem:
From New York to Bangladesh

As has been widely noted, competition in the global apparel industry intensified as a result of the phase-out of quotas on textile products and the resulting explosion of production in China and then Vietnam (Adhikari and Yamamoto 2007; Gereffi and Frederick 2010). These changes in the geography of apparel production occurred alongside changes in the organization of the apparel market in importing countries (Bonacich and Appelbaum 2000). In the United States, consolidation and growth at the retail end of the apparel supply chain over the past several decades have led to "the overwhelming domination of the market by a handful of enormous retailers" (Milberg 2008, 420).

Technological advancements and lean retailing further facilitate the expression of buyer power among major retailers (Abernathy et al. 1999). Today's contractors manage much shorter lead times because retailers, rather than stocking extra items in store inventory, prefer to use point of sale technology to continually track purchases and manage replenishment. One of the most direct impacts of the shift to shorter lead times, more styles, and more volatile orders is in the area of working hours; forced, excessive, and inadequately compensated overtime is an endemic problem in the global apparel industry (Locke 2013; Piore 1997).

Downward price pressure is also a major factor contributing to labor violations in supply chains. In our research, we found that as the real dollar price per square meter of apparel entering the United States declined by 48 percent from 1989 to 2010, there was a corresponding decline in respect for workers' rights in top apparel-exporting countries. That is, as suppliers were increasingly pressured to produce goods more quickly and at a lower price, they experienced greater pressure to violate workers' rights, including the rights to freedom of association and collective bargaining, because labor is the most significant production cost in apparel assembly, and violating these rights reduces workers' ability to increase wages and benefits (Anner et al. 2013, 8–14).

There is a growing consensus, at least among social scientists, that codes of conduct and auditing programs have failed to eliminate, or perhaps even substantially reduce, labor violations in global supply chains (Anner 2012; Esbenshade 2004; IDS 2006; Locke 2013; Seidman 2007). Yet, there is considerable debate about what can be done about this problem. In searching for strategies to clean up supply chains, some scholars emphasize the importance of managerial capacity (Locke et al. 2009), while others look to labor inspectors (Piore and Schrank 2006) or educated consumers (Hainmueller et al. 2015; Robinson et al. 2013) to make a difference. While we see a role for all of the above, our view is that because the commercial dynamics of the current global sourcing model are a primary cause of labor problems, adjustments to this model are necessary for sustained and meaningful improvements in labor compliance. In the final section of our chapter, we examine two developments in Bangladesh, which, as we noted earlier, echo (albeit faintly) developments in New York's garment district following the Triangle fire: the National Action Plan (NAP) and the Accord on Fire and Building Safety in Bangladesh. While the first of these focuses on the role of the state and public governance more broadly, the latter represents a novel system of private governance that pursues lead firm accountability via a binding, enforceable agreement with global brands.

Post–Rana Plaza Solutions in Bangladesh?

Even prior to the Rana Plaza collapse, Bangladesh was the epicenter of a global crisis in garment factory safety. Between 2005 and 2012, more than 500 workers died in a rash of fires and building collapses, stretching from the 64 fatalities caused by the collapse of the Spectrum sweater factory in April 2005 to the fire at Tazreen Fashions in November 2012 in which at least 112 people were killed. Although similar incidents are not unknown in other countries, the frequency and scale of industrial disasters in Bangladesh was unusual. Unlike many major apparel-producing countries where garment factories are generally located in large flat buildings on the outskirts of population centers, Bangladesh's apparel industry is concentrated in multistory buildings in densely populated urban areas. Similar to early twentieth-century Manhattan, where factories like Triangle Shirtwaist were likewise found in multistory tenements, the impetus to build upward stems from a relative shortage of land—a result of extraordinarily high population density in the main urban centers of Dhaka and Chittagong—and the fact that Bangladesh's low altitude and vast network of rivers make the country prone to flooding. Such buildings are more susceptible to dangerous fires and structural failure than low, flat, and/or purpose-built factories.

Throughout this period, myriad civil society groups, both in Bangladesh and in apparel-importing countries, demanded that the Bangladeshi government take action to address the situation. In light of the government's sluggish response, they also began taking such action themselves.[6] In February 2010, following a fire at the Garib & Garib sweater factory that killed twenty-one people, representatives of the International Textile, Garment, and Leatherworkers Federation (ITGLWF)—the Brussels-based international trade union federation of apparel unions, which has since merged with two other global union federations to form IndustriALL—met with Bangladeshi trade unionists to develop a set of proposals to address factory safety. Several international organizations, including the Clean Clothes Campaign (based in the Netherlands), Maquila Solidarity Network (based in Canada), and the International Labor Rights Forum and the Worker Rights Consortium (both based in the United States) further developed these recommendations into a set of "Health and Safety Action Points." Two meetings were held later in 2010, convened by the ITGLWF and Bangladeshi unions; although these were attended by a number of major brands, there was little in the way of concrete outcomes, and Bangladeshi government officials did not respond to an invitation to attend the second meeting.

Shortly after the second meeting, on December 14, 2010, a fire at That's It Sportswear resulted in the deaths of twenty-nine workers. The following April, another meeting was convened in Dhaka, but in addition to the same national and international unions and labor rights groups and global brands that had attended the previous gatherings, this time the main Bangladeshi industry association, the Bangladesh Garment Manufacturers and Exporters Association (BGMEA) and two government agencies, the Fire Safety Department and the Department of Inspection for Factories and Establishments, also sent representatives. At the meeting, participants agreed to draft a Memorandum of Understanding regarding the development of a concrete work program addressing workplace safety. Although the BGMEA and most of the international buyers did not follow through on this agreement, the same coalition of civil society groups that had developed and publicized the "Health and Safety Action Points" worked on drafting the Memorandum of Understanding, along with the ITGLWF and two U.S. brands, Gap and PVH. This memorandum was the basis for the Accord on Fire and Building Safety in Bangladesh.

On November 12, 2012, a factory fire at Tazreen Fashions in Dhaka killed at least 112 people. The scale of the disaster was sufficient to provoke a response from the government of Bangladesh; with the assistance of the International Labour Organization (ILO), it convened a tripartite commission consisting of representatives from the government (Ministry of Labour and Employment), industry (the Bangladesh Employers Federation, the Bangladesh Knitwear Manufacturers and Exporters Association, and the BGMEA), and labor (the National Coordination Committee for Worker's Education and the IndustriALL Bangladesh Council). This committee was tasked with developing a National Tripartite Plan of Action on Fire Safety, which was finalized and endorsed on March 24, 2013.

One month later, Rana Plaza, a large building housing five garment factories, collapsed. The final death of toll of 1,134 workers made it one of the most fatal industrial disasters on record. Again, the ILO sent a delegation to Bangladesh and convened a conversation about workplace safety—this time focused on structural integrity, which the earlier plan of action centered on fire hazards had not addressed. Consequently, the government revised its plan and released a final, consolidated document in July 2013 called the National Tripartite Plan of Action on Fire Safety and Structural Integrity. In the remainder of this chapter, we discuss this plan and the Bangladesh Accord in turn, before concluding with some general reflections on parallels between post-Triangle New York in the early twentieth century and post–Rana Plaza Bangladesh in the twenty-first.

National Tripartite Plan of Action on Fire Safety and Structural Integrity

Like the reforms proposed by the Factory Investigating Commission after the Triangle fire, the National Tripartite Plan of Action on Fire Safety and Structural Integrity (hereafter NAP for National Action Plan) seeks to strengthen the state's capacity to address factory safety. It pursues this goal in two main ways: via changes to the country's labor code and by reforming and strengthening Bangladesh's factory inspection regime.

First, on the labor law front: the NAP called for the government to submit, by July 15, 2013, a "reform package to Parliament . . . [which] must consider inputs of the tripartite partners and should improve protection, in law and practice, for the fundamental rights to freedom of association and collective bargaining, as well as occupational safety and health" (MoLE 2013, 5). On schedule, on July 15, 2013, the Bangladeshi Parliament adopted Bangladesh Labor Law Bill 2013, which included amendments to eighty-seven sections of the Bangladesh Labor Act (BLA) that had been passed in 2006. The amended BLA became official on July 22, 2013, when it was published in the *Bangladesh Gazette*. However, the government's failure to issue the regulations required to put the law into effect severely delayed implementation. In fact, the government did not promulgate these regulations until September 2015—more than two years after the BLA was amended.

A complete evaluation of these government reforms is beyond the scope of this chapter, but we would emphasize that while some of the proposed changes should improve garment worker health and safety, they do not go far enough. On the positive side, requirements regarding fire exits, stairs, and gangways in factories have been strengthened. The amended law also provides for additional safety training, both with regard to the use of mandatory personal safety equipment and with regard to factory fire drills, which are now required every six months in all establishments employing fifty or more workers (Rubya 2015). And it introduces strengthened reporting requirements in the event of industrial accidents or workplace injuries.[7]

Perhaps one of the most significant and closely watched provisions of the post–Rana Plaza reforms mandates the creation of health and safety committees. The 2013 amendments added a section to Article 90 of the BLA, which reads: "Where in any factory, 50 or more workers are employed, there shall be a Safety Committee formed and functioned in the manner prescribed by the Rules." This requirement could serve an important means of empowering workers to monitor and address safety issues in their workplaces, particularly if participating workers are elected by their peers and have a mandate to serve as an independent check on management. The importance of elected health and safety committees is well established in the industrial relations and occupational health and safety literatures (e.g., Weil 1991).

However, when the implementing rules were finally published in September 2015, labor groups were disappointed to learn that they do not require the direct election of workers' representatives to the Safety Committees. Instead, under the rules, in those factories without a union—the vast majority—workers representatives are appointed by factory-level "Participation Committees," which are in principle supposed to provide a forum for dialogue to address worker concerns. Unfortunately, these bodies, which include managers as well as workers, are widely regarded as ineffective in representing worker interests. This is because, although mandated by law, Participation Committees are believed to exist in many factories only on paper, and even where they do exist, the law does not provide adequate protection against the possibility of employer interference in selecting the workers who participate. Since the new regulations give the Participation Committees the right to appoint workers to the Safety Committees, the problems that plague the former are likely to be replicated in the latter. Consequently, the 2015 rules undermine a key provision of the 2013 reforms that could have provided a critical mechanism for ensuring worker safety on an ongoing basis.

The post–Rana Plaza reforms to the labor law also fall far short of securing the associational rights of workers. The 2013 amendments did eliminate a particularly problematic provision of the labor code that required that the names of all workers joining a union were shared with an employer before the union could be recognized, ostensibly so that their employment status could be confirmed. The provision was routinely exploited by managers to rid their workplaces of union supporters.

Left unchanged in the law, however, is the extremely high threshold for union formation; Bangladesh's requirement of 30 percent of workers is one of the highest in the world, and since the workforce in many of Bangladesh's largest factories exceeds 1,000 employees, it is a significant obstacle to unionization. Moreover, the amended Bangladesh Labor Law continues to exclude workers in export processing zones (EPZs), meaning that the 330,000 garment workers employed in EPZs do not have the right to unionize, bargain collectively, or strike. Overall, as the International Trade Union Confederation (ITUC) has documented, Bangladesh took no action or only minimal action in its 2013 reforms to address thirty-one different provisions of the labor law that the ILO Committee of Experts on the Application of Conventions and Recommendations reported were in violation of Conventions 87 (freedom of association) and 98 (collective bargaining) (ITUC et al. 2015).

Despite the reforms' shortcomings, in the immediate post–Rana Plaza period, the number of registered unions increased markedly, from 136 in 2012 to 323 in July 2014. Worryingly, however, this trend has not been sustained. While in 2013 and the first quarter of 2014 only thirty-two union applications were rejected, the corresponding number of rejections from the second quarter of 2014 through the second quarter of 2015 was ninety-six. This trend bears watching because it underscores how precarious the gains are with regard to workers' associational rights, especially as the "spotlight" shone on the industry in the immediate post–Rana Plaza period starts to dim.

Improvements to Bangladesh's factory inspection regime was the other main thrust of the NAP. As was also the case in Triangle-era New York, the division of responsibility among various agencies and the coexistence of multiple standards had undermined the effectiveness of inspection regimes in Bangladesh. Accordingly, the NAP calls for the "development and introduction of [a] unified fire safety checklist to be used by all relevant government agencies." It also requires that all garment-exporting factories be inspected using this common standard for fire, electrical, and structural safety.

This initial phase of inspections has been carried out by three separate programs; two of these are private-sector initiatives (the Accord on Fire and Building Safety in Bangladesh, and the Alliance for Bangladesh Worker Safety), which inspect the factories that supply member brands.[8] Any export factories that do not supply Accord or Alliance member brands fall under the jurisdiction of the third inspection regime, known as the National Initiative, which is a joint initiative of the Bangladesh government and the ILO. Especially compared with the private sector initiatives, the National Initiative got off to a slow start. By the end of June 2014, it had conducted structural assessments of only 178 out of 1,355 factories. Progress remained modest through the rest of that year but accelerated in 2015. According to the Department of Inspections of Factories and Establishments, by October 31, 2015, initial inspections of all factories falling under the National Initiative's jurisdiction at that time (1,475 establishments) had been completed. Most of these inspections were carried out by teams from the Bangladesh University of Engineering and Technology, since the inspection program exceeded the capacity of the government's modest (though growing) building inspectorate.

The NAP not only requires that garment-exporting factories are inspected for fire, electrical, and structural safety; it also requires that companies develop and implement corrective action plans to remediate identified hazards. Although factories vary, most inspections yield findings of at least some hazards, ranging from inadequate fire doors to faulty electrical wiring to missing fire exits or sprinkler systems. Depending on the nature of the problem, remediation can prove costly and difficult. In this context, it is unclear how successful the National Initiative will prove in forcing factories to remediate. Under the Accord or Alliance, progress on remediation is a condition of continuing to supply member brands, and, at least in the case of the Accord, brands are expected to ensure that their suppliers are financially capable of remediating. In contrast, the National Initiative's inspectors have no relationship with the foreign brands that place orders with the factories they inspect. Consequently, they have little leverage, in terms of either sanctions or inducements, to secure factory compliance with safety standards. In practice, the government's sanctions for noncompliance appear to be limited to rare cases where egregious hazards might warrant immediate closure by a government review panel established by the NAP.

Accord on Fire and Building Safety in Bangladesh

As noted above, in 2010, a set of labor rights groups and the ITGLWF began to negotiate a memorandum of understanding on worker safety in Bangladesh, with two U.S. brands, Gap and PVH; later, a European company, Tchibo, joined in. Negotiations of the final draft of the memorandum continued all through 2011 and into 2012. In April 2012, PVH, which also owns the Tommy Hilfiger label, became the first company to sign the memorandum that would become the Accord. Its decision to sign coincided with the airing of a sweatshop exposé by ABC News that revealed the company's link to the fatal That's It factory fire. By the time the segment was broadcast, PVH was able to soften the sting of the negative publicity by announcing that it had signed the memorandum, thus becoming the first company to make such substantial commitments to the safety of Bangladeshi workers. Tchibo became the second company to sign this proto-Accord. Despite extensive participation in the process, at the conclusion of the drafting phase, the Gap declined to sign the agreement, and because it contained a trigger clause requiring a minimum of four signatories to become operational, it was never implemented.

As the Triangle fire had 100 years before, the Rana Plaza collapse in April 2013 created a window of opportunity for meaningful change. The architects of the memorandum moved quickly to recruit new signatories. A group of mainly American companies, led by Walmart and Gap, refused to join, citing concerns that the Accord's dispute resolution mechanism, which enables the union signatories to challenge alleged brand failures to comply via binding arbitration, could expose them to unbounded legal liability. This concern was less salient for European companies, and within a month of Rana Plaza, H&M, the largest global buyer from Bangladesh, signed the Accord. H&M's decision opened the floodgates, with a raft of other major companies following suit, including Carrefour and Tesco (the second- and third-largest retailers in the world), and Inditex (the world's largest fashion retailer and owner of the Zara brand). Eventually over 200 companies from more than twenty countries, including some large American companies such as PVH and Abercrombie and Fitch, signed the Accord. Collectively, they source from factories employing more than two million workers.

Under the Accord, all factories producing for signatory companies must be inspected for electrical, structural, and fire safety; factories are responsible for remediating any hazards that are identified. Accord staff review and approve the corrective action plans for inspected factories, conduct follow-up inspections, and sign off on the remediation process when complete. Importantly, the Accord includes a provision requiring signatory brands to ensure that it is "financially feasible" for supplier factories to complete the remediation process (Accord 2013, 6). The inclusion of this provision was a core priority of unions and labor rights organizations, which have argued that price pressure on suppliers from brands and retailers, and a failure to consider the costs of compliance when setting prices for apparel goods, are key factors explaining the persistence of pervasive violations in Bangladesh and elsewhere. Brands can help ensure the financial feasibility of remediation in a number of ways:

via loans, direct purchase of equipment, or through adjustments to commercial terms of the sourcing relationship. The precise nature of the brands' obligations with regard to financing remediation continues to be discussed and debated within the Accord's steering committee, which includes representatives of both the labor and company signatories to the agreement.

The Accord met its target of conducting initial fire, electrical, and structural inspections at all factories supplying member brands by September 2014, by which time it had conducted inspections of 1,106 facilities. Moreover, this number is increasing over time because, as signatory companies add new suppliers, these factories also become subject to inspection. As of February 2016, the Accord had inspected 1,589 factories of the 1,661 factories on its current supplier list. Of these, the Accord had approved 1,416 corrective action plans for the remediation of identified hazards. The Accord also has a robust ongoing program to monitor progress and verify factory compliance with remediation plans. The number of issues found in original inspections that were either verified as having been corrected or reported as corrected with verification pending stood at 52 percent in February 2016, up from 22 percent one year earlier. In short, while at the time of writing, a massive amount of work remains to be done to bring the base of suppliers into compliance, an impressive amount of progress has been achieved.

Conclusion

We conclude by drawing a number of comparisons between post-Triangle New York and post–Rana Plaza Bangladesh. The first comparison centers on process and time. The battle against sweatshops in the garment district was a bruising and protracted affair waged by workers and their allies over the course of decades. The ILGWU began trying to negotiate jobbers' agreements in the 1920s, but they were unable to institutionalize this model until labor's position was strengthened by the New Deal. The development of the Accord was also a sustained process. Although Rana Plaza was a critical juncture affecting the fate of the Accord, so, too, was it critically important that a draft agreement already existed, thanks to a decades-long anti-sweatshop movement that succeeded in bringing global brands such as Gap, PVH, and Tchibo to the table. The pre–Rana Plaza memorandum enabled post–Rana Plaza negotiations to proceed quickly so that the participation of key signatories could be secured within the window of opportunity opened by the tragedy.

Thus, both the post-Triangle and post–Rana Plaza reforms were products of a much longer arc of history, which includes, in each context, many years of activism and organizing by workers and worker allies. The Triangle fire was a catalytic event that helped mobilize public support for reforms, and this mobilization ultimately succeeded in securing a raft of new safety rules and an enhanced regulatory apparatus for enforcing such measures. More broadly, there was a virtuous cycle between the enabling political environment for workers' rights during the 1930s and the ILGWU's ability to secure jobbers' agreements. In contrast, observers of contemporary Bangladesh have raised legitimate concerns about the willingness and ability of the government to protect garment workers, especially given the apparel industry's outsize importance in the country's political economy. While the technical and financial assistance provided by the ILO and other international sources to the government of Bangladesh after Rana Plaza can help strengthen the state's capacities in this respect, we would emphasize the importance for domestic and global allies to support workers' organizations as well, since a vibrant, independent Bangladeshi labor movement is the best and most sustainable mechanism for improving and maintaining labor standards. This is a long-term prospect, and one that will take much longer than the five-year period envisioned for the Accord to complete its inspection and remediation regime.

More specifically, the Accord itself reflects core principles of the historical jobbers' agreements. It recognizes that, just as New York's jobbers once set the terms and conditions for contractors and their workers in New York, so too do the purchasing practices and policies of today's brands have a profound influence on the thousands of suppliers that fill their orders and the millions of garment workers employed in supplier factories. The commitments that signatory brands make under the Accord are not merely general statements of intent, but as with the jobbers' agreements, contractually enforceable obligations subject to binding arbitration with labor cosignatories. Finally, the Accord's company members include many of the world's leading global brands and retailers sourcing from Bangladesh, and in this sense, like the jobbers' agreements, the Accord covers a broad portion of the industry.

This is not to say, of course, that the parallels are exact. The Accord focuses solely on health and safety, omitting any reference to working hours, wages, benefits, or other matters. By contrast, the jobbers' agreements focused on the full range of issues typically addressed through collective bargaining, though they had relatively little to say about health and safety specifically, as such matters were generally seen as a state responsibility. However, the parallels between these instruments are significant. At its core, the Accord is premised on a modified version of the designated contractor system. Just as the jobbers' agreements sought to protect standards in organized shops by prohibiting the use of nonunion contractors, the Accord circumscribes the use of suppliers by member brands by requiring that they only place orders in Bangladesh with inspected factories that are remediating labor hazards under a set of standards jointly established and monitored with labor representatives. In this sense, the Accord also seeks to put a floor under the race to the bottom in contemporary supply chains, and in so doing provides a foundation on which future efforts can build. Indeed, there is also no reason why the Accord itself and its model cannot be applied to other locales and expanded to address other labor issues.

To be sure, the Accord's full effectiveness has yet to be proven in practice. The agreement is, nonetheless, a massive step forward and the fullest embodiment yet of the jobbers' agreement model in the modern, global era. If successful, the Accord may not only finally address the worker safety crisis in Bangladesh, but also usher in a new paradigm for effectively enforcing global labor standards. We have revisited the battle against sweatshop conditions in one of the first industrial garment districts in the hopes that this history can inform the fight for workers' rights in one of today's largest centers of export-oriented apparel production and beyond.

Notes

1. Mary Leventhal's tasks included distributing among the production workers on the ninth floor of the Triangle the bundled fabric that had been cut on the eighth floor, and recording the garments they returned. She died in the Triangle fire at the age of 22.

2. The Triangle Shirtwaist Company was not among these factories, however, as its owners refused to recognize the union even after the general strike.

3. This section draws from previous research on the history and contemporary significance of jobbers' agreements, especially Anner and colleagues (2013).

4. Between 1947 and 1990, annual average garment worker earnings never fell below 146 percent of the federal minimum wage, and for many years they were more than 200 percent of the minimum.

5. In addition to the workers' earnings (which were specified in the jobbers' agreement), the price that the contractor was to be paid by the jobber included the contractor's overhead and profit. This amount was to be negotiated directly between the jobber and contractor, and subject to binding arbitration in the event of a dispute.

6. This section draws from author interviews and the Clean Clothes Campaign (2013).

7. Yet, as the ILO's Committee of Experts has pointed out, the penalties for violating this and other requirements remain low. For example, the law sets BDT 1000 (an amount equivalent to $12.86) as the maximum fine to be imposed on an employer that fails to report an accident that resulted in serious bodily injury. See http://www.ilo .org/dyn/normlex/en/f?p=1000:13100:0::NO:13100:P13100_COMMENT_ID:3175040. Accessed: July 6, 2016.

8. The Alliance for Bangladesh Worker Safety (the Alliance) is an organization whose members are primarily U.S.-based brands and retailers. Although the broad contours of the Alliance's inspection and remediation program are similar to the Accord, it differs in several important respects; the most significant of these is that unions play no role in the governance of the Alliance.

Bibliography

Abernathy, Frederick H., John T. Dunlop, Janice H. Hammond, and David Weil. 1999. *A Stitch in Time: Lean Retailing and the Transformation of Manufacturing: Lessons from the Apparel and Textile Industries.* New York: Oxford University Press.

Accord on Fire and Building Safety in Bangladesh. 2013. "Accord on Fire and Building Safety in Bangladesh," May 13. Online: http://bangladeshaccord.org/wp-content /uploads/2013/10/the_accord.pdf. Accessed: August 1, 2016.

Adhikari, Ratnakar, and Yumiko Yamamoto. 2007. "The Textile and Clothing Industry: Adjusting to the Post-Quota World." Pp. 183–234 in *Industrial Development for the 21st Century: Sustainable Development Perspectives.* New York: United Nations Development Program (UNDP).

Anner, Mark. 2012. "Corporate Social Responsibility and Freedom of Association Rights: The Precarious Quest for Legitimacy and Control in Global Supply Chains." *Politics & Society* 40(4): 604–39.

Anner, Mark, Jennifer Bair, and Jeremy Blasi. 2013. "Toward Joint Liability in Global Supply Chains: Addressing the Root Causes of Labor Violations in International Subcontracting Networks." *International Labor Law & Policy Journal* 35(1): 1–43.

Bair, Jennifer. 2012. "The Limits to Embeddedness: Triangular Bargaining and the Institutional Foundations of Organizational Networks." Institute of Behavioral Science Institutions Working Paper Series INST2012-10. Boulder, CO: University of Colorado.

Bonacich, Edna, and Richard P. Appelbaum. 2000. *Behind the Label: Inequality in the Los Angeles Apparel Industry.* Berkeley: University of California Press.

Clean Clothes Campaign (CCC). 2013. "The History Behind the Bangladesh Fire and Safety Accord," July 8. Online: http://www.cleanclothes.org/resources/background /history-bangladesh-safety-accord. Accessed: June 29, 2016.

Danish, Max. 1957. *The World of David Dubinsky*. Cleveland, OH: World Publishing.

Dubofsky, Melvyn. 1968. *When Workers Organize: New York City in the Progressive Era*. Amherst: University of Massachusetts Press.

Esbenshade, Jill. 2004. *Monitoring Sweatshops: Workers, Consumers, and the Global Apparel Industry*. Philadelphia: Temple University Press.

Gereffi, Gary, and Stacey Frederick. 2010. *The Global Apparel Value Chain: Trade and the Crisis*. Washington, DC: World Bank Development Research Group.

Greenwald, Richard. 2005. *The Triangle Fire, the Protocols of Peace, and Industrial Democracy in Progressive Era New York*. Philadelphia: Temple University Press.

Hainmueller, Jans, Michael J. Hiscox, and Sandra Sequeira. 2015. "Consumer Demand for Fair Trade: Evidence from a Multistore Field Experiment." *Review of Economics and Statistics* 97(2): 242–56.

Institute of Development Studies (IDS). 2006. *The ETI Code of Labour Practice: Do Workers Really Benefit?* Brighton, UK: Institute of Development Studies.

Industrial and Labor Relations (ILR). 2011. "Remembering the 1911 Triangle Factory Fire: Triangle Fire and ILGWU." Online resource, School of Industrial and Labor Relations (ILR), Cornell University, Ithaca, NY: http://trianglefire.ilr.cornell.edu/legacy/tfandilgwu.html. Accessed: June 20, 2016.

International Trade Union Confederation (ITUC), UNI Global Union, and Industri-ALL. 2015. "An Evaluation of the Bangladesh Sustainability Compact, March 2015 Update." Online: http://www.ituc-csi.org/IMG/pdf/ituc-ia-uni_evaulation_of_the_bangladesh_sustainability_compact_march_final.pdf. Accessed: July 2, 2016.

Levine, Louis. 1924. *The Women's Garment Workers*. New York: Arno.

Life (magazine). 1938. "A Great and Good Union Points the Way for America's Labor Unions." *Life* August 31: 43–44.

Locke, Richard. 2013. *The Promise and Limits of Private Power: Promoting Labor Standards in a Global Economy*. New York: Cambridge University Press.

Locke, Richard, Matthew Amengual, and Akshay Mangla. 2009. "Virtue out of Necessity? Compliance, Commitment, and the Improvement of Labor Conditions in Global Supply Chains." *Politics & Society* 37(3): 319–51.

Milberg, William. 2008. "Shifting Sources and Uses of Profits: Sustaining US Financialization with Global Value Chains." *Economy and Society* 37(3): 420–51.

Ministry of Labour and Employment (MoLE). 2013. "National Tripartite Plan of Action on Fire Safety and Structural Integrity in the Ready-Made Garment Sector in Bangladesh," July 25. Dhaka: Government of the People's Republic of Bangladesh.

Piore, Michael. 1997. "The Economics of Sweatshops." Pp. 135–42 in *No Sweat: Fashion, Free Trade, and the Rights of Garment Workers*, ed. by Andrew Ross. New York: Verso.

Piore, Michael J., and Andrew Schrank. 2006. "Trading Up: An Embryonic Model for Easing the Human Costs of Free Markets." *Boston Review* 31: 1–22.

Quan, Katie. 2008. "Evolving Labor Relations in the Women's Apparel Industry." Pp. 194–210 in *New Directions in the Study of Work and Employment: Revitalizing*

Industrial Relations as an Academic Enterprise, ed. by Charles J. Whalen. Northampton, MA: Edward Elgar.

Robinson, Ian, Rachel Meyer, and Howard Kimeldorf. 2013. "The Strengths of Weak Commitments: Market Contexts and Ethical Consumption." Pp. 140–63 in *Workers' Rights and Labor Compliance in Global Supply Chains: Is a Social Label the Answer?*, ed. by Jennifer Bair, Marsha Dickson and Doug Miller. New York: Routledge.

Rubya, Tamanna. 2015. "The Ready-Made Garment Industry: An Analysis of Bangladesh's Labor Law Provisions After the Savar Tragedy." *Brooklyn Journal of International Law* 40(2): 685–718.

Schlesinger, Emily. 1951. *The Outside System of Production in the Women's Garment Industry in the New York Market*. New York: International Ladies Garment Workers' Unions.

Seidman, Gay W. 2007. *Beyond the Boycott: Labor Rights, Human Rights, and Transnational Activism*. New York: Russell Sage Foundation.

Seidman, Joel. 1968. "The I.L.G.W.U. in the Dubinsky Period." *Labor History* 9: 55–68.

Stein, Leon. 1962. *The Triangle Fire*. Ithaca, NY: Cornell University Press.

———. 1977. *Out of the Sweatshop: The Struggle for Industrial Democracy*. New York: Quadrangle.

Tyler, Gus. 1995. *Look for the Union Label: A History of the International Ladies Garment Workers' Union*. Armonk, NY: M. E. Sharpe.

Von Drehle, David. 2003. *Triangle: The Fire That Changed America*. New York: Atlantic Monthly Press.

Weil, David. 1991. "Enforcing OSHA: The Role of Labor Unions." *Industrial Relations* 30(1): 20–36.

CHAPTER 2

Voluntary versus Binding Forms of Regulation in Global Production Networks: Exploring the "Paradoxes of Partnership" in the European Anti-Sweatshop Movement

Florence Palpacuer

Civil society concerns about the social conditions of workers in global production networks (GPNs) have been channeled toward private forms of regulation, which rely on the voluntary commitment of corporations to oversee compliance with labor rights in their subcontracting factories (Fransen 2011). These soft law instruments, which predominantly take the form of codes of conduct,[1] have been studied and debated in the literature on various aspects such as their processes of formation (Bartley 2005; Hughes et al. 2008; van Tulder and Kolk 2001) and their limited effectiveness (Anner 2012; Barrientos and Smith 2007; Egels-Zandén and Merk 2014). This chapter contributes to the debate by focusing on the role played by anti-sweatshop activists in the rise and diffusion of voluntary regulation schemes in GPNs. Although many codes stem from strictly private corporate initiatives, nongovernmental organizations (NGOs) have also been involved in their diffusion, either by proposing a "model code" to corporations, as did the European activist coalition against sweatshops, the Clean Clothes Campaign (CCC), or by joining multi-stakeholder initiatives (MSIs) where codes of conduct are jointly governed by firms and civil society organizations.

The issue is explored with reference to the European anti-sweatshop movement, with a particular focus on the positions taken by activists regarding the respective role that private voluntary initiatives and legally binding forms of regulation could or should play in GPNs. The issue of combining voluntary and constraining mechanisms applies to two significant aspects of anti-sweatshop activities in Europe: first, the choice to hold corporations, rather than states, accountable for respecting labor rights in GPNs, and second, the choice made by NGOs to work with rule-constrained labor unions in promoting voluntary initiatives.

While the first aspect is typical of the anti-sweatshop movement in Northern markets, including not only Western Europe but also the United States and Canada, the second is more specific to Europe on several grounds (Bair and Palpacuer 2012). For one, organized labor—rather than NGOs—played a lead role in launching the anti-sweatshop movement in the United States by actively supporting the formation of dedicated campaign organizations such as the National Labor Committee or United Students Against Sweatshops. European activism, in contrast, took off under the impetus of NGOs, especially feminist groups such as Women Working Worldwide, who involved labor unions in the formation of anti-sweatshop coalitions. Second, the contrasted characteristics of industrial relations in Europe and the United States have produced quite distinct forms of MSIs. The adversarial American context led to a strong split between the main business-oriented MSI, the Fair Labor Association (FLA), and its union-oriented counterpart, the Worker Rights Consortium (WRC). In Europe the greater institutionalization of social dialogue has allowed instead for the emergence of initiatives based on cooperation between NGOs, labor unions, and corporations, which can be observed in leading European MSIs such as the Ethical Trading Initiative (ETI) founded in 1998 in the United Kingdom and the Fair Wear Foundation established in the Netherlands in 1999.

Another specificity of the European anti-sweatshop movement lies in the strong level of cohesion achieved through horizontal coordination in the Clean Clothes Campaign (CCC), a network of national coalitions of NGOs and labor unions initiated in the Netherlands and the United Kingdom in 1989. The CCC established an international secretariat in the Netherlands and operates in 16 European countries, with approximately 200 partner organizations located in garment-producing countries. The CCC relies on partners in the global South to identify situations of labor abuse on which to launch campaigns, and collaborates with Canadian and American movements to create global campaigns or multi-stakeholder projects aimed at improving workers' conditions.

The simultaneous use of corporate confrontation *and* cooperation is another distinctive feature of the CCC, shared by the Canadian anti-sweatshop movement but contrasting with the strong American divide between the voluntary collaboration of corporations promoted by the FLA and the strategy of corporate confrontation adopted by the WRC (Bair and Palpacuer 2012). In the more cooperative European environment, the CCC has chosen to complement its campaigning activities with a search for concrete, constructive solutions, summed up in the words of one campaigner as, "You can't oppose if you don't propose" (CCC7). This approach has taken the form of a model code of conduct for corporations to apply in their subcontracting networks.

Hence, the empirical focus of this chapter will be on the CCC as embodying the anti-sweatshop movement in Europe, and on discourses and initiatives produced by NGO activists and labor union representatives on the respective roles of voluntary and binding forms of regulation in GPNs. The analysis relies on a number of CCC website documents as well as twenty-six interviews conducted in five countries between 2007 and 2012 with representatives of NGOs and labor unions acting at the European or national level (see Methodological Appendix). The first section reviews the critical literature on private regulation initiatives and identifies an emerging research agenda on the "paradox of partnership[s]" (Hertel 2010) that NGOs have developed with corporations and labor unions by contributing to the widespread diffusion of voluntary forms of regulation. The next two sections turn to the CCC and trace the formation of such paradoxes in the choice made by the CCC to adopt a market-oriented perspective based on codes of conduct, and the choice made by NGOs that initiated the CCC to work closely with rule-constrained labor unions in developing new forms of voluntary action. The fourth section assesses recent initiatives in the anti-sweatshop movement geared toward international organizations or the negotiation of regional framework agreements, in light of their capacity to address some of the limitations of private regulation schemes. The main contributions of this analysis are highlighted in the conclusion.

"Ratcheting Labor Standards" Through Voluntary Initiatives: A Contested Agenda

The rise of private regulation initiatives has generated a great deal of debate in the literature, mobilizing diverse views of the respective role that private and public actors should play, and contrasting assessments of what effects these initiatives could and did produce. This section offers an overview of the debate by opposing two paradigms—the "cooperative" paradigm and the "structural power" paradigm—that respectively emphasize the potentialities of multi-stakeholder cooperation and its failure to address issues of structural power in GPNs.[2]

The cooperative paradigm emphasizes the beneficial nature of these initiatives, nurturing "mutual learning and efforts to attain mutually desirable goals" (Seidman 2007, 41). Also referred to as "public-private partnerships" (Hertel 2010), these initiatives are conceptualized as capable of addressing both state and market failures in the context of economic globalization. In such a view, "collaborative networks" offer a pattern of coordination fostering "continuous innovation and dialogue" and holding the potential to "overcome the regulatory dilemma that markets (which follow the logic of exchange) and states (which follow the logic of command) cannot solve on their own" (Rodríguez-Garavito 2005, 208). MSIs are considered to foster an evolution from confrontation toward "collaboration" between firms and civil society organizations (Arenas et al. 2013), where NGOs facilitate the "ethical learning" of corporations (Hughes et al. 2008). Locke and colleagues (2009, 319) advocate a "commitment-oriented approach" based on "joint problem solving, information exchange, and the diffusion of best practices" to unleash the potential of private voluntary programs. Sabel and colleagues (2000) package this approach as a "ratcheting labor standards" (RLS) model that combines codes of conduct, independent monitoring, and support from international and national regulatory institutions.

Neoliberal, market-oriented values infuse this cooperative paradigm. Market incentives provide an impetus for firms to launch social responsibility initiatives and "compete to capture ethically sensitive customers by bettering their social performance" (Sabel et al. 2000, 2). Hughes and colleagues (2008, 347) proclaim that "knowledge of ethical consumption is challenging and reshaping the governance of GPNs," highlighting the rise of the ethical consumer as a "political figure" blurring the lines between market, state, and civil society. This positive stance on market incentives and voluntarism comes with implicit or explicit skepticism regarding binding forms of regulation established through the state. Seidman (2007, 41) reflects that "NGOs and private agencies are viewed as expression of 'global civil society' and vaguely assumed to be acting on more credible information, propelled by more altruistic motives . . . than more self-interested states." Others present competition as producing greater improvements than binding forms of regulation: "Unlike a fixed-rule regime, which aims to ensure that all facilities exceed minimum thresholds, RLS establishes an on-going competition in which laggards pursue leaders and leaders attempt to out-do themselves because they know that no particular performance level confers lasting ascendancy" (Sabel et al. 2000, 2). On a more neutral ground, proponents of the cooperative paradigm mention a "regulation gap" (Scherer and Palazzo 2008) between the transnational dimension of GPNs and the national scope of public regulation, to justify that private actors should act as "proxy of the state" in enforcing new forms of regulation (Ayres and Braithwaite 1992).

A central criticism of this model by the structural power paradigm lies in its lack of a mechanism to compensate for the deep inequalities embedded in GPNs so as to ensure workers have a voice in defense of their own rights (Bandy and Bickham-Mendez 2003; Esbenshade 2004; Seidman 2007). Rodríguez-Garavito (2005, 210) points out "the absence of institutional designs for including workers as fundamental actors and worker empowerment as a central goal of monitoring." Workers are treated as "passive objects of regulation" (Egels-Zandén and Merk 2014), providing little input in either the governance of private initiatives or their monitoring processes. Empirical studies observed that workers barely knew about codes of conduct at the factories where they were employed (Egels-Zandén and Merk 2014; Sum and Ngai 2005; Yu 2008). Esbenshade (2004, 200) hence considers that private monitoring "institutionalizes workers' vulnerability" by "enforcing manufacturers' accountability for workers without those workers' knowledge or consent." Such failure to enhance workers' capacity to organize and collectively bargain means that although some localized improvements in health and safety, payment of minimum wage, or working hours can be observed thanks to codes of conduct, these instruments do not systemically improve labor conditions (Armbruster-Sandoval 2005; Egels-Zandén and Merk 2014; Esbenshade 2004).

Seidman (2007) further sheds light on fundamental differences between the "human rights" model mobilized in global consumer campaigns and multi-stakeholder initiatives, and the "citizenship rights" approach historically embedded in the construction of labor laws and collective bargaining systems. Rather than fostering the active participation of workers in the elaboration of legal frameworks and collective bargaining systems, the contemporary framing of labor rights as human rights refers to "transcultural, transnational commonalities of human experience." It also entails focusing campaigns on extreme situations of labor abuse where workers tend to be portrayed as powerless victims. This shift from a legalistic to a universal conception of labor rights is reflected in the choice made by the International Labour Organization (ILO) to focus on "core labor standards" in the mid-1990s. While the ILO historically sought to persuade member states to incorporate labor rights into their legal codes and asked them to ratify the conventions drawn up by international conferences, it then turned to "constructing a global standard for labor rights that would be simple and universal rather than specific, multifaceted, or enforced through national legal institutions" (Seidman 2007, 35). Out of the four core labor standards that serve as reference for the codes of conduct of most MSIs, three display a strong "human rights" connotation by addressing immediate harm to victims through child labor, forced labor, or discrimination. Seidman (2007) further discusses how the fourth core convention, on freedom of association, addresses workers' capacity to collectively bargain through a definition that remains difficult to implement notably because obstacles or violations, such as the blacklisting of unionized employees by employers, tend to remain invisible or hard to prove.

The organizational weakness of MSIs' monitoring bodies and their lack of independence from companies paying for the audit of their supply chains have also been criticized (Esbenshade 2004; Wells 2007). More generally, the market-driven rationale of private initiatives is seen as problematic insofar as it induces corporate efforts to promote their image and legitimacy in the market rather than pursuing improvements in the social conditions of manufacturing as a goal per se (Bartley 2005; Egels-Zandén and Merk 2014). Hence, the structural power paradigm underscores the incapacity of private regimes to address the "root causes" of labor abuses embedded in the economic and political structure of GPNs (Hertel 2010). For Esbenshade (2004, 201), "the truth is that no monitoring program can guarantee the rights of millions of workers in tens of thousands of factories and hundreds of thousands of workshops and homes spread through the world." The inadequacy of private initiatives is further highlighted with regard to capital mobility and continuous competition among places and workers in GPNs, which jeopardizes any gains that workers might achieve in working conditions (Wells 2007). Armbruster-Sandoval (2005, 482) concludes his study of campaign cases in Latin America by pointing out that "the contemporary antisweatshop movement's gains will remain ephemeral until neoliberal capitalism, which thrives on capital mobility (companies could still cut and run even if all workers in the Americas were organized) and the attendant race to the bottom, is challenged and ultimately replaced."

According to this paradigm, by reproducing, rather than altering, the power structure of GPNs, private forms of regulation actually operate as "deregulatory strategies that, while serving the needs of image-sensitive transnational corporations (TNCs), are deleterious to the task of protecting workers' rights in the global economy" (Rodríguez-Garavito 2005, 227). Fung and Wright (2003, 265) relate the use of voluntary mechanisms to a "state-shrinking, deregulatory maneuver in which oppositional forces are co-opted and neutralized and the collaborative participation becomes mere window dressing." The "displacement hypothesis" (Bartley 2005), according to which private mechanisms are considered to substitute for public ones, identifies a number of causal factors, including the preference of powerful lead firms in GPNs for "marketing moral-social claims" (Sum 2010, 67) instead of submitting to legal regulation (Cutler et al. 1999) and the active participation of states themselves in promoting voluntary mechanisms. For example, the British Department for International Development (DfID) helped establish the Ethical Trading Initiative as an alliance of companies, NGOs, and trade unions that "epitomised the 'third-way' politics associated with its then new Prime Minister Tony Blair" (Hughes et al. 2007, 497). At the international level, major state-based institutions have likewise chosen to promote voluntary mechanisms such as the OECD Guidelines for Multinational Enterprises, the United Nations Guiding Principles on Business and Human Rights, and the European Commission Strategy for Corporate Social Responsibility.

However, few writers have questioned the role of NGOs in the diffusion of private forms of regulation. Seidman (2007, 40) points out the ambivalence of transnational activists by suggesting that "most proposals recognize the limits of voluntarism, but few see any viable alternative," so that many activists would make such a choice "more out of desperation than out of any conviction that consumer-based campaigns offer an easy alternative" (ibid., 44). Another line of argument rests on trade-offs between short-term and long-term goals: "for most of these groups, codes of conduct and other voluntary forms of regulation are not seen as an alternative to legislation, but as a step towards it" (Connor 2004, 64). Seidman further questions the orientation of transnational activism toward private regulation by highlighting the fundamental distinction between a locally rooted, legal conception of labor rights and a universal approach to human rights, suggesting that NGOs should "shift their efforts to strengthening the institutions of democratic citizenship" so as to work "within the logic of citizenship" rather than "the logic of global competition" (2007, 144). Others see such distinction as lying at the heart of tensions arising between NGOs and labor unions (Braun and Gearhart 2004; Vitols 2011). They depict NGOs as being driven by ideals, seeking to influence firms and seeing codes as a method to prevent violations, whereas labor unions defend the specific interests of their members, aim to actively bargain with employers, and assess codes for their potential to help empower workers through freedom of association and collective bargaining.

Hertel (2010) encapsulates these tensions and contradictions in the "paradox of partnership" formed by NGOs in new forms of advocacy on labor rights. A first paradox revolves around the consideration that states, not corporations, create and enforce labor rights, while states also routinely fail to adequately ensure such rights by lack of capacity or political will. Yet NGOs focus their efforts on pressuring companies—not states—for reforms. The second paradox pertains to the ways in which the structure of MSIs reproduces the social inequalities embedded in GPNs by primarily involving global buyers and lead NGOs from Northern markets while workers in the global South play at best a marginal role, a situation that Hertel (2010) traces to the overall weakness and decline of trade unions worldwide. These considerations offer useful insights into the role played by NGOs in promoting private regulation mechanisms, but do not offer an empirically grounded understanding of the ways in which the "paradox of partnership" has unfolded through the rise of consumer campaigns and multi-stakeholder initiatives. In the following sections, these paradoxes are further explored from the perspective of the inner tensions and debates that they have stirred within the European anti-sweatshop movement both during its phase of emergence and diffusion in the 1990s, and when the movement grew into maturity and institutionalization in the 2000s.

The Paradox of NGO Partnerships with Corporations

The European anti-sweatshop movement has gathered a variety of civil society groups including feminist, fair trade, consumer, and development organizations, as well as labor unions, contributing to a broad and diversified agenda as expressed in the Clean Clothes Campaign (CCC) mission statement: "Since 1989, the CCC has worked to help ensure that the fundamental rights of workers are respected. We educate and mobilize consumers, lobby companies and governments, and offer direct solidarity support to workers as they fight for their rights and demand better working conditions." Yet codes of conduct and MSIs have provided a central means through which the CCC demands improvements in work and employment conditions in companies' supply chains. According to the CCC's core principles: "Brand name garment companies and retailers should adopt a code of labour practice that follows the standards outlined in the CCC model code, commit to implement these standards throughout the garment production subcontracting chain, and participate in credible, transparent and participatory multi-stakeholder verification initiatives in order to develop, guide and oversee code implementation activities" (CCC n.d.).

The decision to promote a code of conduct and engage with MSIs has been an object of debate since the early development of the CCC in the 1990s. Discussions initiated in the Netherlands, where a number of options were being explored: "Should we have a fair trade label, like Max Havelaar, should we have social clauses . . . should we have what we then called a 'charter,' like brands sign a charter and then you get a foundation to inspect their adherence to the charter . . . or should it be a union label?" (CCC7). In the end, a "Fair Trade Charter" was adopted by the Dutch CCC, signaling the movement's preference for a market-oriented perspective. The charter became a reference point in broader discussions when the CCC expanded in various European countries:

> The second half of the nineties was almost automatic growth in the rest of Europe. A lot of discussion then started to take off on codes of conducts and I think in a way, because we already had this whole charter thing, in a way people were really looking for models to deal with supply chain issues . . . then we said, "Look, we should make a process to have one model code of conduct" with the global trade unions, with all our partners, so we finally released that one in '98, it took a long time to get everybody to sign on. That was a model code suggesting for a foundation to oversee the implementation of that code. That became a very strong guidance tool for all the CCC to campaign on. (CCC7)

CCC's model code was central to the campaign's strategy both to dialogue with corporations—that is, to ask for improvement in situations of labor rights violation resisted by Southern workers and activist groups—and to campaign *against* these corporations when they refused to take action. This dual pattern of cooperation and confrontation was developed under the Urgent Appeal (UA) system launched by the CCC in its early days to intervene in support of claims made by workers and activist groups in producing countries. The choice to steer changes with reference to a code of conduct can be framed more broadly as acting through the market and refusing any claim or action detrimental to market growth. Calls for boycotts or protectionism were thus explicitly dismissed in the CCC's core principles, a position that distinguishes the European movement from more radical groups in the United States: "The American movement has tended to be more aggressive, closer to calls for boycott than what we did in Europe, and I think it's still rather the case. We have a constant concern in Europe, not only to make companies act directly through our actions, but also to develop a demand. To dig deeper into the creation of a market that offers social guarantees" (CCC1).

Avoiding protectionist or trade-hampering measures has been a subject of tensions within the movement, particularly with trade unions who leaned in favor of more constraining forms of regulation. This was the case when the incorporation of a social clause in trade agreements was discussed at the World Trade Organization in the mid-1990s, evoking the possibility of applying trade sanctions to the violation of labor rights. The CCC took "a neutral stance" in the debate (Sluiter 2009, 2015), on the grounds that its partners in the global South were strongly opposed to such measures for fear of the impact on employment. More generally, a call for increased government regulation has been considered as impractical, politically unrealistic, or raising issues of legitimacy for the CCC to intervene on:

> It's very difficult to develop a good strategic vision on what you would expect governments to do in terms of legislation or public regulation and by definition on the very long term. It's very difficult. It's much more clear sometimes what others should do than what the government should do, and to have it at least translatable into campaign demands. (CCC7)

> Regulation may well work, but it has to be formulated very clearly. And is it more you want regulation here, or is it more you want to improve regulation in the country where the product is made? (CCC8)

> The role of the anti-sweatshop movement is to create the pressure on the brands. It's very difficult for us as the CCC to create pressures on local governments because they do not have any reason to be accountable to us. At national level, it needs to be national unions that take action, and we support that at the international level. We can lobby

our government, or European representatives, to lobby the Bangladeshi government. (CCC9)

By contrast, codes of conduct offered an immediate, concrete proposition
to take to corporations seeking to improve labor conditions in their supply
chains. Codes of conduct and public regulation were thus cast as complementary rather than competing:

> You support the development of MSIs because you believe that in the
> short term they could do a better job to help workers than what gov-
> ernments could do, while at the same time we would recognize that in
> the long term it has to be included more into accountability or a sort
> of framework. (CCC7)

> I don't think it's an either or. I would say if we didn't have any volun-
> tary initiatives, there wouldn't be pressure for regulation. (CCC8)

At the same time, however, activists have become aware of the limitations of
a strategy that entailed market-oriented responses from corporations, so that
consumers now expected positive messages that were easily provided by corporations and disqualified further critics from activist groups: "The fair trade
movement has been great in using the consumer power base, and give people a
sense of what their consumer power is, but now consumers feel that their only
power is in how they buy, and if there's no positive message they feel powerless,
guilty. They want to know that what they buy does not come from an exploitative model, but that's not the reality. And so it's very easy for companies to
get an ethical line and make people feel it's a real sea change when it's not that
significant. Then when you criticize this kind of initiative you just sound like
the kind of person that's constantly moaning in the corner" (CCC9).

Members of the CCC have even endorsed the "structural power" perspective on private initiatives, acknowledging that the adoption of codes of conduct
failed to alter power relations in GPNs: "Quite often the way [corporations] want
to engage is to ignore political issues and offer technical solutions, they want a
quick fix. The reality of these things is about changing power relations. . . . You
can go in a factory and make sure that the fire extinguisher is there and people
know how to get out of the factory, these kinds of things are technical, but the
fundamental problem is the workers, even if they know their rights they can't
defend them, and that's political and that doesn't change" (CCC9).

Likewise, the MSIs' weakness and lack of implementation in GPNs were acknowledged, in relation to insufficient organizational capacities and lack of independence from corporate funding: "They are so reliant on corporate funding that their whole strategy to grow is to get more corporations in, and there are not enough resources in the unions and NGOs to counterbalance the power of companies" (CCC9).

Despite variations in the operating modes of MSIs, skepticism prevailed over their ability to induce a transformation of corporate sourcing practices both in Europe and the United States:[3]

> ETI, they don't even have to do it on paper, they only do it in projects and blah blah blah. [In the] FLA, brands are supposed to execute a specific number of steps. In real life, half of them I figure don't even know what the steps are that they have to execute. Same with Fair Wear [Foundation], we're on board, I also see happening that same dynamic, Fair Wear says: "we need more members to follow our model," the companies always have an excuse, like this specific supplier only makes bathing suits, or the bathing suits market all just collapsed, you want us to commit for five years but we've only been here for one year, and bathing suits is seasonal, which is true anyway, so how can we commit for more than two seasons, because we cannot project more orders. (CCC7)

Hence, the paradox of NGOs' position toward private initiatives unfolded in a pattern where, having promoted the development of a market-based approach to labor abuses in GPNs, and having discarded market-based sanctions such as protectionism and boycotts, the CCC faced a growing recognition inside the movement of the limitations of private institutional arrangements. An activist expressed her perplexity in such terms in the late 2000s: "The CCC advocates MSIs, the watchword is to push for retailers to enter an MSI, but MSIs do not work! The codes are not applied! Work conditions do not improve! So why should we go in this direction?" (CCC2).

The Paradox of NGOs' Partnership with Labor Unions

A specific feature of the European anti-sweatshop movement is the NGOs' integration of labor unions into the national coalitions that form the organizational backbone of the CCC, and into the partnerships that the CCC developed in producing countries. For the campaign groups that launched and promoted the development of the CCC, labor unions were important partners both in Europe, where workers' organizations already had an established presence in major retail and brand firms, and in the global South, where freedom of association was seen as a major social demand to be supported in view of promoting better working conditions and labor rights: "We can't lead this kind of campaign if there's no one in the South to convey the voice of exploited workers, we can't, and labor unions have a real legitimacy to intervene, they are within corporations, they already conduct negotiations with them. We cannot lobby the top management of a company without involving the labor unions, that would be totally counterproductive" (CCC4).

An important objective for the CCC was to steer North-South connections in a global union movement where such linkages were made difficult by the national structure historically established for workers' representation: "The old structure of labor organizing cannot operate globally. It cannot deal with this regulation gap that developed when these companies started to go global and started to subcontract. That made a big regulation gap in terms of national labor law, capability, international credibility, but also mechanisms for collective bargaining, or for organizing. . . . Often unions are just totally unequipped" (CCC7).

Drawing on historical linkages that feminist, fair trade, and solidarity movements had built in Southern countries, some groups worked from the very early stages of the CCC to establish connections between labor unions in the global North and South. This practice has continued: "We do a lot of 'clearing out' kind of work, bringing various people in touch with each other, through meetings, like we got a meeting with all of our Asian partners not so long ago, just to discuss strategies in Asia, where we want to go in terms of global campaigning work, case work. It's a mix of trade unions and NGOs" (CCC7).

Conversely, European labor unions found a number of advantages in working with NGOs, such as building leverage on their outreach to consumers in Northern markets and to workers' movements in countries where a union presence was not established or labor relationships remained undeveloped:

I believe we need the CCC to work in countries where union activism is repressed and labor activists are jailed or killed, where it can provide a protective shield. This is where we really need the campaign. (UNI7)

We do not always have, from a union perspective, all the elements to explain what's going on in Southern countries and these are areas that NGOs know well. We have some knowledge because of our relationships with labor unions in the South, but there are countries where labor unions are little developed or there's an official, party-based union. So linking up with the NGOs is very important for us to better understand these realities. (UNI5)

The weakness of European unions' international outreach was accentuated by declining union membership and clothing production in Western European countries—which reduced union resources—as well as by a growing focus on national issues at the expense of the "international solidarity work":

In addition to declining trade union density in the sector and the merger of the textile unions into multi-industry unions, the other big factor that's important for understanding the European reality is that the European unions tend to focus on problems in Europe. (UNI1)

In an ideal world this would not be needed and with sufficient trade union strength we would be able to solve problems without a campaign, but in reality the unions in developed countries are weak and fragmented, and therefore I also think we need the campaign. (UNI7)

However, the distinctive features of market-oriented versus rule-based approaches have generated tensions in the ways in which NGOs and labor unions have been able to work together within the CCC. NGOs faced some rigidities and corporatism induced by the predominance of formal rules for bargaining and representing workers in unions, while unions took umbrage with the lack of legitimacy and the informality of consultation and decision making in the functioning of NGOs. Beyond the cultural gap that some activists acknowledged between "the working class organizing base" of labor unions and the "intellectual academic base" of NGOs (CCC9), and the "rather aggressive masculine style of communication" of labor unions that "does not really fit addressing female workers in supply chains" (CCC15), the institutional rules established for labor unions could thus conflict with the objectives and operational modes of NGOs in the CCC. Tensions emerged around the time lag induced by these institutional differences, which was impeding either the fast pace of action needed by NGOs during campaigns, or the bureaucratic processes established for democratic consultation within labor unions:

> In NGOs and labor unions we can see different operating modes; for instance the fact that NGOs are organized in an international network and want to be very reactive, that's less the case for labor unions, especially reactivity, there's still a big difference in the timing of action. (UNI5)

> It takes more time but it builds stronger foundations. . . . Democracy calls for this pedagogy. We can serve to warn NGOs against a certain enlightened avant-gardism that would have decision taken by technocrats that wouldn't be accepted and then would not allow making real progress because in time of action they would be resisted. It's this complementarity with NGOs that we have to look for. (UNI5)

The simultaneous centrality and difficulty of articulating these operational modes is expressed in the CCC's core principles: "Trade unions and NGOs should cooperate nationally, regionally and globally to improve conditions in the garment and sports shoe industries and facilitate worker empowerment. . . . Such cooperation should be based on mutual respect for each other's different roles and methods, open and active communication, participatory consensus building and constructive criticism" (CCC n.d.).

In Southern countries, a problematic situation typically arose when social movements emerged outside of, and competing with, an established labor union formally recognized as legitimate for representing workers' interests. Activist groups would typically support workers' claims for new forms of organizing, while the rules binding the international union federation and its European affiliates would require them to cooperate with established unions: "In cases where union rights exist and in cases where they do not, [NGOs and labor unions] will stand together. The problem is in the intermediate case where there are strong but corrupted unions, so they are a major part of the problem, but for international organizations they are the official partners, and there it's complicated, some labor unions know how to handle this a little, but it's complicated" (CCC3).

In European countries, formal rules recognizing labor unions as legitimate partners in collective bargaining could induce a situation where labor unions would aim to oversee the negotiations engaged in by the CCC, in order to mitigate potentially destabilizing effects on established bargaining positions:

> The CCC goes to see retailers, and they have the right to do so, there's no problem about it, except for the fact that when we have teams inside, they should also be there with the top management and see a little bit what's going on. . . . So it's been done, but not enough, because of wanting to go fast, and because the union people are not into it, that's true. (UNI6)

> Unions are in a very different power position in Europe and production countries. It's always a challenge for someone to upset their own privilege in order to improve the privileges of others! . . . There are cases where we try to get them involved and in the end they consider their relationship with the company to be more . . . they don't want to cause trouble to it on behalf of foreign workers, and I understand that. I've seen it happen in Italy, in Spain, in Sweden. (CCC9)

Significant losses in membership and unionization rates throughout Europe stirred such attitudes by weakening the power and legitimacy of trade unions inside corporations, even though institutional rules still preserved their formal role in collective bargaining. Such situations have been particularly problematic in countries where labor unions acted as important resource providers for the CCC. For instance, in Sweden, "the local coalition had been blocking campaigns on H&M for years, so the decision was made that other national CCCs could campaign H&M" (CCC6). Likewise in France, "[Being hosted by the union] does not mean that the French CCC is stifled, that would be too strong a word, but it puts so many levels of cautiousness to call on companies that sometimes it quite strongly immobilizes the [Clean Clothes] Campaign" (CCC1).

In other countries such as the United Kingdom, differences in the priorities and operating modes of labor unions and NGOs are being played upon in order to develop a complementarity of roles toward corporations, although low levels of joint activity also provided a way out of the tensions that arose elsewhere:

> In the UK, we found it works quite well because on some things they can do very much the active campaigning, attacking the companies a bit and we can play a slightly softer role sometimes of saying "yes but as

a coalition we want to talk to you about how we make these improvements." So occasionally we use the good cop, bad cop approach. (UNI2)

In the UK, the difficulty has been really engaging the union at all in what we do, but we've not experienced any hostility either. (CCC9)

Belgium offered a contrasting case where labor unions had a growing and significant membership base and have been active in campaigning through their members inside corporations. Although their initial involvement required some lobbying on the part of NGOs, over time the trade unions relayed campaigns by mobilizing workers and acting through the internal employees' representation mechanisms of targeted corporations. A strongly symbolic campaign enacted this form of collaboration at Carrefour following the collapse of the Spectrum factory in Bangladesh in 2005, when the union distributed postcards to employees to be sent to the firm's corporate social responsibility (CSR) manager and brought up the case to the Enterprise Committee. Distinctive features of the Belgium CCC included both a high level of workers' unionization in the country and a relative autonomy of the national CCC vis-à-vis labor unions, thanks to a diverse array of large civil society organizations providing resources to the national coalition.

The variety of national situations identified in the collaborations of NGOs and labor unions in the CCC highlights the role of strong workers' representation, both in the North and in the South, for such partnerships to operate successfully. Situations where labor unions are nonexistent, or benefit from institutional rights to represent workers while failing to mobilize workers, either in the global North or South, raised difficulties for the CCC to build convergence among the goals and operating modes of NGOs and trade unions. Tensions in ways of working together arose when the CCC intervened on behalf of workers under the MSI model, which raised issues of legitimacy of the CCC in the absence of a mandate for doing so, or when such a mandate was used by labor unions to defend entrenched interests rather than those of a broader workers' base.

Hence, this paradox could be phrased in terms of NGOs partnering with labor unions in order to promote workers' defense of their own rights, while facing difficulties inherent in the very weakness of workers' unionization in GPNs. The issue similarly affected labor unions' capacity to promote changes through MSIs, as reflected by a labor union representative: "If we had a membership here, the balance of power in ETI would be very different" (UNI2).

Overcoming the Paradoxes of Partnership

Recent transformations in the scope and nature of CCC's activities can be seen as attempts to overcome the paradoxes induced by the partnerships it established during the campaign's first phase of development from the late 1980s to the early 2000s. They include promoting the adoption of broader regulatory frameworks by intergovernmental organizations, and rescaling campaigns from a case-based focus toward regional demands and legally binding framework agreements (see Bair and colleagues this volume).

The first set of initiatives aimed at reaching beyond MSIs by targeting international organizations in view of producing an institutional framework for buyers' responsibility and workers' representation in GPNs. As private initiatives grew in importance and became endorsed by a number of international organizations, the CCC engaged in lobbying for international norms to acquire greater leverage through voluntary *and* legally binding instruments. Some activists situated this strategy as an intermediate option between market-driven codes of conduct and government regulation: "The Urgent Appeal system highlights extreme situations through denunciation, and allows showing that solutions are at times possible. But it's not systemic. So each time we come back to 'we have to move on to the systemic.' And the systemic is not necessarily today right away into regulation because that takes time, it's not about pure codes of conduct either, it's certainly somewhere in between. And that's where all the work on international norms is, the international work of the CCC" (CCC4).

The CCC reacted to the strictly voluntary approach to CSR adopted by the European Commission in the early 2000s by emphasizing the need to "re-establish government influence in the domain of labor conditions and social policy" (CCC 2001) in order to compensate for the deregulatory effects of the rise of GPNs. Here the CCC adopted a cautious stance on MSIs, stating that "they have the potential to improve the implementation, monitoring and verification of codes. However, we also clearly recognise the limitations of these initiatives." Hence the CCC called for "an international legal framework . . . to make sure that companies respect labour standards throughout their supply chain." Specific demands included mandatory reporting on supply chains, the penalization of giving false information to consumers, an extraterritorial application of ILO conventions for both governments and individual companies, and adaptation of national laws by EU member states so that national courts can apply international norms in transnational litigation. No gains were obtained from the commission on such issues, bringing support to the movement's view that progress was "mostly slow and unfruitful" on the front of strengthening "hard law" on labor rights (Sluiter 2009, 225).

A decade later, the international secretariat of the CCC has contributed to the development of the United Nations guideline framework "Protect, Respect, and Remedy." Released in 2011 out of a 2008 report prepared by UN Special Representative John Ruggie, the Framework formalizes (1) states' obligations to respect, protect, and fulfill human rights and fundamental freedoms, (2) the role of business enterprises to comply with applicable laws and to respect human rights, and (3) the need for rights and obligations to be matched to appropriate and effective remedies when breached (United Nations 2011). The CCC insisted on the integration of a grievance mechanism under the "Remedy" principle, and on the extended responsibility of buyers for labor rights in their supply chains, incorporated under the "Respect" principle. Some activists saw these developments as offering new leverage for lobbying for binding regulation at the national level: "I think it's a very good work because it allows us at national level, if there's a work done in terms of regulation, and that is saying a lot of the Ruggie Framework, but it offers a new scale to push for social responsibility beyond the inner workings of the corporation" (CCC1).

This has been the case in France, where Socialist and Ecologist groups have submitted a law proposal to the General Assembly in 2013, backed with important efforts from the French CCC, to establish the "due diligence" of headquarters and buyers on human rights within their supply chains. Following pressures from business groups and the Ministry of Finance, however, the project has been progressively emptied of legal constraints for corporations (Héraud 2015; Petitjean 2014). Likewise, no specific mechanism has been established to ensure the effective implementation of the UN Principles at the international level, generating some skepticism in the CCC as to whether such a tool actually departs in significant ways from MSIs and their codes of conduct: "At the last CCC meeting we spent a whole day discussing about the UN Ruggie Framework, which is a sort of overarching code, about 'can we make use of this at all?' There is a growing skepticism about what can be achieved through codes, and the gap between reality and what's on paper. Spending time on codes of conduct is not necessarily the most relevant" (CCC5).

Labor union representatives expressed their own concerns about the risk that a grievance mechanism would substitute for promoting the organizing capacities of workers on the ground. They emphasized the need for workers to defend their own rights and participate in defining their employment conditions through collective bargaining, an approach that the International Textile, Garment, and Leather Workers' Federation (ITGLWF) had been promoting under the concept of a Mature Industrial Relation System in GPNs (Miller et al. 2011). Hence, while giving a greater role to governmental institutions and greater legitimacy to the principle of workers' rights in GPNs, recent developments in the form of laws and guidelines that lack enforceable mechanisms remain subject to some of the same limitations associated with MSIs and codes of conduct.

Similar nuances were noticeable in the positions of the CCC and global unions at the annual International Labour Conference (ILC) held by the member states of the International Labour Organization in June 2016. While the CCC had remained unsuccessful in its early attempts at lobbying for the emergence of an institutional mechanism to back up MSIs under the auspices of the ILO, the issue of "decent work in global supply chains" was given prominence in the general discussion of the 205th ILC in 2016 in the aftermath of the Rana Plaza collapse. Member states gave a mandate to the ILO to "lead the global call for action to bridge governance gaps in sectoral, national, regional or international supply chains" (ILO 2016), a call that the International Trade Union Federation hoped would be conducive to the adoption of a legal standard (ITUC 2016), while the CCC focused on promoting the adoption of an effective remedy mechanism.

For the first time, the CCC participated in the ILC through a delegation of trade unionists and labor activists to promote adoption of an institutional framework for "effective remedy after and prevention of disasters in global supply chains." The CCC spokesperson stated during a plenary speech: "We knock on the door of the ILO to become involved in overcoming the weaknesses of non-binding initiatives and to enhance collaboration and transparency among the industry partners" (CCC 2016). In another line of action, the CCC has shifted toward broader regional campaigns in order to promote institutional capacity building in particular producing regions. The Asian Floor Wage Campaign launched in 2008 embodied such a reorientation by targeting the actual sourcing practices of buyers rather than their CSR commitments. A distinctive feature of the campaign was the mobilization of a network of more than thirty trade unions and NGOs in fourteen Asian countries. Practical steps included a focus on first-tier suppliers and an operating device offered to calculate a living wage. Although the local embeddedness of this campaign met some of the core expectations of Northern trade unions, the initiative raised some resistance to the legitimacy of the CCC and the risks involved in intervening on such a topic:

> We still did not convince the unions. They have a problem with wages being dictated from the North, they find it something like neo-colonial. Their general position is that there is a problem of principle in the fact that a Danish company should dictate conditions in Bangladesh through its sourcing contract. The local unions should be entitled to negotiate. (CCC5)

> In a way the living wage discussion gets us in a situation where we in the long run risk establishing a global situation of living wage, and so wages in developed countries would have to decline. (UNI7)

The shift in CCC activities further occurred through major sporting events that the CCC started organizing for the 1998 World Soccer Championships in France before involving global unions and Oxfam in the Play Fair Campaign for the 2004 Olympic Games in Athens (Merk 2007). Play Fair demanded that a sectoral framework agreement be signed between the World Federation of the Sporting Goods Industry (WFSGI) and the International Textile, Garment and Leather Workers' Federation (ITGLWF), a demand that the WFSGI declined to satisfy on the grounds that it had no such bargaining authority (Miller 2005). This initiative produced an offspring in the form of the 2011 Indonesia Protocol on Freedom of Association, initially signed by five Indonesian textile, clothing, and footwear unions, four supplier factories, and six sportswear brands including Adidas, Nike, and Puma (Jacobsson 2013). A local union representative emphasized the capacity-building impact of the initiative: "This protocol is important because our law does not cover technical implementation of freedom of association. It also ensures brands take responsibility to ensure respect for union rights" (CCC n.d.). The protocol offered concrete steps to guarantee freedom of association at factory level, including the establishment of local and national committees made of representatives of trade unions, NGOs, suppliers, and buyers. A clause stated that disputes not resolved by these committees could be taken to court, although as emphasized in an NGO assessment report: "it is doubtful whether punishment of offences relating to points in the Freedom of Association Protocol that are outside current legislation would be considered legally binding in a court of law" (Jacobsson 2013, 12).

By far the largest-scale initiative in this geographically focused approach has been the Accord on Fire and Building Safety in Bangladesh (the Accord), which came about in the aftermath of the collapse of Rana Plaza. The formation of the Accord built on preliminary guidelines established by Industri-ALL[4] and Bangladeshi unions after a series of factory fires occurred in the Bangladeshi garment industry in the 2000s. On the basis of these guidelines, the CCC and major North American campaign groups (WRC, Maquila Solidarity Network, and the International Labor Rights Forum) elaborated to propose several "health and safety action points for buyers" in 2010 (CCC and Maquila Solidarity Network 2013). As a result of intense campaigning efforts, the Accord was signed by more than 200 clothing corporations from twenty countries in Europe, North America, Asia, and Australia, two global trade unions—IndustriALL and UNI Global Union—and eight Bangladeshi unions (Accord 2013). The NGOs held an observer role, and the ILO served as chair of a Steering Committee established with the equal participation of (European) companies and labor unions to oversee safety training and inspection programs under the Accord. Practical aspects included specific terms by which signatory buyers would guarantee contract price stability for suppliers who got involved in the program. The Accord conveys contractually enforceable obligations subject to binding arbitration that may be enforced in a court of law of the home country of the signatory party against whom enforcement is sought. The symbolic gains achieved through this Accord in the promotion of labor rights are thus unprecedented both in scope and in magnitude.

As of June 2016, more than 1,600 factory inspections were recorded under the Accord, but a majority of "corrective action plans" for remediation were lagging behind schedule. The next phase would involve establishing "credible labour-management occupational safety and health committees at the factory level" (ibid.) to enhance workers' capacity to exercise bargaining power over their own work and employment conditions. A detailed analysis of the local implementation of the Accord further points to the lack of inclusiveness of unaffiliated Bangladeshi unions in its formulation, and a restrictive technicist focus on safety measures and corrective tasks, which failed to address deeply rooted patterns of worker abuse and very low rates of worker unionization in the local industry (Ashraf this volume).

The actual leverage that such agreements may produce for workers, thus, remains problematic in a context of global economic and political relations of force where the lead firms of GPNs retain a prominent position, and counter powers are not grounded in a strong representation of local workers.

Nevertheless, these evolutions indicate that a new form of integration between voluntary and binding instruments has been promoted by NGOs in the regulation of GPNs, as an attempt to overcome some of the core limitations of voluntary initiatives launched with corporations and labor unions.

Conclusion

By choosing to target corporations rather than states and seeking to address political issues through the market rather than state rules, the transnational advocacy networks reacting to the rise of GPNs have significantly departed from more traditional forms of social contest (Della Porta and Tarrow 2004; Keck and Sikkink 1998; King and Pearce 2010). These initiatives had the innovative capacity to respond to the changing features of production systems by targeting the new sources of economic power lying in market access and brand building, a power that lead firms increasingly exercise through transnational non-equity-based networks rather than nationally bounded direct employment relationships on which the state and collective bargaining systems could exercise countervailing power.

However, by challenging lead firms to perform the role of ensuring respect for workers' rights in GPNs, activists have vested economic institutions with a political responsibility historically assumed by the state, a role that corporations have endorsed by claiming to exercise "corporate citizenship" through private voluntary initiatives in GPNs (Matten et al. 2003; Scherer and Palazzo 2008). As a result, the market-based approach adopted by activists on the sweatshop issue has had the paradoxical effect of increasing the symbolic power of global lead firms as regulatory institutions that nevertheless remain devoid of democratically controlled mechanisms both in decision making and in accounting for the social outcome of their activities. In addition—and in contrast to historical forms of workers' movements that held power over firms' manufacturing resources by resorting to strikes to ensure collective bargaining and the development of workers' rights—the new forms of resistance examined in this chapter have relinquished power over market resources because of a refusal to intervene in ways that potentially could be harmful to international trade. Such a hands-off approach has made it all the more easy for corporations to respond to activist demands by developing market-oriented CSR tools and practices that are increasingly blurring the messages of activists in consumer markets.

Lobbying intergovernmental institutions for legally binding instruments has offered one way out of such a paradox, yet state actors themselves have often engaged in promoting private regulation, as illustrated by the choices made by the European Commission regarding CSR and, to a lesser extent, by the United Nations' endorsement of the Ruggie Framework. A trade-off could thus be identified for the European anti-sweatshop movement between, on the one hand, retaining a capacity to engage with a broad audience including consumers, global buyers, intergovernmental institutions, and NGO partners in the global South while limiting the stakes to trade-friendly demands, and on the other hand, targeting the "root causes" of labor abuses by challenging the global mobility of investment and trade activities, at the risk of becoming marginalized as a contributor to new schemes of regulation in GPNs. Such a trade-off can be illustrated by comparing the approaches chosen by the Clean Clothes Campaign to those taken in the United States by the Worker Rights Consortium (WRC): a proposition for global buyers to commit to a stable base of suppliers under the so-called Designated Supplier Program (DSP), so as to lessen the competitive pressures exercised on manufacturing activities in GPNs. So far the DSP has remained confined to a relatively small group of buyers formed of universities that adhere to the WRC under the pressure of students, and failed to gain a broader influence in corporate spheres (WRC n.d.).

Returning to the paradoxes of NGOs' partnerships highlighted by Hertel (2010), it could be said that, first, the paradox of addressing corporations rather than states to promote workers' rights has produced yet another form of paradox by increasing the very power of corporations that the campaigns aimed to denounce and circumscribe, vesting lead firms with a new form of political authority based on private regulation schemes in GPNs. Second, while the paradox of NGOs working with corporations rather than labor unions to improve workers' conditions does not apply to the Clean Clothes Campaign—where NGOs and labor unions collaborate both in national CCC coalitions and at the international level—the difficulties of combining global NGO-led campaigns with locally rooted, rule-based labor union approaches have been highlighted in the ways in which the formally established and territorially circumscribed representation of workers endorsed by labor unions could conflict with the global voluntary campaigns run by NGOs. Yet regional framework agreements, such as the Bangladesh Accord, that have a legally binding quality while bringing together a diverse array of global and local actors embody an innovative form of institutional transformation in GPNs. Together with the spillover into national laws—even if slow and limited—of global principles endorsed by intergovernmental organizations such as the United Nations or the International Labour Organization, they generate hybrid forms of regulation combining voluntary and binding instruments as well as private and state actors. Whether these initiatives will contribute to giving voice and leverage to production workers so as to alter the structure of economic and political power in GPNs remains an open question.

Methodological Appendix

This chapter draws on interviews completed with twenty-two people over a six-year period in five European countries in the context of various collaborative research projects addressing the rise and dynamics of the anti-sweatshop movement (Bair and Palpacuer 2012; Palpacuer 2008; Vercher 2010). Eighteen interviews were conducted face-to-face, and the remaining eight were done via Skype or phone. All interviews were taped and transcribed. Interviewers included Jennifer Bair, who granted courtesy for the use of one interview undertaken at a global labor union federation in Brussels; Corinne Vercher, who granted courtesy for the use of five interviews conducted with labor union and NGO representatives in France; and Lotte Thomsen, who jointly conducted with the author seven interviews in Denmark and the United Kingdom. The author conducted the remaining half of the interviews alone and is solely responsible for the views and analysis developed in this publication. A particular difficulty encountered in data analysis lay in the exploration of pre-collected data with a research question that was not explicitly addressed in many interviews, even though the central theme of articulating voluntary and binding forms of regulation was present under various aspects discussed in this chapter—for example, avoidance of boycotts, or rules constraining unions'

Table 1. Number of interviews by country and organization type, 2007–2012

	NGO	Labor Union	Total
France	4	2	6
United Kingdom	4	3	7
Netherlands	6	–	6
Denmark	2	1	3
Belgium	2	2	4
TOTAL	18	8	26

operation. This difficulty was attenuated by using the software Maxqdar to code data in an emergent yet systematic way so as to facilitate analytical comparisons across interviews and the elaboration of core ideas. Triangulation was achieved across interviews, CCC statements, as well as previous publications on the movement (Egels-Zandén and Hyllman 2006; Merk 2007; Sluiter 2009).

Notes

1. Codes of conduct typically include a list of labor standards (regarding child labor, forced labor, discrimination, health and safety, etc.) that large buyers commit to follow in their global production chains, and that are verified through private monitoring or "social audit" mechanisms (Wells 2007).

2. This stylized representation of the debate into two "camps" necessarily simplifies the often more nuanced, and at times ambivalent, positions adopted by writers on this topic.

3. The United Kingdom's ETI relies on voluntary initiatives of corporate members to improve supply chain practices, offering social dialogue and training as incentives for doing so, while the American FLA demands an explicit commitment of corporate members to control and improve social conditions in their supply chain and an agreement that supply chains can be audited by the FLA at any time. Involving smaller firms in niche markets, the Dutch FWF has developed a mix of the two approaches, combining the auditing approach of the FLA with learning projects.

4. IndustriALL was formed by the merger of ITGLWF with two other sectoral union federations in 2012.

Bibliography

Accord on Fire and Building Safety in Bangladesh. 2013. "Accord on Fire and Building Safety in Bangladesh," May 13. Online: http://bangladeshaccord.org/wp-content/uploads/2013/10/the_accord.pdf. Accessed: March 16, 2015.

Anner, Mark. 2012. "Corporate Social Responsibility and Freedom of Association Rights: The Precarious Quest for Legitimacy and Control in Global Supply Chains." *Politics & Society* 40(4): 609–44.

Arenas, Daniel, Pablo Sánchez, and Matthew Murphy. 2013. *Different Paths to Collaboration Between Businesses and Civil Society and the Role of Third Parties* (SSRN Scholarly Paper No. ID 2319370). Rochester, NY: Social Science Research Network.

Armbruster-Sandoval, Ralph. 2005. "Workers of the World Unite? The Contemporary Anti-Sweatshop Movement and the Struggle for Social Justice in the Americas." *Work and Occupations* 32(4): 464–85.

Ayres, Ian, and John Braithwaite. 1992. *Responsive Regulation: Transcending the Deregulation Debate*. Oxford: Oxford University Press.

Bair, Jennifer, and Florence Palpacuer. 2012. "From Varieties of Capitalism to Varieties of Activism: The Antisweatshop Movement in Comparative Perspective." *Social Problems* 59(4): 522–43.

Bandy, Joe, and Jennifer Bickham-Mendez. 2003. "A Place of Their Own? Women Organizers in the Maquilas of Nicaragua and Mexico." *Mobilization: An International Journal* 8(2): 173–88.

Barrientos, Stephanie, and Sally Smith. 2007. "Do Workers Benefit from Ethical Trade? Assessing Codes of Labour Practice in Global Production Systems." *Third World Quarterly* 28(4): 713–29.

Bartley, Tim. 2005. "Corporate Accountability and the Privatization of Labor Standards: Struggles over Codes of Conduct in the Apparel Industry." *Research in Political Sociology* 14: 211–44.

Braun, Rainer, and Judy Gearhart. 2004. "Who Should Code Your Conduct? Trade Union and NGO Differences in the Fight for Workers' Rights." *Development in Practice* 14(1–2): 183–96.

Clean Clothes Campaign (CCC). N.d. "About us." Clean Clothes Campaign Website. Online: https://cleanclothes.org/about. Accessed: March 18, 2015.

———. 2001. "Reaction from the Clean Clothes Campaign to the European Commission Green Paper." Press release, December 21. Online: https://archive.cleanclothes.org/newslist/148-reaction-from-the-clean-clothes-campaign-to-the-european-commission-green-paper.html. Accessed: March 18, 2015.

———. 2016. "Clean Clothes Campaign Urges the Establishment of Institutional Frameworks for Remediation and Prevention." Press release, May 30. Online: http://www.cleanclothes.org/news/press-releases/2016/05/30/clean-clothes-campaign-urges-the-establishment-of-institutional-frameworks-for-remediation-and-prevention-1. Accessed: June 17, 2016.

Clean Clothes Campaign (CCC) and Maquila Solidarity Network. 2013. "The History Behind the Bangladesh Fire and Safety Accord." Online: http://digitalcommons.ilr.cornell.edu/cgi/viewcontent.cgi?article=2844&context=globaldocs. Accessed: June 17, 2016.

Connor, Tim. 2004. "Time to Scale Up Cooperation? Trade Unions, NGOs, and the International Anti-sweatshop Movement." *Development in Practice* 14(1–2): 61–70.

Cutler, A. Claire, Virgina Haufler, and Tony Porter (eds). 1999. *Private Authority and International Affairs*. New York: SUNY Press.

Della Porta, Donatella, and Sidney Tarrow. 2004. *Transnational Protest and Global Activism*. Lanham, MD: Rowman & Littlefield.

Egels-Zandén, Niklas, and Peter Hyllman. 2006. "Exploring the Effects of Union–NGO Relationships on Corporate Responsibility: The Case of the Swedish Clean Clothes Campaign." *Journal of Business Ethics* 64(3): 303–16.

Egels-Zandén, Niklas, and Jeroen Merk. 2014. "Private Regulation and Trade Union Rights: Why Codes of Conduct Have Limited Impact on Trade Union Rights." *Journal of Business Ethics* 123(3): 461–73.

Esbenshade, Jill. 2004. *Monitoring Sweatshops: Workers, Consumers, and the Global Apparel Industry.* Philadelphia: Temple University Press.

Fransen, Luc. 2011. *Corporate Social Responsibility and Global Labor Standards: Firms and Activists in the Making of Private Regulation.* London: Routledge.

Fung, Archon, and Erik Olin Wright. 2003. *Deepening Democracy: Institutional Innovations in Empowered Participatory Governance.* London: Verso.

Héraud, Béatrice. 2015. "Projet de loi sur le devoir de vigilance des entreprises: deuxième round." Online: http://www.novethic.fr/. Accessed: March 19, 2015.

Hertel, Shareen. 2010. "The Paradox of Partnership: Assessing New Forms of NGO Advocacy on Labor Rights." *Ethics & International Affairs* 24(2): 171–89.

Hughes, Alex, Martin Buttle, and Neil Wrigley. 2007. "Organisational Geographies of Corporate Responsibility: A UK–US Comparison of Retailer's Ethical Trading Initiatives." *Journal of Economic Geography* 7(4): 491–513.

Hughes, Alex, Neil Wrigley, and Martin Buttle. 2008. "Global Production Networks, Ethical Campaigning, and the Embeddedness of Responsible Governance." *Journal of Economic Geography* 8(3): 345–67.

International Labour Organization (ILO). 2016. "ILO Director-General: 'ILO Sets Course to Promote Decent Work in Global Supply Chains.'" Press release, June 10. Online: http://www.ilo.org/ilc/ILCSessions/105/media-centre/news/WCMS_489199/lang--en/index.htm. Accessed: June 17, 2016.

International Trade Union Confederation (ITUC). 2016. "ILO Conference Takes a Strong Stand on the Future of Work Around Global Supply Chains." *ITUC* (website). Online: http://www.ituc-csi.org/ilo-conference-takes-a-strong?lang=en. Accessed: June 17, 2016.

Jacobsson, Linda Scott. 2013. *Play Fair: A Campaign for Decent Sportswear.* Stockholm: Swedwatch.

Keck, Margaret E., and Kathryn Sikkink. 1998. *Activists Beyond Borders: Advocacy Networks in International Politics.* Ithaca, NY: Cornell University Press.

King, Brayden G., and Nicholas A. Pearce. 2010. "The Contentiousness of Markets: Politics, Social Movements, and Institutional Change in Markets." *Annual Review of Sociology* 36(1): 249–67.

Locke, Richard, Matthew Amengual, and Akshay Mangla. 2009. "Virtue out of Necessity? Compliance, Commitment, and the Improvement of Labor Conditions in Global Supply Chains." *Politics & Society* 37(3): 319–51.

Matten, Dirk, Andrew Crane, and Wendy Chapple. 2003. "Behind the Mask: Revealing the True Face of Corporate Citizenship." *Journal of Business Ethics* 45(1): 109–120.

Merk, Jeroen. 2007. "The Structural Crisis of Labour Flexibility: Strategies and Prospects for Transnational Labour Organising in the Garment and Sportswear Industry."

Presented at the Business, Social Policy and Corporate Political Influence in Developing Countries, Geneva, Switzerland.

Miller, Doug. 2005. "A Play Fair Alliance Evaluation of the WFSGI Response to the Play Fair at the Olympics Campaign." Online: http://fairolympics.org/background /PFOC-eva-WFSGI.pdf. Accessed: December 27, 2016.

Miller, Doug, Simon Turner, and Tom Grinter. 2011. *Back to the Future? A Critical Reflection on Neil Kearney's Mature Systems of Industrial Relations Perspective on the Governance of Outsourced Apparel Supply Chains*. Capturing the Gains Working Paper 2011/08. Manchester: University of Manchester.

Palpacuer, Florence. 2008. "Bringing the Social Context Back In: Governance and Wealth Distribution in Global Commodity Chains." *Economy and Society* 37(3): 393–419.

Petitjean, Olivier. 2014. "Responsabilité des Entreprises: Le Gouvernement Français Avance à Reculons." *Observatoire des Multinationales*, February 13. Online: http:// multinationales.org/. Accessed: March 19, 2015.

Rodríguez-Garavito, César A. 2005. "Global Governance and Labor Rights: Codes of Conduct and Anti-Sweatshop Struggles in Global Apparel Factories in Mexico and Guatemala." *Politics & Society* 33(2): 203–233.

Sabel, Charles, Dara O'Rourke, and Archon Fung. 2000. *Ratcheting Labor Standards: Regulation for Continuous Improvement in the Global Workplace* (SSRN Scholarly Paper No. ID 253833). Rochester, NY: Social Science Research Network.

Scherer, Andreas Georg, and Guido Palazzo. 2008. *Globalization and Corporate Social Responsibility* (SSRN Scholarly Paper No. ID 989565). Rochester, NY: Social Science Research Network.

Seidman, Gay W. 2007. *Beyond the Boycott: Labor Rights, Human Rights, and Transnational Activism*. New York: Russell Sage Foundation.

Sluiter, Liesbeth. 2009. *Clean Clothes: A Global Movement to End Sweatshops*. London: Pluto Press.

Sum, Ngai-Ling. 2010. "Wal-Martization and CSR-ization in Developing Countries." Pp. 50–76 in *Social Responsibility and Regulatory Governance: Towards Inclusive Development?*, ed. by Peter Utting and José Carlos Marques. London: Palgrave.

Sum, Ngai-Ling, and Pun Ngai. 2005. "Globalization and Paradoxes of Ethical Transnational Production: Code of Conduct in a Chinese Workplace." *Competition & Change* 9(2): 181–200.

United Nations. 2011. "UN 'Protect, Respect and Remedy: Framework and Guiding Principles.'" Business & Human Rights Resource Centre. Online: http://business -humanrights.org/en/. Accessed: March 19, 2015.

van Tulder, Rob and Ans Kolk. 2001. "Multinationality and Corporate Ethics: Codes of Conduct in the Sporting Goods Industry." *Journal of International Business Studies* 32(2): 267–83.

Vercher, Corinne. 2010. "Chaînes Globales de Valeur, Mouvement *Antisweatshops* et Responsabilité Sociale des Marques et des Enseignes de l'Habillement en France." *Revue Française de Gestion* 36(201): 177–93.

Vitols, Katrin. 2011. "Strengthening Cooperation Between NGOs and Trade Unions in the Interest of Sustainability." Pp. 185–94 in *The Sustainable Company: A New Approach to Corporate Governance*, ed. by Sigurt Vitols and Norbert Kluge. Brussels: European Trade Union Institute.

Wells, Don. 2007. "Too Weak for the Job: Corporate Codes of Conduct, Non-Governmental Organizations and the Regulation of International Labour Standards." *Global Social Policy* 71(1): 51–74.

Worker Rights Consortium. N.d. Worker Rights Consortium (website). Online: http://www.workersrights.org/dsp/. Accessed: March 18, 2015.

Yu, Xiaomin. 2008. "From Passive Beneficiary to Active Stakeholder: Workers' Participation in CSR Movement Against Labor Abuses." *Journal of Business Ethics* 87(1): 233–49.

CHAPTER 3

Sourcing Ethical Fashion for Collegiate Apparel: "School House" Lessons in Business and Ethics

Caitrin Lynch and Ingrid Hagen-Keith

The April 2013 Rana Plaza garment factory disaster brought renewed worldwide attention to the conditions under which clothes are manufactured, especially in Bangladesh, but also in other low-cost manufacturing locations. In its aftermath, we hear of varied activist- and industry-based efforts to improve and advance the oversight and monitoring of working conditions. We increasingly hear a demand for garment buyers (whose brands adorn the clothing) and retailers to be held responsible for ensuring the ethical treatment of workers in the global garment industry. Garment workers typically face low wages and hazardous working conditions that threaten their livelihoods, health, and safety. What are the successful models of buyers and retailers making a difference in the lives of workers? Between 2008 and 2013, School House LLC aimed to create a brand of ethically sourced collegiate clothing primarily for U.S. consumers. This chapter analyzes the challenges that School House faced when creating a clothing brand that would simultaneously be fashionable for the college consumers and good for workers. By analyzing the difficulties in this instance of acting as an ethical capitalist in a global marketplace, this chapter allows us to imagine a future in which the goals of companies, consumers, and workers can be more closely aligned. Ultimately, with the right lessons learned from previous attempts, we are optimistic that creative and committed entrepreneurs with a solid mission (the desired ideal) and strategy (the mechanism to pursue that ideal) can create a positive economic and social impact for multiple stakeholders in the global garments value chain, including, most importantly, for the people whose sweat goes into producing the clothes.

With the advent of the era of flexible accumulation that began in the 1970s, the manufacture of garments has become increasingly mobile, global, and characterized by a continuous search for cheaper labor and the often accompanying looser regulations on working conditions and environmental impact. Meanwhile, consumers in the global North have become increasingly accustomed to buying inexpensive clothing that they can quickly dispose of: fast-and-cheap fashion is the rule for many. The percentage of household incomes devoted to clothing purchases has been dropping for decades in the global North.[1] Today's quest to create conditions for improving the lives of millions of international garment workers is part of a larger movement for corporate social responsibility, fair trade, and fair labor—a movement that became increasingly popular in the early 2000s. We hear of efforts by corporations across the spectrum of products and services (pharmaceuticals to chocolate; housecleaning to elder care) to "do good while doing well," and corporate marketing efforts encourage consumers to use their consumer habits to positively impact others. Even the coffee that fuels our writing of this chapter boasts this feel-good connection: "Hey, we don't think it's wrong to quest after more—more caring, more connection, more doing what's right. And we especially don't think it's wrong to do it one amazing cup of coffee at a time" (Our [Real] Good Story n.d.).

In garments, ethical consumption is supposed to mean "doing good while looking good." For example, the slogan of one ethical garment brand in the United Kingdom is: "When you wear People Tree, you look good and feel good knowing your unique garment was made with respect for the people and planet" (Dietz 2014). Fashion brands today tend to be "lifestyle brands"— brands that appeal to consumers because they make a statement about the wearer's interests, opinions, and attitudes (Chernev et al. 2011; Helman and De Chernatony 1999, 53–54). In short, for many consumers, donning a lifestyle brand is an aspirational act of identity creation. Savvy marketers seek to create brand loyalty in light of this nexus between consumption and identity, and many garment brands have found ethical garments to be a necessary and attractive marketing hook since the mid-1990s' renewal in consumer concern about "clean" or "ethical" garments.[2]

The world of lifestyle-branded ethical garments raises many questions for people concerned with the health and safety of garment workers. Labor activists, factory owners, and garment buyers often do not even agree on how to define the problem, never mind identify solutions. Many consumers crave a guarantee of fair labor, but who defines what is "fair" or "ethical"? How does the term "ethical" change within different cultural, industrial, or geographic contexts? In the current trend of fast fashion and free trade, garment buyers shift manufacturing to locations with the lowest costs, and suppliers in turn are pressured to decrease all costs, labor included. How can this cycle be broken and what are the responsibilities of each stakeholder in the global supply chain? What is the balance between ethical and profitable? How do stakeholders prioritize one ethical issue over another, and how do stakeholders choose what specific strategy to take to achieve the chosen good?

With these questions as the wider context, this chapter focuses on a small entrepreneurial company's five-year, ultimately suspended, efforts to create a line of ethical clothing. School House was a U.S.-based collegiate apparel company committed to ethical garment production and founded by Rachel Weeks, a Duke University alumnus and a white North Carolinian woman whose grandparents had worked in a cotton mill in Alabama. School House first sourced garments in Sri Lanka in 2008 and then moved to the United States in 2011 to source all labor and components in North Carolina. The company ultimately went out of business in 2013. The School House story provides the opportunity to examine the obstacles faced by a small business owner who wanted to make a difference in the lives of workers in the global garment industry.[3] We use the School House story to imagine a different and better future—this in a context in which entrepreneurs now celebrate failure for the lessons it can provide. As one 2014 *New York Times* article about "failure conferences" among entrepreneurs put it, "Now failure is emerging as a badge of honor among some Silicon Valley start-ups, as entrepreneurs publicly trumpet how they have faced adversity head-on" (Martin 2014, BU1).

Some may argue that business is inherently unethical because it creates profit from the losses of others and profit is never fairly distributed. Our assumption in this chapter is that there *is* value in a company's attempts to be ethical. By examining the story of School House, we want to explore how and if one can be financially successful and ethical at the same time. Stemming from this assumption of the inherent value of ethical businesses, we argue that School House provides lessons on the possibilities of improving the lives of garment workers, and all workers, within the global value chain. In the following sections, we describe School House's mission, strategies, and storytelling techniques and the difficult environments it encountered as a

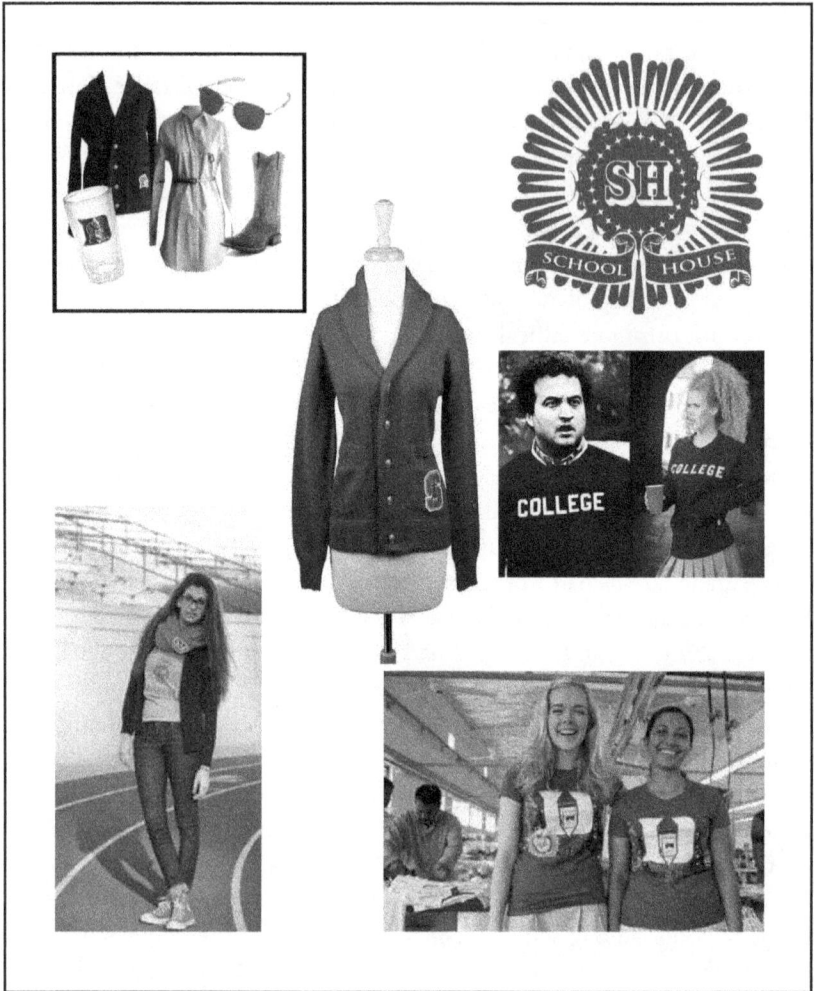

Figure 3.1 School House Product Spread. School House pushed to design fashion-forward collegiate wear. The clothes were frequently compared to Fred Perry's preppy stylings: spunky and classically American. School House sought to appeal to the student with an ethical sensitivity by establishing a personal connection to Weeks and the workers. From top left corner clockwise: shopschoolhouse.wordpress.com, seriousstartups.com, tumblr.com, and whoandwhom.com.

small business working in the collegiate garment industry both abroad and at home. We then discuss the implications of School House's strategy shift for the business's attempts to fulfill its mission of producing ethical garments.

Ethical Narrative

In this section we describe how School House presented itself to consumers, and we focus on its ethical narrative. Weeks launched School House in 2008 with clothing sourced entirely in Sri Lanka. In a 2012 Duke University interview, she described School House as a "socially responsible collegiate apparel line with a mission to bring fashion and fair wages to colleges nationwide" (Burkett 2012). At its peak, its collegiate ware was sold in more than 100 U.S. college bookstores. "I saw a real opportunity to craft a true collegiate lifestyle brand," explained Weeks in a 2012 School House promotional video (Taproot Films 2012). As one writer described the clothing line: "They have carved out a niche for clothing for women that is more stylish (not just male athletic stuff that gets what [Weeks] called the 'shrink and pink' treatment) and upscale. Not surprisingly, this has attracted clients in the Ivy League where image is not driven so much by athletics" (Zenner 2012) (see Figure 3.1).

School House endeavored to market itself as a true lifestyle brand for consumers who want to feel they could "do good while looking good." The extensive marketing material conveys a sense of zest, fun, style, and membership. During its five-year run, School House reached out to college-aged consumers with appropriate marketing methods, language, and images. Some marketing scholars argue that so-called Generation Y consumers respond best to word-of-mouth advertising (Colucci and Scarpi 2013, 4). School House shrewdly employed social media such as Facebook, Tumblr, YouTube, and Twitter. Collegiate blogs frequently mentioned and "tweeted at" the company (among other examples, see Dere and Xie 2010; Landry 2011; McCoy 2012; Mielach 2011; Schwartz 2009). Its dynamic store displays and hangtags (tags that are attached to the garments) advertised its living wages for Sri Lankan workers, and later when the company relocated production to North Carolina they emphasized "Made in America" craftsmanship.

Over a five-year period, School House blog followers could enjoy Weeks's animated posts about her initial factory contacts in Sri Lanka, the latest in geek and chic for MIT students, and the new forthcoming styles of jewelry and socks (Weeks 2012b). The blog evoked fun, fashion, enthusiasm, informality, pluckiness, and—when production shifted to the United States in 2011—patriotism.

In an early post when the company was setting up with a factory in Sri Lanka, Weeks wrote the following, creating a pun to refer to the alternative hip-hop band Jurassic 5's album called *Quality Control* and thus creating inside jokes for those who speak the right language and share the same tastes: "I'm reporting live from the Sri Sri and still trying to figure out how to get photos on my laptop since iPhoto went AWOL on me. So far: new factory is very exciting, Milan, Pradeep and the gang are holding down quality control better than J5, and the curry is even better than I remembered. xoxo R" (Weeks 2009b). And this post, entitled "Abbhaartu Nettha = NO VACANCIES" accompanied a photo of a sign in Sinhala outside a factory: "From Milan [a Sri Lankan employee] . . . The meaning of the Notice is 'Abbhaartu Nettha' which means in Sinhalese as NO VACANCIES! This is the only factory in SL that has a notice informing the public of such a situation as all factories including the multinational plants with larger work forces too have average 30-40 vacancies at any given time!" [Back to Weeks's voice]: "That's our factory, folks!" (Weeks 2010b).

When production later moved to the United States, the blog included regular "Made in America Monday" posts, featuring products made by School House or other companies that share in the patriotic manufacturing vision. Sometimes patriotism was wrapped in fun: one post featured Made in America "cozies," including American flag–motif knitwear for beer bottles and mugs made by a North Carolinian company called Freaker USA. The following post called "Baberaham Lincoln Freaker" (invoking the 1992 hit movie *Wayne's World* and its humorous reference to the U.S. president) described the product: "We just had to include the Baberaham in our School House Collection, lovingly referred to here at SH as the 'Freedom Freaker.' Say goodbye to sweaty bottles and hello to this moisture-wicking sweater for your drink! Tune in to our Twitter on Tuesday, April 9th. We will be giving away two!" (Weeks 2013).

On another Monday, this post linked to the referenced manufacturer's website: "Mitts Nitts is one of our manufacturers that allows School House to proudly be Made in America. Just a short drive from us, Mitts Nitts is one of the last textile factories located in Durham, NC. The company manufactures Military and Law Enforcement Apparel as well as School House apparel. At any visit we can watch our collegiate line being made by hard working Americans. In the picture above you can see the machine that constructs our Majorette Sweater!" (Weeks 2012c).

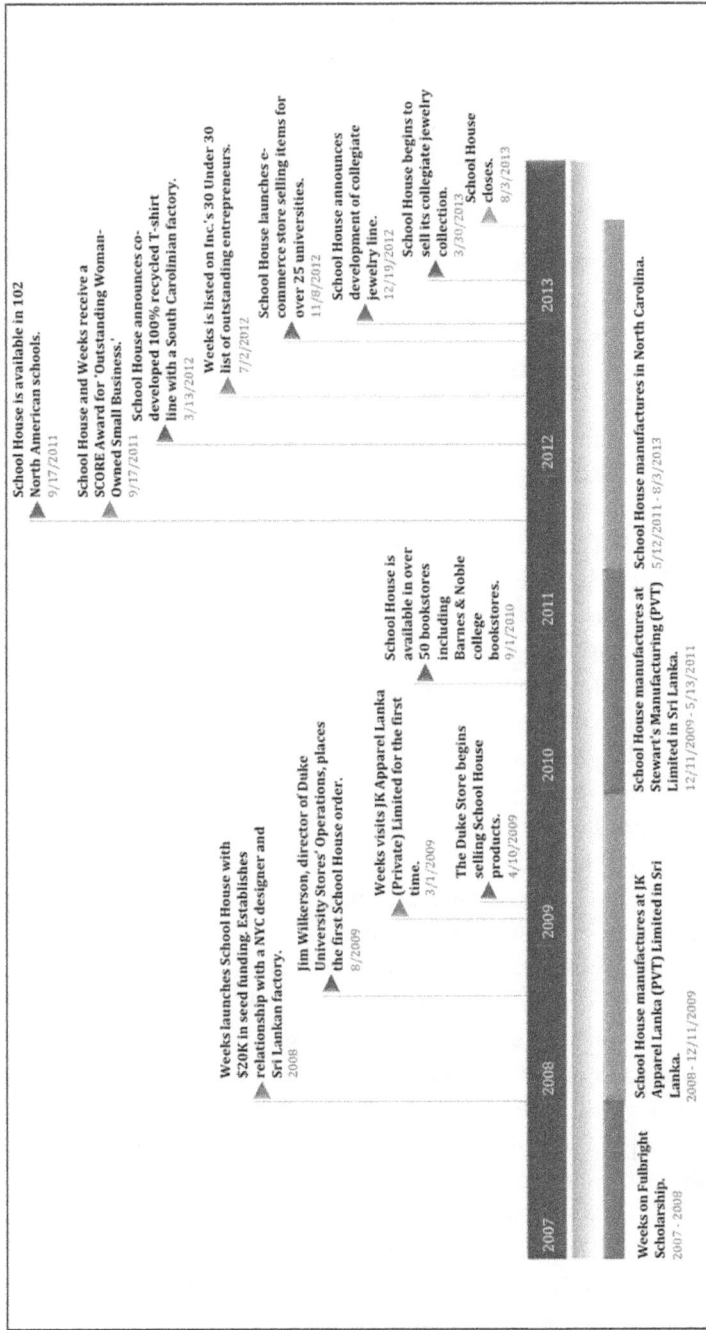

Figure 3.2 School House Timeline

Reading these posts, we can imagine School House's followers feeling membership in a community that resonates with the image they hope to craft of themselves. In all this, we can see the company's attempt at creating a lifestyle brand through creating a certain kind of value that consumers would then mobilize with their purchases.

Behind the Scenes at School House

In this section, we examine the School House strategy to achieve its ethical fashion mission. Whereas the previous section captured some of the company's brand storytelling, this section goes behind the scenes to see how the story was being achieved. In 2007, Rachel Weeks went to Sri Lanka on a Fulbright grant to study industry efforts to produce ethical garments. This led to her launching the company in 2008 with garments manufactured in Sri Lanka; in May 2011, School House moved manufacturing to North Carolina. With this shift, School House altered its focus from providing a living wage for Sri Lankan women workers, to providing business to American manufacturers and invigorating American traditions of craftsmanship. Two years later, School House was out of business (see Figure 3.2).

When studying ethical garments for an undergraduate thesis and as a Fulbright scholar, Weeks conceived of a line of collegiate clothing that could appeal to college students who were concerned both with fashion and fair trade. She decided to focus her efforts on living wages in Sri Lanka after consulting with nonprofit groups, members of labor unions, and workers at every level of garment manufacturing in Sri Lanka. All these groups told her about workers suffering from low wages. In an interview with us, Weeks explained, "They traveled [by foot] three hours to work every day because they couldn't afford the bus, they had all these medical issues—it all came back to not having enough money in their pockets. . . . And so this concept of living wage really appeared to me as a wonderful place to start." The specific monetary value of a living wage varies by country, but School House followed the definition advocated by the Apparel Industry Labour Rights Movement (ALaRM), a local advisory group focusing on labor rights in the Sri Lankan garment industry. The living wage is defined as the wages necessary to cover a worker's basic needs, which include shelter, clothing, transportation to and from work, education for dependents, and proper nutrition. According to a 2008 ALaRM report, a Sri Lankan apparel worker needed to earn Rs. 10,000–12,000 per month as living wages, three times the minimum wage at the time (Atkinson 2008, 21). Weeks clarified to us, "They really looked at what does it take to have a healthy life, to be able to feed yourself in a way that reflects a balanced diet, to travel to and from your job, to have adequate shelter. . . . So that was the baseline. It still wasn't enough, but it was triple what they were making before, which was not enough to live."

Weeks described to us that she drew up a Code of Conduct for her suppliers to sign on to, based on information from nonprofit groups (especially ALaRM), members of labor unions, and workers—and modeled on one widely used by the Worker Rights Consortium. School House's Code of Conduct included requirements for regular and recorded safety and health training; access to clean toilet facilities, potable water, and clean food storage; and sufficient lighting and ventilation. Weeks used $20,000 from personal savings as seed money to hire a designer, Colleen McCann, and create samples to present to Sri Lankan factories (Weeks 2012b). With consultation from a local garment industry expert, Upali Weerakoon, and oversight from ALaRM, she secured her first exclusive supplier: a Colombo factory called JK Apparel Lanka (PVT) Limited (Weeks 2009a, 2014a; cf. Dragovic 2010). The factory agreed to pay workers a living wage, though it did not sign School House's Code of Conduct. Weeks explained to us that she did not feel she had the leverage to insist upon both paying a living wage and adhering to the Code of Conduct, and so she settled on securing a living wage. But we are left to wonder how Weeks, representing a fledging startup, could have convinced a supplier to triple wages. We cannot be sure, but perhaps, due to labor market conditions, the factory owners were already paying close to the rate that Weeks was requesting. In 2010, just two years after School House was founded, some Colombo-area factories experienced labor shortages, which reportedly prompted the factories to pay a prevailing wage of Rs. 20,000 per month as an incentive to attract and maintain the necessary number of workers.[4]

In late 2008, the Duke University Stores director, Jim Wilkerson, a leader in the U.S. movement to demand fair labor in the college clothing market, placed the first order for School House merchandise—$110,000 in wholesale merchandise (Leipziger 2012, 3).[5] Through word-of-mouth, aggressive marketing, success in attracting national media attention, and the receipt of business awards, School House attracted investors and raised funds that allowed it to hire a few employees to develop its brand and business. In 2009, after consistently delayed delivery of orders from JK Apparel, Weeks switched to a different exclusive Sri Lankan supplier, Stewart's Manufacturing (PVT)

Limited (Weeks 2009c). But the delayed deliveries persisted and so, after two more years in Sri Lanka, Weeks, overwhelmed but still committed to School House, relocated operations to North Carolina. She explained to us the rationale behind the move, and her description, with such emotive phrases as "a 'Come to Jesus' moment," shows that this is a woman who was passionate about her mission and trying to figure out if she could implement a strategy shift without losing sight of it. As she said to us:

> I had product that was three months late and no ability to say, "Get this out or else," which you'd imagine you'd have in a buyer-producer kind of relationship. We were the customer, we had the power. But we really didn't. . . . It's really interesting, because I can go back and point, economically, to how and why it should have worked in Sri Lanka. Because it absolutely can, it absolutely can, and the bigger guys, especially, would be fully capable of doing it. The problems that arose, I think, were problems that I was not equipped to overcome alone. . . . We had this sort of "Come to Jesus" moment about what to do as a brand. . . . We were running on fumes from a cash standpoint, and that very thought was overwhelming. And the more that I thought about it, you know, North Carolina has this very rich history in textiles, and the South in apparel manufacturing as well, and I just loved the idea of being locally sourced. Living wage was definitely something that I cared about. It's something that I still care about and am passionate about, but I wasn't expecting to find factories here [in North Carolina] that were paying fifteen bucks an hour. . . . From the beginning, I always had this interest in ethical fashion . . . that was what I went to Sri Lanka to think about and research and propel, and that was really the original vision behind School House. And in Sri Lanka, that issue that really helped us demonstrate the idea of ethical fashion was living wage. . . . And here, in the U.S., it was less *living* as just *proving* that it could be done here in any way. . . . The wages that are already being paid in the U.S. are so far above anything being paid internationally that to prove that you can even do it here on minimum wage is a feat, because that's something that most people in countries around the world, and here, see as impossible.

Weeks and Chief Operating Officer Susan Williams calculated that the security of in-time delivery, savings on time and costs related to shipping and tariffs, plus the costs of in-country administrative staffing (work Weeks could do herself onsite in North Carolina) would outweigh the increased labor costs in the United States (Leipziger 2012, 1). Weeks divulged to us that she later discovered that the U.S. manufacturing focus attracted investors across the political spectrum who were interested in the lower environmental impact and the prospect of rebuilding the U.S. manufacturing sector. The company's marketing focus became the incomparable quality of "Made in America" and the importance of reinvigorating the suffering North Carolina textile and garment industry (ShopSchoolHouse 2011). With the move to North Carolina, School House advertised its ethical angle to be about generating jobs in a state that at the time had an unemployment rate of 10.3 percent, high by U.S. standards (North Carolina Employment Rate n.d.).

When School House sourced from Sri Lanka its ethical focus was on living wages; when it moved to the United States, the ethical focus shifted to "Made in America" and providing jobs in a state with high unemployment. The company did not consider paying living wages in North Carolina because of the high labor costs and the pressing need for basic employment-generation programs. The notion was that simply providing basic jobs in North Carolina—even if below a living wage—is of social and ethical value. Although the same styles of fashion-forward collegiate clothing were made in two different locations, the story School House told consumers about the ethics of their brand was radically different for the two locations. What was the ethical context for School House's production in these two settings?

Sri Lanka

In 2006, the Sri Lankan garment industry's Joint Apparel Association Forum responded to an early 2000s global push for fair trade garments by launching its "Garments Without Guilt" (GWG) program (Lopez-Acevedo and Robertson 2012; Ruwanpura 2014). GWG advertises Sri Lanka as an ethical production site and boasts the empowerment of women, development of eco-friendly apparel manufacturing, and production of quality apparel. As of June 2010, 20 percent of factories in Sri Lanka were GWG certified (Goger 2011, 17). Geographer Annelies Goger argues that "it is clear from the complex set of strengths and weaknesses of Garments Without Guilt that the process of becoming more 'ethical' is long, unstable, costly, and fraught with risks" (Goger 2011, 21). Goger suggests that some factories opt out of the certification process because it does not promise a price premium and incurs an annual audit fee from a Swiss-based third-party firm, SGS, ranging from $500 to $2000.[6] Among the program's limitations, Goger found that GWG does not address effectively the issues of freedom of association and collective bargaining, and it has not alleviated long-extant adversarial relations between the industry and unions and between unions and local NGOs. Furthermore, it is unable to guarantee that workers across all sites enjoy the same protections, and it can reinforce the patriarchal forms of control that characterize many Sri Lankan factories.

Though GWG has produced some positive change, Sri Lankan garment workers still do not universally earn living wages or enjoy freedom of association or access to collective bargaining. Sri Lankan garment workers are mainly young unmarried women whose income is a critical means of family support (Hewamanne 2010; Lynch 2007). These young women are rarely paid a living wage, often because employers erroneously assume that their wages are merely pocket money or supplemental to family support. These wages, already low, are also irregularly earned across a work year, so workers cannot rely on a consistent wage. Typically, wages change according to the production season. During the low season, workers are often given paid days off but are expected to "cover" (make up) for the days off by later working overtime without the appropriate overtime pay. As a result, workers are unable to pay for adequate meals even for themselves, never mind family members whom they may be supporting. Geographer Kanchana Ruwanpura has found that Sri Lankan garment workers would only be able to achieve a living wage when overtime, plus the extra wage they can earn by achieving incentive targets, is taken into account (Ruwanpura 2012, 19; see also Hewamanne this volume).

North Carolina

Meanwhile, the labor situation in North Carolina is not much better. North Carolina, a textile and garment manufacturing giant until the early 1990s, today faces low revenue and high unemployment. Outsourcing is one source of the problem, but another is that the state's manufacturers are slow on technological innovation and struggle with marketing themselves as a good option for garment buyers (Aframian 2013). Between 1996 and 2006, the North Carolina apparel industry experienced a 70 percent decline in jobs as U.S. clothing companies outsourced orders to overseas manufacturers with lower labor costs (Duke University n.d.; Gemberling and Only 2014). Referring to South Carolina and Kentucky, anthropologist Ann Kingsolver in 2012 described how unemployment is commoditized and marketed by these southern states to potential employers because of assumptions about an isolated, low-wage, fairly captive and nonunionized labor force. Kingsolver quotes a Kentucky Chamber of Commerce pamphlet aimed at potential investors: "There are no unions in Nicholas County—they're not needed. Low cost of living allows a workforce to offer you the most reasonable manufacturing wage in the region. They're eager to make you a part of their community and anticipate the benefits accrued from mutual appreciation and service" (Kingsolver 2012, 4).

Here we see that cheap nonunionized labor is being offered as an incentive to potential employers. Kingsolver shows that in South Carolina, Foreign Trade Zone permits are provided, especially in rural areas "where the unemployed and underemployed are considered plentiful and wages are low" (Kingsolver 2012, 8). Though North Carolina and South Carolina have different economic policies and labor force compositions, similar labor-force characteristics may have accounted in part for School House's perceived benefit of moving manufacturing to the U.S. South.

Why Did School House Fail?

School House appears to have been adept at crafting a lifestyle brand that consumers could use to build their own identities. So, if it was receiving new orders, cultivating a loyal social media following, and attracting investors, why did it fail? Weeks has been generous in sharing her experiences with us, and our conversations and research suggest to us that School House's demise resulted from the company's responses to a set of highly complex production and trade environments that did not actively support ethical labor practices. These environments include being a small business in an industry dominated by larger players, working within the collegiate apparel industry, operating without a means of leverage on behalf of workers, and coming up against American consumer attitudes toward "Made in America." In this section we detail those environments; in the conclusion we argue that those specific environments contributed to School House's shift in strategy, which in turn may have led to its demise.

Small Business, Little Power

School House was a small startup in the global garment industry: a difficult context to navigate where staffing, order size, and consistency are important sources of negotiation power for buyers. Weeks alone headed School House, and the company included a shifting core team of between three and six people. During its five-year span, one person led design and another led finances and internal operations. Weeks was in charge of attracting investors, liaising and coordinating with manufacturers, and selling to educational institutions, as well as any task that was not otherwise being done. Weeks notes that she was spread too thin and that the business suffered as a result. She described to us what this looked like: "I was either raising money in order to keep the business afloat, in order to hypothetically go out selling. And then I wasn't selling when I wasn't doing that so the revenue was never where it needed to be because whenever I was raising money, I was not meeting my sales forecast. So then when I didn't meet the sales forecast I would have to go back and disappoint all of the investors I had just raised money from. And then I was out on the road selling but never selling enough to get up to profitability in the right amount of time and consistently because of the way the apparel industry works."

Ultimately, this process was not financially sustainable and took its toll on Weeks, who invested her savings and all her energy into the effort.

Weeks noted that as a small business, School House struggled to maintain a powerful voice with its suppliers and sellers. Small businesses that wish to do social good frequently suffer from weak negotiation power and leverage (Heledd Jenkins 2006, 249; Lepoutre and Heene 2006, 264–65). Because they place small orders that lack style and volume consistency, small business are often unable to be selective in choosing suppliers. School House struggled during negotiations with factories domestically and abroad. Sri Lankan factories continually bumped the company's orders in favor of orders from larger and more consistent customers, and those larger customers may have been attracted to a factory that was offering triple wages—and easy access to a hook for corporate social responsibility. In the United States, Weeks found that very few factories were willing to collaborate and innovate to meet her needs. Weeks described to us obstacles to working with some of the North Carolinian manufacturers (who were hard to find anyway, few having a Web presence, many relying on word-of-mouth):

I tell them I have a T-shirt order. And they are like, "Well, we make pillowcases." Like well, you know, "Have you ever thought of making, well you know, T-shirts because I know . . . the machines that you make a pillowcase on and they're the machines that can make T-shirts." "We make pillowcases and we do 500 in the same color." And that's it. That's what the conversation is. There's not a lot of vision at all in many factories and I think that's the key to the huge problem. Vision in terms of growing outside their product base, vision in looking at partnering with a startup which may . . . be placing a fifty-piece order with you today, but you can invest in each other's businesses, so it's an opportunity to grow. And we worked with a great factory . . . [that] made our sweaters and they are quality. They made really low minimums but a delivery date was not existent. They could not deliver on a specific date. It got to the point where I would give them a date five weeks before I needed them shipped because I knew it would take five weeks of back-and-forth begging them before they would ship.

In this story, we hear Weeks exasperatedly explain that with such small orders, and no established name, she did not have any ability to convince U.S. manufacturers to experiment and innovate, and when she did manage to place an order, she did not have the leverage to get the orders made on time.

School House was operating in the context of an unforgiving and unpredictable garment industry that presented challenges both abroad and at home. Beginning in the 1970s, the culture of fast fashion broke from the now-archaic two-season cycle to a more unpredictable and flexible set of small orders with short lead times. Originally established by Toyota, lean manufacturing (whose aim is to eliminate as much waste as possible from a supply chain) is today employed by fashion mega-powers such as Zara and Gap, which have redefined the meaning of a "season." Goger, in an analysis of the global impetus for lean restructuring in Sri Lanka, explains how lean has impacted garment buyers and manufacturers. Because customers have come to expect flexible seasons, even smaller clothing companies have begun to employ lean manufacturing. Such a shift has created an extremely competitive atmosphere in which buyers emphasize production costs, reliability, and quality, as well as faster lead times, social and environmental compliance, design capability, and inventory management. All these expectations in turn prompt factories to prioritize fast production of moderate orders by established companies (Goger 2013, 2636–37; cf. Memic and Minhas 2011, 12; Ruwanpura 2014, 12). Weeks shared with us that as School House was frequently unable to meet sales projections, it placed smaller orders, and then the suppliers routinely bumped its orders in favor of established companies with larger orders.

Collegiate Ethical Fashion

Weeks admitted to us that when she chose to create a line of collegiate apparel, she had not anticipated the special challenges this niche poses. Any brand working in collegiate apparel, where the college or university name appears on the clothing, must collaborate with the institution to ensure image fit, and with licensing bodies (such as the Collegiate Licensing Company and Fermata College) to ensure authenticity.[7] Licensing can become quite expensive, costing between $500 and $1,000 to gain and maintain licensing standards for only one school (Vagnomi 2010, 78–80). Restrictions on public university spending may have been another source of pressure for School House. According to the Duke University Stores director Jim Wilkerson, "most public universities are required by policy or law to accept the lowest price" (Wilkerson 2009, 5). While private universities are not legally required to accept the lowest prices, there are still pressures to select garments that may provide the greatest profit margin to the institution. Within the context of collegiate ware, School House had limited ability to increase their garment's unit prices to create a sustainable profit. So, despite its unique look and expression, School House faced stark competition with larger and more established collegiate-ware brands that were able to sell their garments at a lower price than School House. One competitor was Knights Apparel, a leader in collegiate clothing, which in response to the activism of the Worker Rights Consortium created a living wage factory called Alta Gracia in the Dominican Republic. This factory pays workers "nearly 340% higher than the factory's required minimum wage" (Kline 2010, 18).[8]

Additionally some consumers may have preferred to buy from companies like Knights Apparel that are Fair Trade Certified—which School House was not.[9] A Fair Trade product must follow a set of standards regarding price, premiums, advanced payment, long-term contracts, democratic cooperatives, and sustainable environmental practices (Castaldo et al. 2009, 6). In a study of consumer perception of socially oriented companies, marketing professor Sandro Castaldo and co-authors have argued that certified Fair

Trade products foster consumer trust for two reasons. Consumers believe that Fair Trade retailers wish to maintain their reputation and therefore would be unlikely to "renege on promises" (Castaldo et al. 2009, 6). And, consumers believe that Fair Trade companies are more likely to be transparent as their supply chain is heavily documented through "ethical accounting, sustainability reports, codes of conduct and the like" (ibid.). However, studies show that consumption practices do not necessarily align with consumers' social conscience when a price increase is associated with a more "ethical" product.[10] This may be especially true for college students on a budget. School House may have been at a relative disadvantage because its consumers are less financially secure than other consumer groups and so for them, after style, it is price that consumers look to when selecting garments (Lynch 2009). So although students express a social conscience (Hyllegard and Yan 2009) and rely on clothes as a method of self-expression (Noble et al. 2009, 620), perhaps college students lack the income to consistently follow through on these values (though it certainly could be profitable to reach out to parents who often make purchases for college students).

Consumers of ethical fashion live at a juncture of contradictory forces: there is a direct tension between a culture of fast fashion and a culture of social justice for garment workers abroad. Even Weeks began to wonder about this tension. Referring to college students, she said to us, "Everybody says they are so cause-oriented and they put their dollars where their mouth is and they want to support charitable brands.... It is so hard to actually measure that and I think there is a big gap between people who will say that when we ask them, but what they end up buying is totally different. And I think that is where the power of brands comes into play." And, as we discuss below, this is where School House's shift in the story behind the brand may have done it damage.

Sri Lanka: No Code, No Leverage

The pressures that School House experienced were also colored by the ethical context of the two manufacturing locations, Sri Lanka and North Carolina. First, we will discuss Sri Lanka. Though Sri Lanka has a comparatively strong record in treatment of its factory workers (Ruwanpura and Wrigley 2011, 1041), workers still struggle to earn a living wage,[11] to exercise the right to freedom of association, and to engage in collective bargaining (Ruwanpura

2012, 4). School House appears to have succeeded in securing a living wage
for its workers. To address rights to freedom of association and collective
bargaining, as well as everyday health and safety measures, School House
had planned to rely on its Code of Conduct (which was to be overseen by
monitoring organizations). However, it could not convince either supplier to
sign a code, and so it moved ahead without any leverage for ensuring worker
protection. Perhaps the suppliers had already signed several codes and were
suffering from code fatigue.

Note, though, that even if it had a code in place, scholars and activists
have shown the weakness of establishing a Code of Conduct or achieving
Ethical Trading Initiative approval. These bureaucratic auditing measures sel-
dom represent the needs of workers (Pearson and Seyfang 2001; Ruwanpura
2012, 2014; Thomas 2011). Kanchana Ruwanpura and Neil Wrigley (2011,
1039) suggest that buyers should take into account the local context when
constructing or assessing a Code of Conduct. As anthropologist Geert De
Neve argues, these codes are often paternalistic. Referring to South India,
he writes: "Buyer representatives in Tiruppur make it clear that they are the
ones who 'taught' local suppliers how to produce quality garments in a professional manner" (De Neve 2009, 12). Sociologist Mark P. Thomas suggests
that in order to avoid creating paternalistic Codes of Conduct and associated
behaviors, buyers should seek joint discussions of labor practices with the factories, and buyers should actively encourage granting often-neglected rights
to workers (Thomas 2011, 284; cf. De Neve 2009; Esbenshade 2009; Pearson
and Seyfang 2001; Ruwanpura and Wrigley 2011; Ruwanpura 2012). Furthermore, codes are often only acquired via intimidation (De Neve 2009, 10–14;
Ruwanpura and Wrigley 2011, 1044), and Sri Lankan suppliers report that
they have low motivation to sign on because they contend that signing Codes
of Conduct and ethical certification agreements rarely guarantees higher
prices, new business, or consistently larger orders from buyers (Ruwanpura
and Wrigley 2011, 1040–44). In light of these caveats about Codes of Conduct, we speculate that had School House approached their sourcing efforts
in Sri Lanka from a more collaborative angle, partnering with the manufacturers and workers and NGOs, they might have met a different future where
their orders were not consistently late. In this case, perhaps School House
could have created a situation of leverage on behalf of workers *without* a
Code of Conduct. For example, a study by political scientists Richard Locke
and Monica Romis (2006, 35–40) examines the role of Codes of Conduct
in improved working conditions and enforced labor rights. Comparing two

garment factories in Mexico that use the same Nike Code of Conduct, they argue that the drastically different worker experiences in the factory can be attributed to the different ways in which workers are allowed to feel ownership of their work. We suggest that the role of the unions may also provide an explanation for the differences.

North Carolina: American Attitudes Toward "Made in America"

North Carolina also posed unique challenges to School House. Weeks noted concern to us about School House's carbon footprint from sourcing abroad; she asserted that a switch to a completely domestic supply chain was more environmentally advantageous. She also hoped that domestic sourcing would ultimately be more economical, in part because of saving on shipping and staffing costs overseas. However, in truth, this move may have been a net expense, for a number of reasons. School House would not have been able to take advantage of government incentives for foreign trade. Furthermore, though School House sought to create collaborative relationships with its suppliers (Tracey and Vonderembse 2000), and though she is quoted in a *USA Today* article saying that inshoring increased the company's profit margin between 7 and 12 percent (Davidson 2013, n.p.), we suspect that she could have improved this margin by domestically sourcing a percentage of her product as opposed to all of her product.[12]

Weeks described some of the difficulties she encountered once she shifted the production to North Carolina. Weeks entered the North Carolina apparel trade at a time when apparel manufacturing in the United States was limited and shrinking, and as a small business she had little leverage to choose suppliers or influence their wage rate.[13] Because School House struggled to find factories it could afford, it did not focus on providing a living wage to the American workers nor did it require its sourcing factories to sign a Code of Conduct. According to Weeks, "It's such a challenge to think about all the factories we wanted to work with. It was almost the same story all over again where there is only a handful of options for shirt factories in the entire country that are left. If you want to work with them you have to meet their standards in some ways. As a small player, you still go into it not in the driver's seat. . . . It is such a huge hurdle because you're not in the driver's seat and you are having to follow their rules to get the product that you want out. And that was really challenging."

In this same interview with us, Weeks said that ultimately this experience of sourcing in North Carolina was "enlightening." It gave her the opportunity to see why the industry has suffered in the United States: "Because we didn't innovate technologically, we did not come in with customer service, fast turnaround. I think that this industry fell out from underneath us."

Another barrier to School House's success may have been the following: Weeks may have encountered an oft-unacknowledged attitude-behavior gap regarding domestic manufacturing. Many American consumers and American policymakers may value "Made in America" and the associated profits, and yet they do not value the work and welfare of American factory workers. Some may argue against this assertion, citing the apparent resurgence in 2014–2015 of domestic manufacturing (Plumer 2013a, n.p.; Schurenberg 2012, n.p.; Sirkin et al. 2013, n.p.; Tankersley 2013b, n.p.) and consumer opinion.[14] However, the investment banking firm Goldman Sachs points out that the recent success of American manufacturing is less connected to American appreciation of "Made in America" by an American factory worker and more connected to the global trend toward increasing domestic manufacturing exports and profit *regardless of country* (Plumer 2013a). The American factory worker is likely not benefiting from these fluctuating global manufacturing profit trends because unions and American trade and labor policies do not protect their rights or wages (Establishing a Living Wage in Rural North Carolina 2009; Glasmeier 2016; Jason R. Jenkins 2006; Karjanen 2010; Kingsolver 2012) and because American manufacturing is becoming increasingly automated, resulting in fewer new hires (Matthews 2013, n.p.; Tankersley 2013a, n.p.). School House's blog boasts that it was able to provide work for 2,784 workers in North Carolina (ShopSchoolHouse 2011, 23), but it is silent on whether School House provided jobs to *new* workers or if it focused on protecting or improving the rights of these workers. North Carolina is one of twenty-five states to have right-to-work laws that restrict union power. As of January 2014, North Carolina had the lowest union membership of any U.S. state, at 3 percent of the working population (Union Members Summary 2014, fig. 5). Journalist Jim Tankersley (2013b) suggests that as large plants become more automated, workers are less likely to be unionized, and anthropologist Ann Kingsolver (2010) and others argue that the lack of unions is often to the detriment of the workers (Establishing a Living Wage in Rural North Carolina 2009; Jason R. Jenkins 2006). All this leads us to believe that some policymakers and consumers who champion the "Made in America" movement may in fact value American *manufacturing profits* more than American *worker rights and welfare.*

School House sought to provide work to North Carolinians but it did not pay a living wage due to concerns about profitability. Weeks told us that even without a living wage for U.S. workers, the cost of wages for the company would have been more in the United States than in Sri Lanka. This decision reveals another aspect of the ways in which American manufacturing workers are valued. Many scholars refer to the global economy since the 1970s as a "post-Fordist" period. Social theorist David Harvey (1991) describes the current moment as a phase of "flexible accumulation" that began roughly with the 1970s recession. This phase is characterized by flexible labor and capital, with corporations moving operations internationally with the aid of globally connected transportation, communications, and financial systems. The ability of workers to afford the commodities they produce is the exception rather than the rule, and lifetime pensions and affordable benefits are elusive to many. Instead, there is a prevalence of part-time workers ineligible for health and retirement benefits.

All this is the context for the labor situation in North Carolina when School House arrived. This post-Fordist phase is characterized by a devaluation of mass manufacturing work, a rise in neoliberal conceptions of competition, and increasing sentiments of American exceptionalism. North Carolina is one of twelve states with the state minimum wage set to the federal minimum wage (Kingsolver 2010, 36). The living wage in North Carolina in 2016 was $10.53/hour for one adult while the minimum wage was $7.25/hour (Glasmeier 2016). As manufacturing becomes more automated and trade is made more "free," the American factory worker is becoming devalued: the work of several factory workers can be accomplished by one machine for less money (Tankersley 2013a, 2013b). The neoliberal political economic approach contends that automation facilitates innovation. Though this may be the case from one vantage point, new technologies have yet to fulfill the promise of more jobs (Plumer 2013b), and the jobs they may eventually generate will undoubtedly require new training. In a study of public perception regarding living wages, anthropologist David Karjanen (2010, 12–13) analyzes American exceptionalism and American conceptions of economic competition and opportunity: Americans feel that wage floor policies would be "un-American" because they would oppose what they consider a hallmark of American society, the free market economy.

All this means that when School House shifted its mission from providing a living wage to Sri Lankan workers to providing jobs to North Carolinian workers, their consumers perhaps unconsciously valued North Carolinian workers less than foreign workers due to the prevalence and strength of post-Fordist, neoliberalist, and exceptionalist attitudes in the United States.

Conclusion

Garment workers worldwide routinely face hazardous working conditions that threaten their health and safety. With such an unjust global system impacting thousands of workers, there is a need for creativity and collaboration among multiple stakeholders. A small company that aims to make a change in a complex and unjust system would benefit from understanding the pitfalls and challenges that are apparent in the School House story. These include small businesses' lack of influence, collegiate apparel restrictions, lack of pro-worker leverage, and the contradictory appeal of "Made in America." As School House floundered and tried to come up with survival strategies, these specific constraints were the context for the shift in School House's strategy that may have in turn led to the company's demise. In an interview with us, Weeks explained how she understands the term "ethical fashion": "[It is a term] I use to conceive of a wide variety of efforts in this industry, whether it's eco-friendly fashion, locally sourced clothing, repurposed vintage buys, living wage garments. That word for me has been kind of my vehicle to think about those efforts. I don't know if that's right or wrong but that's how I think about it. Because I think there are so many different ways people are tackling this industry for the better."

In this comment Weeks identifies a range of ways in which she understands the concept of "ethics." This diversity of perspectives and her own acknowledgment of the flexibility around how "ethical fashion" can be realized may have contributed to School House's ultimate decline.

School House's *mission* was to provide ethical and fashionable collegiate ware.[15] This mission did not change over time. But what did change was the specific *strategy* it employed to achieve its goals. School House could not ultimately translate its values into profit, and no business will make an impact if it cannot profit and stay in business. A company must try to simultaneously satisfy customers but also create a brand that is sustainable from a business perspective.

Companies often face a time when growth requires trade-offs, and sometimes growth inadvertently leads to a compromise on the company's basic values. School House gained increasingly more investors and orders from colleges and universities, but it could not sustain production—and it encountered specific unanticipated pitfalls of global garment manufacture. Could it have had more long-term success by committing to stay small? What if it, in effect, had chosen to do a smaller amount of good (for example, only serving a few colleges), but over a longer period of time? Perhaps School House experienced an unanticipated setback in its growth: in shifting its strategy, it may have ultimately lost customer trust.

School House made a radical change when it moved from Sri Lanka to North Carolina. This strategy shift may have eroded consumer trust. Studies have shown that consumers are likely to trust products that are deemed "ethical" when they can trust the company's reputation and transparency (Castaldo et al. 2009; Rode and Vallaster 2005). Even if this new strategy attracted more investors, as Weeks claims, consumer trust may have eroded with the move. School House's switch from living wage to domestic job creation may have attracted a completely different set of consumers—patriotic consumers—and may have lost the original customers who were concerned with living wages of women in the global South. Therefore rather than expanding its consumer base by shifting its ethical strategy, it may have inadvertently replaced it with a new but insufficient consumer base.

School House's strategy shift may have caused consumers to question the company's commitment to ethical manufacturing. Even if, as we have seen, Weeks's own definition of "ethical fashion" is flexible and open, consumers tend to buy into a brand's story. School House started with a very specific strategy in Sri Lanka, and it worked tirelessly to communicate this strategy and the underlying values to customers. With powerful storytelling it cultivated a brand following around living wages for Sri Lankan women. So when it found the business was struggling in the Sri Lankan apparel-manufacturing context, the choice to pivot to a new manufacturing location may have led to customer confusion. We can imagine this incredulous consumer response, riffing off Weeks's enthusiastic blogged abbreviation for Sri Lanka: "What's this? I care about Sri Sri, not N.C.!!!" The original customers may have felt that it was actually *unethical* not to pay a living wage but instead embrace a patriotic attitude (Kleinig et al. 2014; Stearns et al. 2003, 519–20).

Storytelling and image building are important in company growth, but School House began telling a story that may have been too different from a consumer perspective. We can see in School House's marketing material considerable effort to create a lifestyle brand whose story reflects its unique strategies. However, the new strategy may have been too different from the old one. Even if the new strategy also has some underlying good, any change can come across as disingenuous to customers who may already be skeptical about whether any business can make a difference in workers' lives.

Ultimately, what are the School House lessons? School House shows us that a small new business cannot assume that there is an inherent quality in and value to its products and its approach. It must work to tell a consistent story, to scale it appropriately, and to work creatively to partner with allies who may be able to help it achieve its mission. What originally moved Rachel Weeks was a concern about the workers behind clothing labels; we share that concern and are optimistic that future small entrepreneurs in ethical clothing will be able to learn from these School House lessons.

Acknowledgments

Thanks primarily to Rachel Weeks for sharing the School House story with us. Thanks also to Geert De Neve, Rebecca Prentice, and Peter Luetchford for detailed written comments on a draft of this chapter, and to the participants at the 2014 University of Sussex workshop on health and safety in the global garment industry. For feedback and discussion, thanks also to Andrew Corbett, Michael C. Davis, Elizabeth Ferry, Annelies Goger, Kent Jones, Sarah Lamb, Lawrence Neeley, Smitha Radhakrishnan, and Cinzia Solari.

Notes

1. Between 1901 and 2003, the percentage of clothing expenditures in U.S. households decreased from 14 percent to 4.2 percent (Chao and Utgoff 2006, 68–69).

2. For a fashion-industry definition of "ethical fashion," see Bumpus 2010.

3. This chapter is based on analysis of School House marketing materials (including the company's consumer-facing website and blog), press coverage, and interviews we conducted with Rachel Weeks in 2014.

4. In a March 2015 conversation with us, Annelies Goger explained this connection between labor shortage and the prevailing wage, based on unconfirmed reports from factory managers. She refers in passing to Colombo-area garment workers earning Rs. 20,000 per month (Goger 2013, 2640).

5. In the mid-1990s in the United States and Europe, collegiate apparel clothing brands began to address the issue of ethical manufacturing; one important impetus for these efforts was the organization called Students Against Sweatshops, started in 1997 at Duke University. This movement grew to include multiple university student labor rights groups, and the United Students Against Sweatshops (USAS) group was formed in 1998. In 2000, USAS joined with others to form the Worker Rights Consortium (WRC), a monitoring organization that works with NGOs, human rights organizations, and local labor groups to investigate the working conditions at factories where apparel (but especially collegiate ware) is produced. As of July 2016, WRC's membership includes more than 180 universities in the United States, Canada, and the United Kingdom. See http://www.workersrights.org/about/as.asp.

6. SGS is the only auditing firm for the GWG program (see Bair et al. 2013; Goger 2011; SGS n.d.).

7. See http://www.clc.com/, http://fermatacollege.com/.

8. In his study of Alta Gracia, business professor John Kline notes that the consumer prices of Knights Apparel garments were not notably higher than those of competitors such as Nike and Adidas (Kline 2010, 34). In 2015 Hanesbrands acquired Knights Apparel, but Alta Gracia remained an independent subsidiary.

9. Fair trade is distinct from ethical trade (see Ethical Trade and Fair Trade 2010 and Smith 2011).

10. Attitudes about fair trade do not always translate into behavior. In a study by De Pelsmacker and colleagues (2005) on whether consumers are willing to pay extra for fair trade items, the authors determined that consumers are willing to pay a 10 percent premium price for a fair trade–labeled item and that only 10 percent of 808 Belgian respondents were willing to pay the current 27 percent price premium for fair trade coffee.

11. The majority of Sri Lankan garment workers are female and the issue of living wage is a heavily gendered subject (Bao 2001; Freeman 2001; Lynch 2007; Mills 2003).

12. We thank Kent Jones for discussion about the possible financial implications of leveraging foreign trade agreements.

13. In 2013, the apparel industry employed only 0.05 percent of the working population in the United States (Platzer 2014, 19). Between 2001 and 2010, the number of private apparel manufacturing firms decreased from 15,478 to 7,855 (BLS Spotlight on Statistics: Fashion 2010, 4).

14. According to Wu and Fu, consumers view products that are made in America by an American firm more favorably than the same product from the same firm made in a developing country (Wu and Fu 2007, 345). In another study, researchers found that 20–25 percent of American survey respondents were willing to pay an 8 percent price premium for American-made athletic shoes (Sirkin et al. 2013, n.p.).

15. We cannot find a clear articulation of School House's mission; our analysis is based on marketing materials (including the School House consumer-facing website and blog), press coverage, and our interviews with Rachel Weeks (all listed in the Bibliography).

Bibliography

Aframian, Mor. 2013. "Textiles in North Carolina: The Economic Benefits of Supporting the USA's Apparel and Textiles Industry." *Redress*. Online: http://redressraleigh.com /blog/2013/1/23/textiles-in-north-carolina-the-economic-benefits-of-supporti .html. Accessed: January 24, 2015.

Atkinson, Jeff. 2008. "Analysis of an Oxfam International Campaign on Garment Workers in Sri Lanka, 2002–2007." London School of Economics: NGPA Working Paper Series.

Bair, Jennifer, Doug Miller, and Marsha Dickson, eds. 2013. *Workers' Rights and Labor Compliance in Global Supply Chains: Is a Social Label the Answer?* New York: Routledge.

Bao, Xiaolan. 2001. *Holding up More Than Half the Sky: Chinese Women Garment Workers in New York City, 1948–92*. Urbana: University of Illinois Press.

Blisstree Staff. 2010. "Game-Changers: Entrepreneurs and Social Change Q&A with Rachel Weeks of School House." Blog. Blisstree. Online: http://www.blisstree.com /2010/05/20/sex-relationships/game-changers-entrepreneurs-and-social-change -qa-with-rachel-weeks-of-school-house/. Accessed: February 13, 2014.

BLS Spotlight on Statistics: Fashion. 2010. U.S. Bureau of Labor Statistics. Online: http:// www.bls.gov/spotlight/2012/fashion/pdf/fashion_bls_spotlight.pdf. Accessed: January 7, 2015.

Bumpus, Jessica. 2010. "Buy Right." *Vogue UK*, April. Online: http://www.vogue.co.uk /news/favourites-of-vogue/2010/04/ethical-and-sustainable-fashion-shopping. Accessed: June 12, 2014.

Burkett, Melanie. 2012. "Alumna Profile: Rachel Weeks '07." Duke University. Online: https://globaladvising.duke.edu/pointers/advice/2012/02/13/alumna-profile-rachel -weeks-07. Accessed: May 28, 2014.

Castaldo, Sandro, Francesco Perrini, Nicola Misani, and Antonio Tencati. 2009. "The Missing Link Between Corporate Social Responsibility and Consumer Trust: The Case of Fair Trade Products." *Journal of Business Ethics* 84(1): 1–15.

Chao, Elaine L., and Kathleen P. Utgoff. 2006. "100 Years of U.S. Consumer Spending— Data for the Nation, New York City, and Boston." U.S. Department of Labor and U.S. Bureau of Labor Statistics, Report 991. Online: http://www.bls.gov/opub/uscs /report991.pdf. Accessed: March 10, 2015.

Chen, Monica. 2011. "School House 'Inshoring' Jobs from Sri Lanka to Wendell." *Triangle Business Journal*. Online: http://www.bizjournals.com/triangle/print-edition/2011 /05/13/school-house-inshoring-jobs-from-sri.html. Accessed: February 13, 2014.

Chernev, Alexander, Ryan Hamilton, and David Gal. 2011. "Competing for Consumer Identity: Limits to Self-Expression and the Perils of Lifestyle Branding." *Journal of Marketing* 75(3): 66–82.

Colucci, Mariachiara and Daniele Scarpi. 2013. "Generation Y: Evidences from the Fast-Fashion Market and Implications for Targeting." *Journal of Business Theory and Practice* 1(1): 1–7.

Concepting: Designing a School-Specific T-Shirt. 2011. Online: http://www.youtube
.com/watch?v=qct781ZdmUg&feature=youtube_gdata_player. Accessed: February
23, 2014.

Davidson, Paul. 2013. "Some Apparel Manufacturing 'Reshoring' to USA." *USA
Today*, July 5. Online: http://www.usatoday.com/story/money/business/2013/07
/04/some-apparel-manufacturing-returns-to-us/2454075/. Accessed: February
13, 2014.

De Neve, Geert. 2009. "Power, Inequality and Corporate Social Responsibility: The Politics of Ethical Compliance in the South Indian Garment Industry." *Economic and
Political Weekly* 44(22): 63–71.

De Pelsmacker, Patrick, Liesbeth Driesen, and Glenn Rayp. 2005. "Do Consumers Care
about Ethics? Willingness to Pay for Fair-Trade Coffee." *Journal of Consumer Affairs*
39(2): 363–85.

Dere, Kathryn, and Jenny Xie. 2010. "School House Brings Ethical Fashion to MIT."
The Tech Online Edition. Online: http://tech.mit.edu/V130/N37/schoolhouse.html.
Accessed: February 13, 2014.

Dietz, David. 2014. "Introducing People Tree: Pioneers in Ethical Fashion (Just Ask
Emma Watson)." MODABLOGI. Online: http://blog.modavanti.com/2014/01/12
/introducing-people-tree-pioneers-in-ethical-fashion-just-ask-emma-watson/.
Accessed: June 10, 2014.

Dragovic, Ana. 2010. "Teen Vogue: Fair Wear." *Women Thrive Worldwide*, August.
Online: http://womenthrive.org/media-resources/pressroom/news/teen-vogue-fair
-wear. Accessed: January 23, 2015.

The Dress That Started It All. 2011. Online: http://www.youtube.com/watch?v=
tx013FkNzuk&feature=youtube_gdata_player. Accessed: February 23, 2014.

Duin, Steve. 2011. "Steve Duin: Rachel Weeks' School House Clothing Line: Just a Girl
with a Great Idea." *The Oregonian—OregonLive.com*, November 19. Online: http://
www.oregonlive.com/news/oregonian/steve_duin/index.ssf/2011/11/rachel_weeks
_school_house_clot.html. Accessed: February 21, 2014.

Duke University. N.d. "Key Industries: Textiles & Apparel." *Learn NC*. Online: http://
www.learnnc.org/lp/editions/nchist-recent/6259. Accessed: May 26, 2014.

Duke Women's Studies Undergraduates. 2013. "A Great Internship Opportunity
and LOCAL Business Founded by Women's Studies' Own Rachel Weeks!" Facebook Page. Online: https://www.facebook.com/DukeWSUndergraduates/posts
/516756138358810. Accessed: March 27, 2014.

"Durham NC Startup: School House Apparel; Collegiate Home Grown Apparel with
Purpose." N.d. *Nibletz*. Online: http://nibletz.com/2012/04/16/durham-nc-startup
-school-house-apparel-collegiate-home-grown-apparel-with-purpose/. Accessed:
February 13, 2014.

Esbenshade, Jill Louise. 2009. *Monitoring Sweatshops: Workers, Consumers, and the
Global Apparel Industry*. Philadelphia: Temple University Press.

Establishing a Living Wage in Rural North Carolina. 2009. University of North Carolina Center for Health Promotion and Disease Prevention. Online: https://depts.washington.edu/ccph/pdf_files/Living_Wage.pdf. Accessed: January 8, 2015.

Ethical Manufacturing in Sri Lanka. 2011. Online: http://www.youtube.com/watch?v=n3INlePmz4Y&feature=youtube_gdata_player. Accessed: February 23, 2014.

Ethical Trade and Fair Trade. 2010. Ethical Trading Initiative. Online: http://www.ethicaltrade.org/in-action/issues/ethical-trade-fairtrade. Accessed: January 7, 2015.

Fair Fashion. 2010. Online: http://www.youtube.com/watch?v=xehD28Zr5gA&feature=youtube_gdata_player. Accessed: February 23, 2014.

Fashion's Future: Rachel Weeks, Founder and CEO of School House. 2011. *Truth Plus.* Online: http://truthplusblog.com/2011/12/07/fashions-future-rachel-weeks-founder-and-ceo-of-school-house/. Accessed: February 13, 2014.

Fenn, Donna. 2012a. "How Manufacturing on Home Turf Pays Off. American Express: OPEN Forum." Online: https://www.openforum.com/articles/how-domestic-manufacturing-pays-off/. Accessed: February 20, 2014.

———. 2012b. "Fashionable, Fresh . . . & Made in USA." *Inc.com,* July 2. Online: http://www.inc.com/30under30/donna-fenn/rachel-weeks-founder-of-school-house.html. Accessed: February 13, 2014.

Freeman, Carla. 2001. "Is Local:Global as Feminine:Masculine? Rethinking the Gender of Globalization." *Signs* 26(4):1007–37.

Gemberling, Kyra, and Jordan Only. 2014. "Dwindling North Carolina Textile Industry Hopeful." *The Pendulum,* April 8. Online: http://www.elonpendulum.com/2014/04/north-carolina-textile-industry-hopeful/. Accessed: January 24, 2015.

Glasmeier, Amy. 2016. "Living Wage Calculation for North Carolina." Poverty in America: Living Wage Calculator. Cambridge, Mass: MIT. Online: http://livingwage.mit.edu/states/37. Accessed July 6, 2016.

Goger, Annelies. 2011. "Going More Local with Global Governance: Lessons from Ethical Branding in Sri Lanka." Online: http://betterwork.com/global/wp-content/uploads/Session-6-Going-More-Local-With-Global-Governance.pdf. Accessed: January 6, 2017.

———. 2013. "From Disposable to Empowered: Rearticulating Labor in Sri Lankan Apparel Factories." *Environment & Planning A* 45(11): 2628–45.

Greenhouse, Steven. 2010. "An Apparel Factory Defies Stereotypes, but Can It Thrive?" *New York Times,* July 17: 1.

Harvey, David. 1991. *The Condition of Postmodernity: An Enquiry into the Origins of Cultural Change.* Cambridge, MA: Wiley-Blackwell.

Helman, Deborah, and Leslie De Chernatony. 1999. "Exploring the Development of Lifestyle Retail Brands." *Service Industries Journal* 19(2): 49–68.

Hermes—Craftsmanship. 2010. Online: http://www.youtube.com/watch?v=g6HOhqaVXW0&feature=youtube_gdata_player. Accessed: February 23, 2014.

Hewamanne, Sandya. 2010. *Stitching Identities in a Free Trade Zone: Gender and Politics in Sri Lanka.* Philadelphia: University of Pennsylvania Press.

The Hot Gear Team. 2013. "College Kids Are Falling in Love with School House Apparel and Accessories." Hot Gear Direct Blog. Online: http://blog.hotgeardirect.com/2013/08/school-house-apparel-and-accessories/. Accessed: February 13, 2014.

Hyllegard, Jennifer Ogle, and Ruoh-Nan Yan. 2009. "The Impact of Advertising Message Strategy—Fair Labour v. Sexual Appeal—upon Gen Y Consumers' Intent to Patronize an Apparel Retailer." *Journal of Fashion Marketing and Management: An International Journal* 13(1): 109–27.

Jenkins, Heledd. 2006. "Small Business Champions for Corporate Social Responsibility." *Journal of Business Ethics* 67(3): 241–56.

Jenkins, Jason R. 2006. "A Living Wage for North Carolina: An Introduction." *North Carolina Council of Churches*. Online: http://www.ncchurches.org/wp-content/uploads/2010/07/Living-Wage-for-NC-Report-Final.pdf. Accessed: January 8, 2015.

Karjanen, David. 2010. "Opposition to the Living Wage: Discourse, Rhetoric, and American Exceptionalism." *Anthropology of Work Review* 31(1): 4–14.

Kingsolver, Ann. 2010. "Living Wage Considerations in the Right-to-Work State of South Carolina." *Anthropology of Work Review* 31(1): 30–41.

———. 2012. "Unemployment Commodified: In/Visibility of Rural Unemployment in South Carolina and Kentucky." Paper presented in the session Anthropologies of Unemployment: Disciplinary Borders and Crossings in the Study of Unemployment. American Anthropological Association meetings, San Francisco. November 16.

Kleinig, John, Simon Keller, and Igor Primoratz. 2014. *The Ethics of Patriotism: A Debate.* Chichester, UK: John Wiley & Sons.

Kline, John M. 2010. *Alta Gracia: Branding Decent Work Conditions.* Research Report, Kalmanovitz Initiative for Labor and the Working Poor. Washington, DC: Georgetown University.

Landry, Lauren. 2011. "School House Brings Socially Conscious Clothing to Boston's College Campuses." *BostInno.* Online: http://bostinno.streetwise.co/2011/09/22/school-house-brings-socially-conscious-clothing-to-bostons-college-campuses/. Accessed: February 13, 2014.

Leipziger, Deborah. 2012. "School House." Aspen Institute. Online: www.caseplace.org/pdfs/SchoolHouse.pdf. Accessed: January 23, 2015.

Lepoutre, Jan, and Aimé Heene. 2006. "Investigating the Impact of Firm Size on Small Business Social Responsibility: A Critical Review." *Journal of Business Ethics* 67(3): 257–73.

Locke, Richard, and Monica Romis. 2006. "Beyond Corporate Codes of Conduct: Work Organization and Labor Standards in Two Mexican Garment Factories." MIT Sloan School of Management. Online: http://mitsloan.mit.edu/newsroom/pdf/conduct.pdf. Accessed: April 2, 2015.

Lopez-Acevedo, Gladys, and Raymond Robertson, eds. 2012. *Sewing Success?: Employment, Wages, and Poverty Following the End of the Multi-Fibre Arrangement.* Washington, DC: World Bank Publications.

Love, Maggie. 2010. "Duke Apparel Supplier Pays Ethical Wages." *Duke Chronicle*. Online: http://www.dukechronicle.com/article/duke-apparel-supplier-pays-ethical -wages. Accessed: February 22, 2014.

Lynch, Caitrin. 2007. *Juki Girls, Good Girls: Gender and Cultural Politics in Sri Lanka's Global Garment Industry*. Ithaca, NY: Cornell University Press.

Lynch, Meghan. 2009. "The Power of Conscious Consumption." *Journal of Culture and Retail* Image 2(1). http://services.library.drexel.edu/static_files/dsmr/lynch.pdf. Accessed: January 7, 2015.

Made In North Carolina. 2011. Online: http://www.youtube.com/watch?v=iWTWCu 2EURg&feature=youtube_gdata_player. Accessed February 23, 2014.

Martin, Claire. 2014. "Wearing Your Failures on Your Sleeve." *New York Times*, November 8: BU1.

Matthews, Dylan. 2013. "This Chart Will Change How You Think About Manufacturing." *Washington Post*, March 21. Online: http://www.washingtonpost.com /blogs/wonkblog/wp/2013/03/21/this-chart-will-change-how-you-think-about -manufacturing/. Accessed: January 9, 2015.

McCoy, Maxie. 2012. "Friday Future Leaders: Meet School House's Rachel Weeks, Learn the Can-Do (with a BA in Women's Studies) Attitude." *Levo League*. Online: http:// www.levo.com/articles/uncategorized/friday-future-leaders-meet-school-houses -rachel-weeks-learn-can-do-with-ba-womens-studies-attitude. Accessed: February 13, 2014.

Memic, Mersiha, and Frida N. Minhas. 2011. "The Fast Fashion Phenomenon. Master in Fashion Management, The Swedish School of Textiles–University of Boras." Online: http://bada.hb.se/bitstream/2320/9241/1/2011.13.9.pdf.

Mielach, David. 2011. "Entrepreneur Brings Manufacturing Back Home to N.C." *BusinessNewsDaily.com*. Online: http://www.businessnewsdaily.com/1542-apparel -manufacturing-school-house.html. Accessed: February 13, 2014.

Mills, Mary Beth. 2003. "Gender and Inequality in the Global Labor Force." *Annual Review of Anthropology* 32(1): 41–62.

Needleman, Sarah E. 2010. "For Mark Zuckerberg Wannabes, Sometimes It's Easy to Lose Face." *Wall Street Journal*, September 9. Online: http://www.wsj.com/articles /SB10001424052748703453804575480260973065920. Accessed: December 27, 2016.

Noble, Stephanie M., Diana L. Haytko, and Joanna Phillips. 2009. "What Drives College-Age Generation Y Consumers?" *Journal of Business Research* 62(6): 617–28.

North Carolina General Statute. N.d.   95.78-84. Online: http://www.nrtw.org/right -work-states-north-carolina. Accessed: January 8, 2015.

North Carolina Unemployment Rate. N.d. Y-Charts. Online: http://ycharts.com /indicators/north_carolina_unemployment_rate. Accessed: May 8, 2014.

Our (Real) Good Story. N.d. Online: http://zookeeperapp.com/0afe69f9b929ab3e 513a5af2. Accessed: March 20, 2015.

Pearson, Ruth, and Gill Seyfang. 2001. "New Hope or False Dawn?: Voluntary Codes of Conduct, Labour Regulation and Social Policy in a Globalizing World." *Global Social Policy* 1(48): 49–77.

Platzer, Michaela D. 2014. "U.S. Textile Manufacturing and the Trans-Pacific Partnership Negotiations." CRS Report 7-5700. Washington, DC: Congressional Research Service. Online: http://fas.org/sgp/crs/row/R42772.pdf. Accessed: July 25, 2015.

Plumer, Brad. 2013a. "Goldman Sachs: Sorry, U.S. Manufacturing Isn't Coming Back." *Washington Post*, March 25. Online: http://www.washingtonpost.com/blogs/wonkblog/wp/2013/03/25/goldman-sachs-sorry-u-s-manufacturing-isnt-coming-back/. Accessed: January 8, 2015.

———. 2013b. "Is U.S. Manufacturing Making a Comeback—or Is It Just Hype?" *Washington Post*, May 1. Online: http://www.washingtonpost.com/blogs/wonkblog/wp/2013/05/01/is-u-s-manufacturing-set-for-a-comeback-or-is-it-all-hype/. Accessed: January 8, 2015.

Rachel Weeks-SCORE Awards 2011. 2011. Online: http://www.youtube.com/watch?v=GZKIWLMeJjs&feature=youtube_gdata_player. Accessed: February 23, 2014.

Rode, Verena, and Christine Vallaster. 2005. "Corporate Branding for Start-Ups: The Crucial Role of Entrepreneurs." *Corporate Reputation Review* 8(2): 121–35.

Ruwanpura, Kanchana. 2012. "Ethical Codes: Reality and Rhetoric—A Study of Sri Lanka's Apparel Sector." University of Southampton. Online: http://eprints.soton.ac.uk/337113/1/ESRC-EndofProjectReport2012.pdf. Accessed: April 28, 2014.

———. 2014. "Garments Without Guilt? Uneven Labour Geographies and Ethical Trading—Sri Lankan Labour Perspectives." *Journal of Economic Geography* 25(2): 1–37.

Ruwanpura, Kanchana N., and Neil Wrigley. 2011. "The Costs of Compliance? Views of Sri Lankan Apparel Manufacturers in Times of Global Economic Crisis." *Journal of Economic Geography* 11(6): 1031–49.

School House—Founder and CEO Rachel Weeks. 2012. http://vimeo.com/42360601. Accessed: February 13, 2014.

School House Photo Shoot: Behind the Scenes. 2010. Online: http://www.youtube.com/watch?v=X7wFaLxp2Y4&feature=youtube_gdata_player. Accessed: February 23, 2014.

The School House Production Process. 2011. Online: http://www.youtube.com/watch?v=5ayQKO0YaVY&feature=youtube_gdata_player. Accessed: February 23, 2014.

Schurenberg, Eric. 2012. "What Is 'Made in America' Worth?" *Inc.com*, December 2. Online: http://www.inc.com/eric-schurenberg/what-is-made-in-america-worth.html. Accessed: January 8, 2015.

Schwartz, Judith D. 2009. "Buying Local: How It Boosts the Economy." *Time*, June 11. Online: http://content.time.com/time/business/article/0,8599,1903632,00.html. Accessed: June 5, 2014.

SGS. N.d. Audit. SGS. Online: http://www.sgs.com/en/Service-by-Type-Path/Audit.aspx. Accessed: January 24, 2015.

ShopSchoolHouse. 2011. "School House : Made in America." *Business*, August 31. Online: http://www.slideshare.net/ShopSchoolHouse/school-house-made-in-america. Accessed: June 5, 2014.

Sirkin, Harold L., Michael Zinser, and Kate Manfred. 2013. "That 'Made in USA' Label May Be Worth More Than You Think." BCG Perspectives by the Boston Consulting Group. Online: https://www.bcgperspectives.com/content/commentary/consumer_products_retail_that_made_in_usa_label_may_be_worth_more_than_you_think/. Accessed: January 8, 2015.

Smith, Alastair. 2011. "Fair and Ethical Trade: An Explanation." *WIEGO*. Online: http://wiego.org/sites/wiego.org/files/resources/files/Global-Trade-What-Fair-and-Ethical-Trade.pdf. Accessed: January 7, 2015.

Stearns, James M., Shaheen Borna, and Gillian Oakenfull. 2003. "Buying for Love of Country: Assessing the Ethics of Patriotic Appeals in Advertising." *Business and Society Review* 108(4): 509–21.

Tankersley, Jim. 2013a. "As Manufacturing Bounces Back from Recession, Unions Are Left Behind." *Washington Post*, January 16. Online: http://www.washingtonpost.com/business/economy/as-manufacturing-bounces-back-from-recession-unions-are-left-behind/2013/01/16/4b4a7368-5e88-11e2-90a0-73c8343c6d61_story.html. Accessed: January 8, 2015.

———. 2013b. "Innovation: The Jackpot for American Manufacturers." *Washington Post*, April 29. Online: http://www.washingtonpost.com/postlive/innovation-the-jackpot-for-american-manufacturers/2013/04/29/dacb0f56-acf9-11e2-a8b9-2a63d75b5459_story.html. Accessed: January 8, 2015.

Taproot Films, dir. 2012. School House—Founder and CEO Rachel Weeks. http://vimeo.com/42360601. Accessed: February 13, 2014.

Thomas, Mark P. 2011. "Global Industrial Relations? Framework Agreements and the Regulation of International Labor Standards." *Labor Studies Journal* 36(2): 269–87.

Tracey, Michael, and Mark A. Vonderembse. 2000. "Building Supply Chains: A Key to Enhancing Manufacturing Performance." *American Journal of Business* 15(2): 11–20.

Union Members Summary. 2014. Bureau of Labor Statistics, U.S. Department of Labor. Online: http://www.bls.gov/news.release/union2.nr0.htm. Accessed: January 9, 2015.

Vagnomi, Dave. 2010. "License to Play." *Counselor Magazine*, June: 75–80.

Weeks, Rachel. 2008. "Freshman Year." Blog. SCHOOL HOUSE. Online: http://schoolhouseblogs.blogspot.com/2008_12_01_archive.html. Accessed: February 22, 2014.

———. 2009a. A Big Day. Tumblr. SCHOOL HOUSE INC. Online: http://schoolhouseblogs.blogspot.com/2009/03/big-day.html. Accessed: January 23, 2015.

———. 2009b. Live from Sri Lanka It's Friday Morning! Tumblr. SCHOOL HOUSE INC. Online: http://schoolhouseinc.tumblr.com/post/278384404/live-from-sri-lanka-its-friday-morning. Accessed: January 23, 2015.

———. 2009c. Happy Girls Make Happy Garments! Tumblr. SCHOOL HOUSE INC. Online: http://schoolhouseinc.tumblr.com/post/278879634/happy-girls-make-happy -garments. Accessed: January 23, 2015.

———. 2010a. School House Has Moved!

———. 2010b. Abbhaartu Nettha = NO VACANCIES from Milan . . . The . . . Tumblr. SCHOOL HOUSE INC. Online: http://schoolhouseinc.tumblr.com/post/410408665 /abbhaartu-nettha-no-vacancies-from-milan-the. Accessed: January 23, 2015.

———. 2012a. Need Your Help! School House Kickstarter Campaign.

———. 2012b. Tumblr. SCHOOL HOUSE INC. Online: http://schoolhouseinc.tumblr .com/?og=1. Accessed: February 22, 2014.

———. 2012c. Made in America Monday Mitts Nitts. Tumblr. SHOP SCHOOL HOUSE. Online: http://shopschoolhouse.tumblr.com/post/38159274343/made-in-america -monday-mitts-nitts. Accessed: February 23, 2014.

———. 2013. American Made Coozies! Tumblr. SHOP SCHOOL HOUSE. Online: http://shopschoolhouse.tumblr.com/post/47291267456/american-made-coozies. Accessed: January 23, 2015.

———. 2014a. Interview with Rachel Weeks 2/23/2014. February 23.

———. 2014b. Interview with Rachel Weeks 3/31/2014. March 31.

———. N.d. Shop School House Tumblr. Tumblr. SHOP SCHOOL HOUSE. Online: http://shopschoolhouse.tumblr.com/ Accessed: February 22, 2014.

———. N.d. "Duke Global Advising Profiles: Rachel Weeks '07." *Duke Global Advising Profiles*. Online: http://globaladvising.duke.edu/pointers/profiles/weeks. Accessed: February 13, 2014.

Who We Support, How & Why. N.d. "Who We Support, How & Why." Bull City For-ward. Online: http://bullcityforward.org/overview/who-we-support/. Accessed: February 21, 2014.

Wilkerson, Jim. 2009. "Best Practices in University Sweatfree Licensing and Lessons for Government Procurement." Presentation Notes presented at the SweatFree Pro-curement Forum for Purchasing Officials, March 26. Online: http://digitalcommons .ilr.cornell.edu/cgi/viewcontent.cgi?article=2359&context=globaldocs&sei-redir =1&referer=http%3A%2F%2Fscholar.google.com%2Fscholar%3Fhl%3Den%26q %3Dcollegiate%2Bgarments%2Blicensing%26btnG%3D%26as_sdt%3D1%252C38 %26as_sdtp%3D#search=%22collegiate%20garments%20licensing%22. Accessed: January 6, 2015.

Wu, Jian, and Guoqun Fu. 2007. "The Effects of Brand Origin Country and Made-in Country on Consumers' Product Evaluations and Purchase Intention." *Frontiers of Business Research in China* 1(3): 333–50.

Zenner, Jay. 2012. "Program Report: Rachel Weeks and School House Apparel." *Rotary Club of Durham*. Online: http://durhamrotaryclub.org/2012/04/schoolhouse/. Accessed: February 13, 2014.

PART II

From Structures to Actors, and Back

CHAPTER 4

Capital over Labor: Health and Safety in Export Processing Zone Garment Production since 1947

Patrick Neveling

The textile and garment industry is one of those sectors in which the globalization of sourcing, production, and retailing has been closely linked with the worldwide spread of export processing zones (EPZs) (Neveling 2015d).[1] It is impossible to understand the global proliferation of EPZs to more than 3,500 zones with more than 70 million workers in 130 or so nations (Boyenge 2007) without reference to the textile and garment industry and the working conditions of its more than 60 million workers, and vice versa. This chapter traces the link between EPZs and the textile and garment industry in regard to health and safety concerns. From the opening of the world's first EPZ in Puerto Rico in 1947 onward, the zones have had considerable impact on labor relations in the global garment sector. In fact, EPZs may be regarded as a mode of governing labor conditions in their own right, and this mode maintains low standards of health and safety for labor and high standards of safety for return on capital investments.

Linking the historical development of EPZs with that of the global garment sector is not a common genealogy. So far the sector's infamously unsafe and unhealthy working conditions have mainly been regarded in the light of a salient and catchy term, the "sweatshop." From Ellen Rosen's outstanding monograph *Making Sweatshops: The Globalization of the U.S. Apparel Industry* (Rosen 2002) to Naomi Klein's highly popular *No Logo* (Klein 2000), the genealogy of sweatshops is commonly traced back to the textile and garment businesses that emerged in New York's Lower East Side in the late nineteenth century. While such linkages are undeniable, an overemphasis on them has nurtured a decoupling of EPZs—where the majority of garment factories are located globally—and the industry itself. This enables pro-EPZ lobbyists to praise the rapid growth of EPZs in Bangladesh and to recommend replicating its EPZ program in African nations (e.g., Farole 2011, 83) without even mentioning how Bangladesh's EPZ growth rates thrived on unsafe and unhealthy labor conditions that created the amazing profit margins attracting investors.

As the following shows, abandoning the U.S.-centric analytical angle and inserting the historical spread of EPZs into the sweatshop genealogy enables us to link the killings of workers in the Rana Plaza factory—and the plight of tens of millions of garment workers and their families—to EPZs as a particular mode of capitalist exploitation. This does not take the sweatshop out of the equation, but instead shows how powerful coalitions of actors and institutions from World Bank research departments to private consulting corporations and UN agencies have collaborated over considerable periods of time to create EPZs as a particular global economic condition that is now embedded in social structures worldwide. Based on this analytical shift, the genealogy offered in this chapter seeks to understand global processes and the particularities they generate in space and time. For such processes have contributed to the collapse of the Rana Plaza factory building in Bangladesh in 2013, where the national government has promoted EPZs, often as bonded warehouses, since the 1970s (Rhee 1990), as much as to the 1911 Triangle Shirtwaist Factory fire in New York City in 1911, which is often cited as the paradigmatic historical example for the worst of sweatshop conditions (Rosen 2002, 1; Bair et al. this volume). At the same time, EPZs often have an undeserved reputation as a policy tool that creates miraculous economic growth. Zones have often been compared to the Californian and earlier gold rushes, the famous Klondike, and the infamous El Dorado. Obviously, workers in the zones hardly stand a chance to amass unforeseen riches overnight. Rather, EPZs are a standard feature in nation-states wishing to achieve economic growth by attracting export-oriented industries; the set of policies that makes an EPZ is first and foremost designed to assist national and multinational capital (Neveling 2014c).

Unfortunately, mainstream development policy reviews of EPZs never get to the bottom of these important structural determinants. The definitions of EPZs and SEZs (special economic zones) they offer are technical at best, and the examples that they feature are success stories throughout. Browsing through such pamphlets one encounters partial descriptions of ever-the-same success cases (e.g., Akinci et al. 2008, 29–31). Therefore, we need better definitions, and this is what the first section of this chapter develops based on empirically verifiable features of seventy years of EPZ operations, which still apply today, such as in the bonded warehouse facilities granted to all textile and garment companies operating in the Rana Plaza building before its collapse.

The second section retraces the emergence of EPZs in Puerto Rico in 1947. The third section sketches how EPZs went global in the decades after, with a special focus on health and safety policies and on South Asia. In sum, these sections offer a historical anthropology of a global neoliberal regime, which enables anthropology to analyze health and labor issues in garment factories on a global scale. Such an approach progresses from the discipline's current investment in "worm's eye view" (Cross 2010, 358) methodologies, which consider factories as isolated social units with culture-specific "relations in production" and which produce workers without history and zones without history, toward a comparative and historical analysis of the "relations of production" present in all those factories (see Burawoy 1983). The historical anthropology proposed here then moves beyond a moralist empathy for the plight of EPZ workers toward an anthropological contribution to the struggle against the ongoing global attack on garment workers' health and safety by producing comprehensive evidence of structural patterns of exploitation and abuse. Such evidence highlights the very existence of a global EPZ regime, which was the product of often coincidental interactions of national, transnational, and global players since the late 1940s—those actors and institutions are the "Natives" that have determined whether an interest in health and safety in EPZs was with the health and safety of capital or that of labor.

In line with a global historical anthropology approach, which I detail elsewhere in regard to methodology and theoretical implications (Nevel-ing 2016), the concluding remarks offer examples that illustrate the limits of workers' rights movements over more than seventy years of EPZ operations. I juxtapose a long-standing, strong concern with capital's health and safety with an equally long-standing lack of concern for labor's health and safety. Finally, I revisit briefly the relations between capital, state, and labor that continue to enable this difference in concern.

Verifiable Definitions of EPZs as Main Production Sites
for the Global Textile and Garment Industry

Definitions of EPZs are dominated by the research departments of international organizations such as the World Bank and the International Labour Organization (e.g., Akinci et al. 2008; Boyenge 2007). Because their ambition is often to promote the global spread of these zones, these definitions focus on technical and legal aspects and have little concern for the historical reality of EPZ operations. We therefore need better definitions—definitions that represent EPZs as having a history and workers in the zones as having histories that have produced legacies of struggle. I identify six defining features of EPZs that are rooted in the historical development and present-day expressions of relations between capital, state, and labor since the late 1940s. For the relations of these meta-actors dominate social and economic interaction in the zones and their factories. Such relations change, but as with any other cultural setting, they also persist and are therefore crucial determinants in a global setting that saw the Rana Plaza killings in Bangladesh unfold in 2013.

First, national governments, and often also regional administrations, offer tax and customs breaks for a given number of years to encourage the relocation of manufacturing capital. This means that the regions establishing EPZs declare themselves and their workforce unworthy/undeserving of manufacturing investment in the first place and, in reverse, portray taxes and customs as a burden for capital, from which it deserves "holidays" (Neveling 2012, 347–89). This, like all the following defining features of EPZs, has considerable impact on how workers in textile and garment factories are treated, and the notion of an unworthy/undeserving workforce severely restricts the bargaining position of workers and their representatives.

Second, development agencies, funded by the state and/or public-private partnerships, cultivate land and build so-called "turnkey factories" in industrial estates and zones, which are then offered at low leases to investors wishing to set up manufacturing and other enterprises. States, in other words, put up significant investments in fixed capital in EPZs and thereby become entrepreneurs who take on a substantial share of the risks involved in the competitive realm of global capitalist production.

Third, in the past, this risky entrepreneurial activity of national governments was aggravated when developing nations guaranteed exchange rates of their currencies against "hard" currencies such as the U.S. dollar, creating a flat world for transactions by EPZ investors. In the volatile global currency market of the post–Bretton Woods regime, such guarantees turned out to be an entre-preneurial gamble. Such high-risk monetary policies remain in place as national development banks offer comparatively low-interest loans for the acquisition of means of production (Rosen 2002, esp. 33–35; cf. Neveling 2014b).

Fourth, most national EPZ laws lowered minimum wages for the zones, banned collective bargaining and unionization, and protected investors from nationalization of industries by any future government. One effect of these EPZ measures is super exploitation, meaning that wages are insufficient to reproduce labor power. This creates what I call "exploitation chains" because households, extended kin-groups, and modes of self-help activated by EPZ workers ultimately contribute to investor profits (Fröbel et al. 1981; Latimer 2015; Neveling 2015a).

Fifth, EPZs are a one-way street into sustained misery for developing nations with few exceptional success stories (for example, the Shenzhen region). One reason for this is export-oriented production, which means insecurity as no nation without command over a superior armed force can be sure to maintain its export markets. Efforts to catch up with industrially advanced nations have distorted effects, as ever lower-cost labor enters the assembly lines of multinational and local corporations, retailing or subcon-tracting the production of garments. Directions of exports may have changed over the past seven decades, but the bulk of EPZ garments moves from poorer to richer people and regions. The beneficiary of EPZ incentives is capital, not labor or the overall wealth of nations.

Sixth, whether nations advance or decline from consumer to producer or vice versa has (had) less to do with EPZ incentives than with the structura-tion of the global trading system, where bilateral and multilateral trade agree-ments and regional trading blocs define which garment exporting nations have access to important markets. Examples include the 1974 Multi-Fiber Arrangement (MFA), the current U.S. African Growth and Opportunity Act, the European Union (EU), and the North American Free Trade Area (NAFTA) (Carswell and De Neve 2014; Gereffi et al. 2002; Neveling 2015a).

So far, social science research has not fully come to terms with these six defining features that make for a global EPZ regime. Often, researchers stick to definitions from international organizations, which focus on the technical and legal aspects of EPZs as ideal types. Such ideal types neither reflect the relations on the ground, in a given zone or a given zone factory, nor do they reflect the relations on wider scales, such as in a national economy with a high share of EPZ output, or how EPZs shape relations of production in the global textile and garment industry. In short, it is the actors within the global EPZ business that provide the funding for such definitions and their focus on technical and legal matters, which means that the definitions have no superior authority but they are a "Native's Point of View" (Carrier 2012) as good as any other. In order to deepen an alternative understanding, it is now time to assess the global spread of EPZs since 1947 and how their diffusion has shaped health and safety standards in the global textile and garment industry.

Capital, State, and Labor Relations in the Global EPZ Regime Since 1947

All of the above definitions highlight the particular relations between capital, state, and labor in EPZs and, thus, in the global garment sector. That these definitions are axiomatic for any assessment of health and safety concerns in the sector has to do with the fact that EPZs went global and became a regime in the process of diffusion. Zones set up in the past seven decades all, in one way or another, emerged from the first EPZ established in Puerto Rico in 1947. The zone model refined itself as it spread globally. The following illustrates, by way of example, which variations stuck with a particular zone and which were added to the global EPZ regime that millions of workers have been subjected to.

The historical development of intransparent production and transactions is particularly evident within the garment-EPZ nexus. This is evidenced also in other chapters in this volume (Ashraf this volume; Bair et al. this volume), which show how the Rana Plaza killings put a spotlight on the sector's global sourcing strategies. Today, even multinational retail corporations such as Primark and H&M can claim to be unable to see the myriad trajectories of commodity chains that end in their retail stores. Surprisingly, though, social scientists with their much slimmer research budgets can point out how these chains incorporate subcontracting firms, individual (women's) home labor, or putting out style production (Prentice 2008; Mezzadri this volume). Also, according to expert estimates I collected during many years of research on the global spread of EPZs, most garment orders today are placed through "middleman" agents such as Hong Kong's Li & Fung.

This ramification of commodity chains in the global textile and garment industry, which allows for retailers' false claims of intransparency, can be traced back to the very beginnings of the EPZ model. Already in 1947, sourcing agents, albeit of a different kind, were indispensable for establishing what would be the world's first EPZ and rapidly expanding garment businesses. Some historical background is needed for understanding the conjunctures on which their operations blossomed. Back then, Puerto Rico, a Caribbean island and a U.S. dependency since 1898, showed all the symptoms of the neo-Malthusian dilemma that became a leading explanatory device in development policies during the era of the Cold War and decolonization. Population size nearly tripled between 1900 and the 1950s, whereas agriculture, increasingly driven by U.S. trusts controlling sugar cane, tobacco, and coffee plantations and milling, remained the island's mainstay economic activity. A needlework industry emerged in the 1920s. Production and sales to the U.S. mainland increased rapidly. Nevertheless, employment figures of 60,000 workers in that industry were insufficient to counter rising unemployment among an increasingly unhappy youth. Tens of thousands of Puerto Ricans migrated to U.S. mainland cities on the East Coast, where they were employed under sweatshop conditions, if at all. Anti-colonial ideas from India, the Soviet Union, Latin America, and elsewhere soon made their way from mainland Puerto Rican communities back to the island. During the 1930s, a new political party, the Partido Popular (later Partido Popular Democratico, PPD), rose to power and won elections in 1940. The blow to U.S. mainland capital's interests this served was short-lived, though (Neveling 2015b). Early New Deal–style measures that the PPD leadership put in place after establishing an alliance with the Roosevelt administration and the American governor of Puerto Rico, Rexford Tugwell, soon came under assault from a Puerto Rican version of what has been described for the U.S. mainland as a "businessmen's crusade against the New Deal" (Phillips-Fein 2009).

In order to understand the success of that crusade it is important to highlight another movement. This is the spread of ideas for a different political economy from the U.S. "Silicon Valley" of its day, the Boston/Cambridge region with its university campuses at the Massachusetts Institute for Technology (MIT) and Harvard. Puerto Rican New Deal money initially went into establishing a set of local government agencies, such as a planning board and an industrial development corporation (initially Fomento Industrial, later widely known as Puerto Rican Industrial Development Corporation, PRIDCO). Import-substitution industries were promoted, aiming to produce locally what might otherwise be expensive imports from the mainland, such as shoes, cement, and garments. Another initiative, which never came to completion, was for a government-owned sugar mill that would offer an alternative outlet for small planters and give them independence from the U.S. trust-owned mills and, this way, challenge the trust's capacity to dictate purchase prices and milling fees. Instead of all this coming to fruition, import-substitution policies were scrapped to privatize state-owned enterprises on a large scale. As the *Wall Street Journal* put it, a "Puerto Rican lure" (Diefenderrer 1946) was set up, with the island's government offering what later became the central features of EPZs: low-cost leases or purchases of government-owned factories, tax and customs exemptions, backed by an all-out promotion campaign also highlighting cheap and docile workers and the pleasant Puerto Rican climate. This was masterminded by the Boston consulting company Arthur D. Little Incorporated (now ADL), which, among a plethora of services, supplied the relocation of a leading U.S. textile and garment manufacturer by way of kinship networks to Puerto Rico (Neveling 2015a).

This was Royal W. Little, the nephew and later the adopted son of Arthur D. Little, owner of ADL. His company, Textron Limited, was among the first to relocate from the U.S. northeast heartlands in New Hampshire and Massachusetts to Puerto Rico, seeking greater competitiveness in a heated market with lots of mergers among U.S. textile and garment manufacturers during and after the Second World War. According to an internal Fomento study, Royal Little had a "[g]old rush psychology [that] is apparently still a part of the American scene and the possibility of making a killing seems to be much more of an attraction to many businessmen than does the rather high probability of a more moderate return" (quoted in Fernandez 1992, 168–69).

However, without the shift from import-substitution to export-oriented EPZ policies, backed by a coalition that encompassed local government and federal agencies, consulting corporations, and, ultimately, investors, no Royal Little ever would have descended on Puerto Rico, or, possibly, on any other setting. In fact, a much more significant global conjuncture helped maintain the Puerto Rican scheme and, at the same time, spread it to other parts of the world, thereby creating the island's ultimate downfall.

After the Second World War, development through industrialization became popular in many postcolonial nations as they sought to overcome the status of suppliers of raw materials for manufacturing industries located in industrialized capitalist nations. An important aspect of this was the Prebisch–Singer thesis, formulated in 1950, which pointed out this particular relationship as well as the fact that it was one between former colonizers, benefiting from the deal, and former colonized, suffering from the deal (Bair 2009). Several years later, this was framed by dependency theory and world systems theory scholars as a persistent and global pattern of unequal exchange. By then, the Puerto Rican model had already provided a triumph for neoclassical development economists, as it seemed to prove that their policy measures could generate rapid growth. The model quickly spread into national and international development agencies as proof for the famous Kuznets curve predictions that a rising tide of economic growth would lift all boats.

Such triumph had to do with the fact that since the late 1940s, successive U.S. administrations had promoted Puerto Rico to young postcolonial nations, praising the island's short takeoff phase as a road to sustainable industrialization, fueled by cheap labor, tax incentives, and government subsidies. Puerto Rican politicians were sent around Latin American capitals to praise the benevolence of the U.S. government and mainland capital—an all-out better ally than Moscow. ADL won contracts with Caribbean development agencies. The company sold the same package of tax incentives, state-funded infrastructure for industries, promotion campaigns, and so forth, again and again and received substantial financial backing from U.S. government development programs for developing nations and Latin America in the 1950s and 1960s. Some country programs were designed to counter socialist-leaning political movements—in Egypt and Honduras, for example. Elsewhere, the aim was to back anticommunist bastions, like the Republic of China under Chiang Kai-Shek and the Philippines, with EPZ programs. In the early 1960s, ADL also co-designed those Mexican EPZs in border cities with the United States that the 1990s anti-sweatshop campaign would make infamous globally as *maquiladoras* (Neveling 2015b; cf. Kahn 1986).

An irony of history is that the EPZ "gold rush" capitalism increased the future need to battle unhappy, socialist-leaning workers. Royal Little, for example, used relocations to Puerto Rico to downsize an empire of textile and garment factories he had built during the Second World War. He fired 10,000 unionized workers in New Hampshire in 1948 and moved some of the production to a PRIDCO-funded factory in Ponce. Hailed a hero in Puerto Rico, he came under attack on the mainland, but was able to brush off a U.S. Senate subcommittee inquiry in 1948, citing time-motion studies as proof of lower worker productivity in the U.S. northeast and generously "saving" 1,000 jobs in a New Hampshire sheeting mill.

The shape that EPZs took in Puerto Rico thus furnished one group of actors—investors/capital—with significant gains in bargaining power over another group of actors—workers/labor. The U.S. federal government and the local Puerto Rican government facilitated this by acting as if governments had "to compensate investors for setting up production facilities and for exploiting workers" (Neveling 2015a, 172).

Health and Safety in the Global EPZ Regime

In such a climate, the health and safety of workers was of little concern. A fire in the changing rooms of a Textron factory in Ponce in August 1954 received minor newspaper coverage. The focus was on $2,000 financial damage despite the fact that the cigar that reportedly started the fire could have caused a much larger blaze that might well have cost the lives of workers (Rivera 1954).

In a study contracted by PRIDCO for the tenth anniversary of the EPZ incentives schemes, we encounter an even more striking imbalance between an interest in the safety of capital and securing profit margins for investors on the one hand and the safety of workers on the other hand. The 1957 PRIDCO report listed all government institutions and agencies involved, which reveals that among the specialized and well-funded agencies catering for the EPZ, none were concerned with health and safety. Instead, the positive evaluation of PRIDCO focused solely on attracting investors and boosting their exports from Puerto Rico to the mainland (Stead 1958, 61–62). The evaluation category "industrial failures" only meant closures and not accidents and worker injuries (ibid., 74–78), despite indications that few or no safety inspections were in place. Investors, for example, complained about limited contact with government officials once plants were running and about a labor force trained "through a crash program of vocational training and by many ingenious methods of on-the-job training" (ibid., 82). Other sections acknowledged health and safety concerns, only to contradict the very existence of such measures a few pages further on. For example, one section stated that "[i]n general, working conditions are very good. The new factories conform to modern codes of health, sanitation, and safety—all carefully enforced by the Departments of Labor and Health" (ibid., 92), while it was soon stated that the very same government Departments of Labor and Health handled their EPZ tasks inefficiently compared with "corporations" such as PRIDCO (ibid., 112–24).

With these particular features—maximized safety for capital and minimized safety for labor—the Puerto Rican model went global (Neveling 2015a, 2015b, 2015d). Of course, concern for capital's and workers' health and safety would spread unevenly in the process, and there may well have been a racist element to this. The first European EPZ in the Republic of

Ireland benefited from a national setting dominated by paranoid anti-communism and a solid grounding in the capitalist bloc. Therefore, from its opening in 1959, workers in the Shannon Free Zone (SFZ) had fairly strong unions and the Shannon Free Airport Development Corporation (SFADCo) ran the zone with an ombudsman system in place to mediate between workers, their unions, and multinational capital (personal conversation with SFADCo staff, August 2010). In Taiwan, where the Kaohsiung Export Processing Zone (KEPZ) was one of the first Asian EPZs, anticommunism came in the form of a dictatorship that preached development as a national effort. The health and safety aspects of KEPZ were much closer to those in Puerto Rico than to those in Shannon. The KEPZ became operational as part of a large international container harbor in 1965, built upon advice from the U.S. Agency for International Development (USAID) and funded by USAID and United Nations technical assistance money. Taiwan, like any other U.S.-leaning developmental dictatorship in East and Southeast Asia, until today regards the environmental damages, the poor health and safety conditions in factories operated by Japanese, U.S., Hong Kong, and homegrown multinationals as essential sacrifices on the road to economic prosperity and world-market production.

This is best illustrated by juxtaposing the following historical snapshots and their uneven representation in the present. On the one hand, Kaohsiung is home to the burial tomb of twenty-five young women EPZ factory workers who drowned in 1973 when the overcrowded ferry that took them to work each morning sank. On the other hand, Kaohsiung is the location for a 1978 production by the Central Motion Picture Corporation, celebrating their stamina and sacrifices in *The Story of a Female Worker*. The colorful, high-quality print book celebrating the forty-fifth anniversary of setting up an EPZ in Taiwan mentions only the official movie, although the other event also has nationwide renown, not least because of a famous ghost story that has one dead "maiden" taking a taxi from the tomb to the EPZ and back in search of a husband (Export Processing Zone Administration [MOEA] 2011; Lee and Tang 2010).

In sum, Puerto Rico, Shannon, and Kaohsiung have been central sites for the distribution of the EPZ model from the 1950s to the 1980s. Despite the variations mentioned above, this model has had a consistently negative impact on workers' health and safety and a consistently positive impact on capital's health and safety. It is now time to find out how this uneven concern for health and safety traveled along with the EPZ model.

In Puerto Rico, a well-networked group of individual EPZ experts emerged. They provided similar kinds of training for Shannon and Kaohsiung bureaucrats, and in the late 1960s all three groups of trained EPZ experts found their way into the United Nations Industrial Development Organization's (UNIDO) consultancy books. UNIDO played a crucial role in establishing what macro-sociologists, who counted seventy-nine operational EPZs in 1975 in more than twenty countries with 725,000 workers, called "The New International Division of Labour" (Fröbel et al. 1981). And, in that division, health and safety—unless they were for investors and their money—remained a minor concern for the next two decades. Based on a 1970 global survey of zones, UNIDO codified what in practice already was a global EPZ regime. A 1971 brochure on "Industrial Free Zones as Incentives to Promote Export-Oriented Industries" (UNIDO 1971) was soon followed by the first edition of a "Handbook on Export Free Zones," commissioned by UNIDO's Export Promotions Division (EPD) and written by a SFADCo employee (Kelleher 1976).

The handbook itself was based on the training workshops that UNIDO had organized in Shannon and elsewhere. Safety, to UNIDO, was foremost the safety of investors. As one Indian EPZ official, who contributed his experience from the establishment of Kandla Foreign Trade Zone (KFTZ) in Western India to UNIDO's pool, put it: "A free trade zone or an export processing zone must be visible to the world at large as being essentially one of government initiatives backed by the full force of government authority, with *assurances and guarantees regarding the safety of investment* against any moves of nationalization. The nature of government must be permanent, in the form of legislative enactment, ensuring a climate in which export industries can develop" (Singh 1974, 49 of PDF document, emphasis mine).

UNIDO's EPD operated in an international setting still largely defined by the Cold War in the 1970s, albeit shaped by the increasing decline of the non-aligned movement (NAM). Leading NAM nations had called for limiting the power of multinational corporations and for introducing better global labor standards. But many of the administrations involved in these calls had been hit by U.S.-backed coups, which brought right-wing parties, backed by religious movements, to power, for example in Indonesia in 1965 and in Chile in 1973. There, as elsewhere, setting up EPZs was the order of the day. Even in the lost case of Saigon the U.S.-backed South Vietnamese government sought UNIDO and other technical assistance for an EPZ as late as 1974 and 1975 (UNIDO 1975).

South Asia, which today is home to major EPZs with textile and gar‐
ment production, showed a somewhat diverse trajectory, although its zones
replicate the regime's global defining features. The decoupling of EPZs as a
miraculous development policy on the one hand and the textile and garment
industry as a problematic sector on the other hand is strikingly evident in
the South Asian zones. India was officially the first Asian country to have
an EPZ up and running. This was the Kandla Foreign Trade Zone (KFTZ),
which opened in 1965 under an Indian government administration that was
commonly regarded as socialist leaning. The KFTZ is yet another example
showing that neoliberalism did not emerge from a radical rupture in the
1970s. Instead, EPZ regimes emerged much earlier from neoliberal states,
which privatized public enterprises and acted as entrepreneurs to facilitate
capital mobility and profit. In the Indian setting, this "untimely coincidence
of neoliberalism with other capitalist modes of production" (Neveling 2014b,
24–25, 2014c) was fueled by U.S. expertise that informed the establishment
of KFTZ and of Santacruz Electronics Export Processing Zone (SEEPZ) in
Mumbai, while there was also a continuity of institutional arrangements from
the colonial period (Maruschke 2015).

U.S. involvement and colonial continuities in the Indian zones also point
to what I propose to call a "myth of independent invention" of EPZ regimes.
This myth does excellent service to pre-scientific claims that inhumane health
and safety were caused by weak regional or national structures of governance
or by rogue individuals and corporations. It is for good reason that such a
myth of independent invention is strikingly visible in writings on Bangla‐
desh's EPZs. A story first published by a World Bank consultant has a Ban‐
gladeshi army general, Noorul Quader, as incidental hero and catalyst for the
takeoff of the Bangladesh ready-made garment (RMG) industry in the 1970s.
Daewoo, a South Korean *chaebol* founded in 1967, is Quader's business part‐
ner. The South Koreans want to do business in Bangladesh but obstacles only
disappear after Quader somewhat randomly passed by at Daewoo's Euro‐
pean headquarters in Paris in the mid-1970s, and the two sides agreed on
the opening of the Desh Garment Company and the training of 130 Bangla‐
deshi workers in Daewoo's plant in Pusan, South Korea (Rhee 1990, 335–40).
Ever since, the rise of Quader to leading entrepreneur in Bangladesh has been
explained by an ingenious Schumpeterian spirit. He and his daughter emerge
as the human faces of self-made entrepreneurs keeping the Bangladeshi gar‐
ment sector afloat (Bradsher 2004; Hossain 2013). Now, how is such a myth of
independent invention relevant to the issue of health and safety in the global

garment industry? And in what ways can demystification inspire a "better" anthropology—openly and analytically at odds with the vicissitudes of EPZ capitalism?

First, demystification highlights the nexus between the trajectory of anthropological research on EPZs and the future-oriented policy prescriptions of international development organizations that I have outlined above. The attraction of journalists and development planners to such myths of independent invention as the Bangladeshi one reveals the analytical limits of a focus on individuals or on developments in single factories and zones. It is as if one would allow capital to decide on the roles, the plot, and the cast of actors in a play and then only analyze a single performance with a focus on nothing but the stage, while behind the scenes, it is the global EPZ regime that determines the dramatic structure and variations of the plot, as the Cold War setting changes, ends, and at the same time survives in its neoliberal drive to increase global inequality in favor of capital. Writings on Bangladesh "forget" that Quader served as an army general in a military dictatorship that emerged from mass killings and environmental disasters, which, in many ways, fertilized the ground for an EPZ infrastructure. Without this infrastructure and the provision of preferential export quotas under the MFA, no RMG sector could have risen to what it is in the present.

Importantly, an anthropology interested in demystifying independent invention is required to venture into the archives and into the published outputs of international organizations involved in setting up the EPZ in Bangladesh. For example, one former World Bank consultant detailed in a journal article that it was in fact Robert McNamara, acting World Bank president and former director of Ford Motor Company and U.S. Secretary of Defense, who recommended establishing an EPZ to the president of Bangladesh in 1976 (Dowla 1997, 562). Another obvious contradiction to the myth of independent invention comes to light from research in the archives of UNIDO. In 1980, Peter Ryan, head of EPD's institutional successor, emphasized that UNIDO's 1973 pre-feasibility study (jointly funded with the Irish government) and its funding for a study tour for Bangladeshi government officials to India, Ireland, the Republic of Korea, and the Philippines in March 1979 led the Bangladeshi government to build the Chittagong EPZ. Ultimately, this would become a UNIDO flagship project, with an Irish consultant sitting in the Dhaka Sheraton and typing reports on hotel paper sent by international carbon copy to Vienna (Ryan 1980). Given this central role of UNIDO in Bangladesh and most other EPZs planned and realized since the 1970s, it is important to take a look at the organization's concerns for workplace health and safety.

As already mentioned, UNIDO was closely linked to the non-aligned movement initiative of the 1960s and, in fact, it needed several years of political pressure from those nations before the UN Council approved the establishment of the agency. When UNIDO was inaugurated at an international conference in Athens in 1967, the agency explicitly put workers' health and safety standards on the agenda (cf. UNIDO and ILO 1967). However, not all of its fourteen internal groups made this the mainstay of their activities. The EPD's handbook on EPZ establishment did not feature such concerns. Safety comes in the form of recommendations to bury power supply cables underground when cultivating industrial land, whereas health appears as a possible cause of extra production costs in zones with regional climatic conditions that could "influence worker productivity or incur additional costs on such things as special health care services, air conditioning and dust control" (Kelleher 1976, 26 and 36).

It is thus no wonder that for the 1970s, UNIDO's vast Industrial Development Abstracts database only shows a single EPZ-related document with "safety" as a keyword (and none with "health"). This is about workers' "Safety, Health and Welfare" in the Malaysian pioneer EPZ of Petaling Jaya, which was a redevelopment of an industrial estate adjacent to a 1950s British colonial rehousing program for Kuala Lumpur's squatters. The newly founded Petaling Jaya Development Corporation added EPZ features in the 1960s. By 1967, 264 factories employed 10,000 workers on the estate (Neilson 1976, 20). Despite the document title, the section on health and safety has only one page, which reprints government statistics and commends the Factories and Machinery Act of 1970 for regulating "Fencing of Machinery and Safety" and "Safety, Health and Welfare," "enforced by inspectorate with offices in most estates" (ibid., 31–32). What comes as "success statistics" is a reduction in the annual number of accidents per 1,000 workers from 19.5 in 1968 to 16.0 in 1972. Although no major accidents are listed, the absolute number of fatal accidents per annum is high. Their peaks in 1972 amounted to seventy-five dead workers. Still, the UNIDO consultant praised a number of achievements: "good guarding of moving parts," safety clothing provisions in large factories, widespread use of goggles, and those regulations prescribing medical facilities, such as first-aid cabinets with specified dressings in smaller establishments, a "clinic with a trained full-time attendant and visiting or resident doctor" serving the entire EPZ, and additional clinics maintained by larger factories that are also open to workers' families (ibid., 31).

UNIDO's 1970s and 1980s technical assistance projects in the EPZ realm (or in the garment sector) are too numerous to assess here. Even in the 1990s, after it had incurred significant financial losses from the United States, Canada, and other Western nations cancelling their non-mandatory membership in this specialized UN agency, UNIDO still played an important role in establishing EPZs in Eastern Europe and supporting China's booming industrial sectors. Since the late 1980s, workers' health and safety was central to UNIDO technical assistance, although working groups promoting EPZs picked this up a bit later (as happened with UNIDO's turn to "sustainability" and the Rio Agenda, see Luken 2009). A 1978 Handbook on Industrial Estates emphasized that they facilitated keeping factories in check (UNIDO 1978, 86), and a 1987 reprint recommended, "[w]ithout authorization no changes in the purpose of buildings, subletting or alterations may take place" (UNIDO 1987, 39).

In sum, then, an analysis of UNIDO consultancy papers, myths of independent invention, and the lack of attention to historical continuities reveals how national and international EPZ development policy guidelines offered little in regard to health and safety measures for workers up to the late 1980s. Although UNIDO and other organizations (the World Bank followed in the 1990s) took a more cautious approach to EPZ promotion from then on, it is striking that this was applied to new zones only. In fact, there was never any larger international initiative to refurbish and upgrade zones established in the 1960s and 1970s, many of which remain operational today.

Concluding Remarks: The Politics of Foxes Guarding Henhouses (with Codes)

The global spread of EPZs sketched above reveals a gradual shift, at best, from a sole concern with the health and safety of capital and capitalists to a consideration of the health and safety of workers. Recent efforts acknowledge the need for governments to properly monitor the operations of investors and enforce restrictions on their practices in EPZs—and here is the Catch 22 situation for any government operating an EPZ. Most investments in EPZs are not made because those moving money, machinery, production, and knowledge arrive to better the lives and times of workers. What they want is to better their own lives, the lives of their shareholders, their leading personnel, and possibly the lives and times of their customers, who, for the most part of the history of the global EPZ regime, have been shoppers in Western advanced capitalist nations. So, if anyone involved in the operations of a given EPZ wanted to enforce the regulations for health and safety laid out in that UNIDO handbook, for example, they would have to do so within a global setting that offers investors thousands of competing EPZs for relocation. And relocations are encouraged because it is governments that put up fixed capital, not investors.

This particularity of capital mobility and the logic of industrial relocation in EPZs has, for many decades now, meant that any emphasis on health and safety concerns for workers in textile and garment factories does not incentivize relocation or subcontracting to a given EPZ, but instead would appear as a disincentive and thus reduce that very EPZ's competitiveness in a global market, pitting the zones against each other in bids for industrial relocations and subcontracting. These findings are vividly exemplified in one 1977 UNIDO report. In that report, the chairman administrator of the Export Processing Zones Authority (EPZA) of the Philippines describes in detail and frames as policy advice how his EPZA stripped the local municipality of all its rights to regulate the Bataan Export Processing Zone (BEPZ). This happened after the municipality had tried to enforce various regulations in the EPZ, among them health and safety measures. Once investors refused to comply, violent confrontations erupted between municipal police and zone police, acting on behalf of the investors (Pena 1977). EPZA then delegated rights for regulation back to individual zone authorities, not least the right for policing. The following example from the 1990s illustrates how, in the long run, this introduced highly abusive modes of rule by EPZ authorities in the Philippines: "The Subic Bay EPZ in the Philippines . . . was built on an abandoned U.S. Army airbase. Richard Gordon, who ran the zone, established a military style regime, forcing job seekers to work several months without wages in order to qualify for employment. Radio features of the German journalist Karl Roessel tell of a Subic Bay zone workforce that had to wear T-shirts praising Gordon, EPZ factory managers, and investors, as they were forced to participate in regular street parades" (Neveling 2014a).

Given what I have said in this chapter and given the range of actors that I discussed, many readers may be inclined to ask: "What about labor and resistance in the face of all these grave injustices?" That is a valid question, but the answers are not enchanting.

First, post–Second World War Puerto Rico was not just a testing ground for globalizing EPZ regimes. As many U.S. investors came with trade unions in tow that gave little support to workers, Puerto Rico was also the testing ground for what has been analyzed as a "Secret War against Developing Countries' Workers" by the American Federation of Labor and the Congress of Industrial Organizations (AFL-CIO) (Scipes 2010). Collaboration with the U.S. Central Intelligence Agency during the Cold War meant that the AFL-CIO's five big labor research centers for Asia, Africa, Latin America, Southern Europe, and the global solidarity campaigns largely operated to support anti-communist dictatorships in developing nations.

Second, the ILO could have campaigned against the emerging global EPZ regime from the 1960s onward. However, by then the ILO was no longer the sole auditor for social and welfare issues, which it had been under the League of Nations system. When the UN created more and more agencies from the 1950s, this weakened the ILO. UNIDO was set up in 1966 to better the global positioning of developing nations. It took over ILO's policy fields and, in the long run, developed a neoliberal industrialization agenda with little regard for worker health or workplace safety. The ILO rather accidentally became aware of the EPZ regime in the early 1970s, when one Japanese freelance consultant pointed out that Japanese enterprises operated in South Korean and Taiwanese EPZs and were now relocating to Mexican *maquiladoras* to fetch better export quotas to the United States.[2] In the late 1970s, the ILO stepped up its research on EPZs in concert with the United Nations Centre on Transnational Corporations (UNCTC), only for the UNCTC to be scrapped after sustained attacks from U.S. neoliberal policy powerhouses (Bair 2009). This triggered a policy shift from the 1970s ambitions to oblige multinational corporations to honor certain production standards, to a 1990s "global compact" with a weak self-imposed and self-regulated corporate commitment.

Instead, in South Korea, Mauritius, and elsewhere, nationalist discourses of the 1970s portrayed EPZ labor as a necessary sacrifice in the development process. Often, workers in textile and garment factories in EPZs were subject to malevolent double-movements. Such movements became manifest as religious and right-wing factions in postcolonial societies sought to dislocate themselves from the impact that EPZ labor relations had on households and society more generally. Dislocation came by way of discriminating against female workers because they were women and therefore "deserved" lower wages than men and because they worked in the EPZ, which was regarded as an arena of moral decline (Neveling 2015c; cf. Hewamanne this volume). Capital initiated its own double-movement. In EPZs, this extended beyond pressure groups in national economies. Instead, an ever-increasing number of multinational corporations produced myriad replica of Royal W. Little's relocation from New Hampshire to Puerto Rico and farther afield. Like Royal, even today, multinational corporations commonly move elsewhere once their ten-year "tax holidays" in a given EPZ come to an end (Neveling 2014c).

In the face of such powerful alliances, workers' resistance was confined to the factory or the region for many years. Global resistance emerged only in the 1970s and 1980s and from an international grassroots level as activists and scholars jointly analyzed and battled the new international division of labor (Chisolm et al. 1986; Fröbel 1981; War on Want 1985[1984]). A turning point came when in 1996 the International Conference of Free Trade Unions published a survey of global EPZ operations that described patterns of killing trade unionists, intimidations, and generally antisocial behavior of EPZ corporations (ICFTU 1996). This, again only briefly, limited World Bank and UNIDO promotions of EPZs until the World Bank's public-private partnership wing, the IFC, embarked on a massive campaign to whitewash what were EPZs with the new label SEZ (Neveling 2015d).

Social anthropologists have only had a limited influence on anti-EPZ campaigns since the 1980s cultural turn subjected the discipline to a neoliberal, postmodernist backlash (Carrier 2012; Neveling 2016). Now, anthropologists again deconstruct high-flying and low-achieving notions such as "corporate social responsibility" (De Neve 2014), and the contributions of this volume will surely strengthen this focus. My contribution to this renewed alliance of anthropologists and labor activists reveals the particular relationship between capital, state, and labor established in EPZs that devalues labor outright, while capital is misrepresented as a benevolent donor. Under such circumstances, it has been and will be impossible to arrive at standards that are sufficient to guarantee the long-term health and safety of workers in the textile and garment industry. As the many recent nonfatal and fatal accidents in the textile and garment industry show, the introduction of self-imposed ethical codes for corporate capital can never be more than the fox guarding the henhouse.

For this relationship to change, there needs to be an end to the myths of independent invention, and to the legends of foreign exchange earnings and of the great leaps forward that the zones are said to enable. The social sciences often sustain such legends by turning away from history and toward "newness," the false coins of neoliberal dreams, which can only be desecrated when the focus is on the global praxis of neoliberal and other capitalist regimes (Baca 2005; for EPZs in particular Neveling 2006).

The global reality of EPZs is one historical example of neoliberal praxis. EPZs have created a race to the bottom in corporate taxation and in labor standards. This has been facilitated in part by the fact that the history of EPZs is constantly rewritten in a very particular way. The present generation of SEZs is promoted with reference to the People's Republic of China's establishment of such zones since the late 1970s and the promise that opening an SEZ will enable any nation to follow in the footsteps of its economic boom. What is not said is that the zones in the People's Republic of China were built on an earlier model, that of the Irish zones first emerging in Shannon, and how these zones were built with the consultancy of Arthur D. Little based on the Puerto Rican experience. If the latter were emphasized, it would be a lot more evident that the sacrifices of export-oriented, EPZ-driven development are not in the interest of national development or for the betterment of the social and economic conditions of future generations. Instead, such sacrifices are called for by the false preachers and fake healers of global capitalism—those neoliberal development economists and capitalist corporations promoting the spread of EPZs. It is such corporations that in Puerto Rico in the 1970s and in Ireland in the 2010s moved on and left the local populations queuing for food stamps, while the legacies of bustling EPZs with poor health and safety conditions for workers evaporated and vanished.

Notes

1. I here use "export processing zone" as the umbrella term for special economic zones (SEZ), free trade zones (FTZ), foreign trade zones (FTZ), free enterprise zones (FEZ), bonded warehouses, and so forth. For several decades, EPZ was the common term among academics and practitioners (Boyenge 2007; Murayama and Yokota 2008). Recently, the International Finance Corporation (IFC), the public-private partnership arm of the World Bank, started promoting SEZ as the new label. I deal with this misguided, neoliberal usage in detail elsewhere (Neveling 2015d).

2. The history of ILO engagement with EPZs remains to be written (Neveling in preparation). Early engagement, which is largely driven by the Japanese consultant Susumu Watanabe, is documented in the following folder in the ILO Archives in

Geneva: ILO-BIT, Registry/150496, MULTI RCH 3–8, 1975–1982, "Multi Enterprises Programme—Research—Export processing zones."

Bibliography

Akinci, Gokhan, James Crittle, and FIAS/World Bank Group. 2008. *Special Economic Zones: Performance, Lessons Learned, and Implications for Zone Development.* Washington, DC: World Bank Group.

Baca, George. 2005. "Legends of Fordism: Between Myth, History, and Foregone Conclusions." Pp. 31–46 in *The Retreat of the Social: The Rise and Rise of Reductionism,* ed. by Bruce Kapferer. New York: Berghahn.

Bair, Jennifer. 2009. "Taking Aim at the New International Economic Order." Pp. 347–85 in *The Road from Mont Pèlerin: The Making of the Neoliberal Thought Collective,* ed. by Philip Mirowski and Dieter Plehwe. Cambridge, MA: Harvard University Press.

Boyenge, Jean-Pierre Singa. 2007. ILO Database on Export Processing Zones (Revised). *ILO Working Papers,* 251. Online: http://www.ilo.org/public/english/dialogue /sector/themes/epz/epz-db.pdf. Accessed: November 27, 2009.

Bradsher, Keith. 2004. "Bangladesh Is Surviving to Export Another Day." *New York Times,* December 14.

Burawoy, Michael. 1983. "Between the Labor Process and the State: The Changing Face of Factory Regimes under Advanced Capitalism." *American Sociological Review* 5: 587–605.

Carrier, James G. 2012. "Anthropology After the Crisis." *Focaal* 64: 115–28.

Carswell, Grace, and Geert De Neve. 2014. "T-shirts and Tumblers: Caste, Dependency and Work under Neoliberalisation in South India." *Contributions to Indian Sociology* 48(1): 103–31.

Chisolm, Nick, Naila Kabeer, Swasti Mitter, and Stuart Howard. 1986. *Linked by the Same Thread: The Multi-Fibre Arrangement and the Labour Movement.* London: Tower Hamlet International Solidarity and Tower Hamlet Trade Union Council.

Cross, Jamie. 2010. "Neoliberalism as Unexceptional: Economic Zones and the Everyday Precariousness of Working Life in South India." *Critique of Anthropology* 30(4): 355–73.

De Neve, Geert. 2014. "Fordism, Flexible Specialization and CSR: How Indian Garment Workers Critique Neoliberal Labour Regimes." *Ethnography* 15(2): 184–207.

Diefenderrer, M. M. 1946. "Puerto Rican Lure." *Wall Street Journal,* June 7.

Dowla, Asif. 1997. "Export Processing Zones in Bangladesh: The Economic Impact." *Asian Survey* 37(6): 561–74.

Export Processing Zone Administration (MOEA). 2011. *Carrying on from Generation to Generation (Export Processing Zone 45th Anniversary Edition).* Taipei: Export Processing Zone Administration (MOEA).

Farole, Thomas. 2011. *Special Economic Zones in Africa: Comparing Performance and Learning from Global Experiences*. Washington, D.C.: World Bank; London: Eurospan.

Fernandez, Ronald. 1992. *The Disenchanted Island: Puerto Rico and the United States in the Twentieth Century*. New York: Praeger.

Fröbel, Folker, Jürgen Heinrichs, and Otto Kreye. 1981. *The New International Division of Labour: Structural Unemployment in Industrialised Countries and Industrialisation in Developing Countries*. Cambridge: Cambridge University Press.

Gereffi, Gary, David Spener, and Jennifer Bair (eds). 2002. *Free Trade and Uneven Development: The North American Apparel Industry After NAFTA*. Philadelphia: Temple University Press.

Hossain, Anushay. 2013. "Made in Bangladesh, Not in Bangladeshi Blood." *Forbeswoman*, February 5. Online: http://www.forbes.com/sites/worldviews/2013/05/02/made-in-bangladesh-not-in-bangladeshi-blood/. Accessed: February 6, 2013.

International Conference of Free Trade Unions (ICFTU) 1996. "Behind the Wire—Antiunion Repression in the Export Processing Zones" (A survey prepared by Jean-Paul Marhoz, with Marcela Szymanski). Bruxelles: ICFTU.

Kahn, E. J. 1986. *The Problem Solvers: A History of Arthur D. Little, Inc.* Boston: Little, Brown.

Kelleher, Thomas. 1976. *Handbook on Export Processing Zones*. Vienna: United Nations Industrial Development Organization (UNIDO).

Klein, Naomi. 2000. *No Logo: Taking Aim at the Brand Bullies*. London: Flamingo.

Latimer, Amanda. 2015. "Super-exploitation, the Race to the Bottom, and the Missing International." Pp. 1136–50 in *The Palgrave Encyclopedia of Imperialism and Antiimperialism*, ed. by Immanuel Ness and Zak Cope. Basingstoke: Palgrave Macmillan.

Lee, Anru, and Wen-hui Anna Tang. 2010. "The Twenty-Five Maiden Ladies' Tomb and Predicaments of the Feminist Movement in Taiwan." *Journal of Current Chinese Affairs* 39(3): 23–49.

Luken, Ralph A. 2009. "Greening an International Organization: UNIDO's Strategic Responses." *Review of International Organizations* 4(2): 159–84.

Maruschke, Megan. 2015. "Are There Connections Between Previous Free Port Practices and Current Special Economic Zones? The Case of Mumbai's Ports." *TraFo (Transregionale Forschung)*, April 1. Online: http://trafo.hypotheses.org/2112. Accessed: April 29, 2015.

Murayama, Mayumi, and Nobuko Yokota. 2008. "Revisiting Labour and Gender Issues in Export Processing Zones: The Cases of South Korea, Bangladesh and India." *IDE Discussion Paper* 174. Online: http://www.ide.go.jp/. Accessed: February 26, 2009.

Neilson, A. 1976. "Evaluation Report on Industrial Estates No. 9, Malaysia." (Paper for Expert Group Meeting on Evaluation and the Effectiveness of Industrial Estates in Developing Countries, Vienna, Austria, December 1976, *United Nations Industrial Development Organization Archives*, Industrial Development Abstracts, 007246).

Neveling, Patrick. 2006. "Spirits of Capitalism and the De-alienation of Workers: A Historical Perspective on the Mauritian Garment Industry." *Graduate School for Societies and Cultures in Motion: Working Paper Series*. Online: http://www.scm.uni-halle
.de. Accessed: April 14, 2010.

———. 2012. *Manifestationen der Globalisierung: Kapital, Staat und Arbeit in Mauritius, 1825–2005 (DPhil Thesis, Engl.: Manifestations of Globalisation: Capital,
State, and Labour in Mauritius, 1825–2005)*, Halle/Saale: Martin Luther University Library.

———. 2014a. "Capitalism: The Most Recent Seventy-Two Years." *FocaalBlog*, July
17. Online: http://www.focaalblog.com/2014/07/17/capitalism-the-most-recent
-seventy-two-years-by-patrick-neveling. Accessed: November 28, 2014.

———. 2014b. "Structural Contingencies and Untimely Coincidences in the Making of
Neoliberal India—The Kandla Foreign Trade Zone, 1965–1991." *Contributions to
Indian Sociology* 48(1): 17–43.

———. 2014c. "Three Shades of Embeddedness: State Capitalism as the Informal Economy, Emic Notions of the Anti-market and Counterfeit Garments in the Mauritian
Export Processing Zone." *Research in Economic Anthropology* 34: 65–94.

———. 2015a. "Export Processing Zones and Global Class Formation." Pp. 164–82 in
Anthropologies of Class: Power, Practice, Inequality, ed. by James Carrier and Don
Kalb. Cambridge: Cambridge University Press.

———. 2015b. "Export Processing Zones, Special Economic Zones and the Long March
of Capitalist Development Policies During the Cold War." Pp. 63–84 in *Negotiating
Independence: New Directions in the Histories of the Cold War and Decolonization*,
ed. by Leslie James and Elisabeth Leake. London: Bloomsbury.

———. 2015c. "Flexible Capitalism and Transactional Orders in Colonial and Postcolonial Mauritius: A Post-Occidentalist View." Pp. 207–34 in *Flexible Capitalism:
Exchange and Ambiguity at Work*, ed. by Jens Kjaerulf. Oxford: Berghahn.

———. 2015d. "Free Trade Zones, Export Processing Zones, Special Economic Zones
and Global Imperial Formations 200 BCE to 2015 CE." Pp. 1007–16 in *The Palgrave
Encyclopedia of Imperialism and Anti-imperialism*, ed. by Immanuel Ness and Zak
Cope. Basingstoke: Palgrave Macmillan.

———. 2016. "Beyond Sites and Methods: The Field, History, Global Capitalism."
Pp. 72–91 in *Routledge Companion to Contemporary Anthropology*, ed. by Simon
Coleman, Susan B. Hyatt, and Ann Kingsolver. London: Routledge.

———. In preparation. "The ILO and Export Processing Zones: A Different Story of
Development and Decolonisation."

Pena, T. Q. 1977. "How to Organize an Industrial Free Zone." (Report for the Seminar
on Co-operation between Industrial Free Zones in the Arab Region, Alexandria,
February 21–March 1, 1977, *United Nations Industrial Development Organization
Archives*, ID/WG.244/5).

Phillips-Fein, Kim. 2009. *Invisible Hands: The Businessmen's Crusade Against the New
Deal*. New York: W. W. Norton.

Prentice, Rebecca. 2008. "Knowledge, Skill, and the Inculcation of the Anthropologist: Reflections on Learning to Sew in the Field." *Anthropology of Work Review* 29(3): 54–61.

Rhee, Yung Whee. 1990. "The Catalyst Model of Development: Lessons from Bangladesh's Success with Garment Exports." *World Development* 18(2): 333–46.

Rivera, M. 1954. "Cigarrillo Causa Fuego en Textron." *El Mundo*, August 5.

Rosen, Ellen Israel. 2002. *Making Sweatshops: The Globalization of the U.S. Apparel Industry.* Berkeley: University of California Press.

Ryan, P. 1980, undated. "Note for the File—Bangladesh." *United Nations Industrial Development Organization Archives*, Folder DP:BGD:80:022_a/Subset BGD066.

Scipes, Kim. 2010. *AFL-CIO's Secret War against Developing Country Workers: Solidarity or Sabotage?* Lanham, MD: Lexington Books.

Singh, Rajinder. 1974. "Organization of Export-oriented Free Zones and Free Ports: Study Based on Shannon (Ireland), Masan (Republic of Korea), and Hong Kong." October 5–11, *United Nations Industrial Development Organization Archives*, ID/WC.185/6, Regional Export Working Group Meeting on Industrial Free Zones.

Stead, William H. 1958. *Fomento—The Economic Development of Puerto Rico (A Staff Report).* Washington, D.C.: National Planning Association.

United Nations Industrial Development Organization (UNIDO). 1971. *Industrial Free Zones as Incentives to Promote Export-Oriented Industries.* Vienna: UNIDO.

——. 1975. *Assistance à la société nationale pour le developpement de zones industrielles (SONADEZI)—Rapport final.* DP/RVN/78/006.

——. 1978. *Guidelines for the Establishment of Industrial Estates in Developing Countries.* Vienna, New York: UNIDO, United Nations.

——. 1987. *Industrial Estates—Principles and Practice.* Vienna, New York: UNIDO, United Nations.

United Nations Industrial Development Organization (UNIDO) and International Labour Organization (ILO) 1967. *Planning for Industrial Safety and Health in the Place of Work* (Proceedings of the International Symposium on Industrial Development, Athens, 1967). UNIDO-ID/CONF.1/B.6; UNIDO-ID/CONF.1/35.

War on Want 1985 (1984). *Women Working Worldwide: The International Division of Labour in the Electronics, Clothing and Textiles Industries.* London: War on Want.

CHAPTER 5

Discourses of Compensation
and the Normalization of Negligence:
The Experience of the Tazreen Factory Fire

Mahmudul H. Sumon, Nazneen Shifa, and Saydia Gulrukh

In this chapter we discuss how industrial disasters in Bangladesh's ready-made garment industry have become normalized by regimes of compensation for survivors and the families of the dead. We argue that international and national efforts to compensate Bangladeshi victims of factory fires and building collapses have drawn attention away from the negligence of factory owners (a punishable offence under national law) and foreclosed redress in the courts. We write as three members of a Bangladeshi activist group called Activist Anthropologist,[1] which in the wake of the November 2012 Tazreen Fashions factory fire in Dhaka staged several public protests to call for the arrest of its owner, Mohammad Delwar Hossain, for negligence in protecting the health and safety of his workers. After months of inaction by the government, Activist Anthropologist filed a Public Interest Litigation (PIL) in the High Court of Bangladesh to charge the factory owners with negligence.

In the immediate aftermath of an industrial disaster, workers need financial support of various kinds. With few savings or assets, garment workers injured on the job or made suddenly unemployed by a factory fire or building collapse require prompt relief to meet basic needs. Injured and disabled workers may have long-term requirements for costly medical care and disability supports; dependent family members, including children and the elderly, need financial compensation for the loss of earnings when a relative is killed or gravely injured at work. In the absence of state enforcement and oversight of short-term and long-term payments, what has emerged in Bangladesh is a complex web of private initiatives from industry, NGOs, and the state. Payments may be given to affected workers and their families as charity in the form of "cash assistance" or "humanitarian relief," or as compensation to which workers are legally entitled. According to the International Labour Organization (ILO), victims of workplace injury should expect payment for medical expenses and loss of wages, and compensation for emotional pain and suffering (Kazmin 2013). Compelling foreign fashion brands to contribute funds for victims of industrial disasters has been a major part of NGO campaigning, both in Bangladesh and globally.

As Bangladeshi activists collecting information on the Tazreen fire and its aftermath while also organizing and participating in public demonstrations and legal action, we have been troubled by the narrowing down of the public debate to issues of compensation. The culpability of factory owners in the preventable deaths and injuries of workers has been almost completely ignored, while what has emerged is what we call a "regime of compensation," in which hegemonic debates about compensation preclude consideration of any other forms of justice. The power of this regime of compensation to preempt other avenues of justice was encapsulated by the words of the Tazreen Fashions factory owner, Mohammad Delwar Hossain. At the first hearing of our PIL case against him, Hossain remarked to a newspaper reporter outside the courtroom: "Don't know which NGO has filed this case; they won't be able to do anything to me. I have given money to all the affected workers."

"Glocal" activism in the wake of the Tazreen fire, and later after the Rana Plaza factory collapse in 2013, has emphasized the need to compensate victims and their families. We examine various and sometimes competing forms of compensation that became available after the Tazreen fire, discussing patterns that were first developed in response to the Spectrum building collapse in 2005, which killed sixty-two workers and injured eighty-four workers in the Savar industrial district of Dhaka (Miller 2012, 28–29). We also explore how since the Spectrum collapse, activist discourses have come to echo this issue of compensation to the neglect of broader structural issues and criminal negligence. We are troubled by this narrowing and depoliticization of issues of health and safety in the garment industry, and we trace the ways in which compensation has come to dominate debates on postdisaster justice.

"Burned Alive": The Factory Fire in Nishchintapur

On November 24, 2012, a little after the *Maghreb* (evening prayer), a fire broke out at the nine-story Tazreen Fashions factory in Nishchintapur, a village on the outskirts of Dhaka. Workers in the building later described a fire alarm sounding about ten minutes before they began seeing smoke. Recounting that night, an injured worker named Molina Khatun[2] said,

> I was a sewing operator on the fifth floor. The fire alarm started ringing. I managed to get down to the third floor, then the factory manager, Rajjak Shaheb, told us, "Nothing happened, go back to work." Then we said, "But we can see smoke, we want to go." He insisted, "Nothing happened, don't run around unnecessarily." We said, "No, we saw smoke. There is fire." We begged him, urged him to help us so [our family members] could find our dead [bodies]. Somehow I came to the sample room on the third floor and saw boys breaking the window. The [gates on each floor] were locked. We were running around in pitch-black darkness. I jumped through a window, broke my backbone and left ankle. Now I am incapacitated for life. (February 18, 2014)

The fire started on the ground floor, where flammable fabrics and threads were stored (Sarkar 2013). Since there were no emergency exits, and the floor gates were locked, workers ran for their lives, running toward the windows, breaking exhaust fan holes or windows, and jumping off the building from the fourth, fifth, and even sixth floors. At least six workers were killed jumping from windows and those who survived were severely wounded. When fire trucks arrived, approximately two hours after the fire began, the absence of an adequate water source made it difficult for the firefighters to extinguish it.

All night long, with horror and anguish, relatives of workers stood by the factory gate. The fire was ablaze from the evening until the following morning. On November 25, 2012, it was reaching nearly *Zahr* prayer time (around 1:00 p.m.) when rescue workers began to bring out dead bodies in white body bags. According to the Bangladesh Fire Service, 102 bodies were recovered from the factory and kept at the Nishchintapur School premises for identification. Bodies were burned beyond recognition, leaving no traces for relatives to identify them. In the end, sixty-eight charred bodies of Tazreen workers were taken to Dhaka Medical College Hospital.[3] Later that night, the government declared that the unidentified bodies would be buried at Dhaka's Jurain Public graveyard and it would use a DNA[4] testing method to identify the bodies.

Rahima Begum and her husband, Badiur Rahman, had worked in various garment factories over the previous seven years. The night of the fire, Badiur was working at Tazreen. Rahima, eight months pregnant, was at home from her job at the Knit Asia Limited factory when her husband called at 6:38 p.m. He said, "There's a fire at the factory. Pray for me." He called again at 7:02 p.m.: "I am stuck on the third floor. I don't think I'll be able to get out." At 7.33 p.m., he called her for the last time. He whispered, "I am dying. Forgive me."

When we met Rahima Begum less than a month after the fire, she was outraged by the safety measures at the factory. She contrasted her own workplace with Tazreen Fashions, saying, "When an alarm goes off in our factory, we come down within two minutes. But my husband was stuck in the building for the whole night. Why couldn't he come out? My whole life is burned to ashes now; my child lost its father before birth. We had come to Dhaka driven by need; we have been so neglected, but does that mean they would have to kill us?" (December 3, 2012).

Rahima Begum was not alone. Immediately after the fire, many survivors raised similar questions. Why did the floor managers lock the collapsible gates once the fire alarm started ringing, as they were alleged to have done? Why was factory management, especially the factory owner, so negligent about ensuring worker safety? As we walked through Nishchintapur, grieving families and injured workers asked the same questions. More than 119 workers were killed, and at least 150 workers were injured.[5] When we walked into the fire-ravaged factory, safety violations were in plain sight. The nine-story building had no proper fire exits or stairways. Interior stairs were used as "fire exits" and the ground floor was used as a storage space, blocking the exit. There were few tools on hand for fighting fire, and most workers would not have known how to use them. Lists of safety violations at the factory began appearing in national newspapers and investigative reports in the days following the fire, and it was revealed that the factory lacked an up-to-date fire safety certificate (Ain o Salish Kendra 2012; Manik and Yardley 2012). Walmart, one of many foreign buyers—including C&A, Disney, and Sears—that knowingly or unknowingly sourced garments from Tazreen Fashions, had reportedly identified "high risk" violations of working conditions during a social audit of the factory more than twelve months before the fire (Bajaj 2012).

A History of Impunity

Within days of the fire, rumors began circulating around Nishchintapur about its cause. Some accused the owner of Tazreen Fashions Ltd., Mohammad Delwar Hossain, of intentionally setting his factory ablaze. A national daily newspaper even published a brief story claiming that Hossain had filed a report with the local police station on the very night of the fire, describing his material loss as close to BDT 10 million (US$128,500). The suspicion was that the fire provided an opportunity to claim insurance money. The Home Minister, after visiting the site, read political motives in the incident, speculating to the press that the fire could be an act of sabotage designed to discredit the government.

In the context of major international and national outrage and swirling accusations, the government was compelled to set up a committee to investigate the cause of the fire. A week later, Hossain admitted in an interview being unaware of the specifics of the factory building code relating to fire exits. In another interview, an executive from the fire safety department confirmed that the Tazreen Fashions fire safety certificate had expired in June 2012. Those who were responsible for ensuring workers' safety were publicly talking about their failure. But the only arrests that were made were of some mid-level managers (who had prevented workers from leaving their stations once the fire alarm sounded) and a security officer. The people of Nishchintapur wanted to see justice done, but were not surprised that Hossain himself had not been arrested. A grieving mother who had lost her son spoke of a culture of impunity for the factory-owning class: "The law is for the elite; injustice done to the poor needs no redress."

In 1990, more than thirty workers, mostly women, were killed when fire broke out at Saraka Garments in Mirpur (*The Daily Star* 2010; Zaman 2001, 155). Since then, fires and collapses in export-oriented garment factories have continued to kill workers with alarming frequency (Miller 2012, 40). In almost every case, no factory owners or government officials have been tried for negligence in ensuring worker safety. The one exception was the April 11, 2005 Spectrum sweater factory collapse in Palashbari. Public outrage led to the arrest of the Spectrum factory owner and director, although the case file went missing once the initial media attention died down. More than ten years later, both remain out on bail and no progress has been made on this case. According to Doug Miller (2012, 38, 44), culpability for the Spectrum collapse may reside less with the factory owners than with the negligence of the construction company that had poorly constructed the factory's under-girding, and with systemic failures of the Chief Inspectorate of Factories and Establishments (CIFE). With tragic irony, CIFE, like other institutions for safeguarding health and safety, may have failed to identify the danger of building collapse because they were more focused on the growing problem of factory fires than on infrastructural integrity.

The Ministry of Home Affairs announced the initial findings of its investigation in December 2012, stating that legal action should be taken against Hossain and nine managers and supervisors who had prevented evacuation (Manik and Yardley 2012; Sarkar 2013). In so doing, the ministry breached an unofficial agreement between the business elite and the government. The powerful Bangladesh Garment Manufacturers and Exporters Association (BGMEA) is a cornerstone of political patronage in Bangladesh. Besides, there are other widely known techniques that industry owners use to protect themselves: they have staggering financial resources at their command, they can bribe the police to influence the investigation process, or they can seek to silence affected workers by paying them compensation money. Threats of disappearing and killing workers and labor leaders are not unknown either.

Filing a Public Interest Litigation

But could any redress be achieved through Public Interest Litigation (PIL)? PIL is a type of class action lawsuit that petitioners can raise in instances where fundamental rights under the Bangladesh Constitution have been violated (Miller 2012, 54). Although a PIL must be filed by an "aggrieved person," this standing is interpreted widely, allowing individuals and organizations to instigate proceedings in the name of the public interest or to "enforce human rights of common people who could not otherwise activate judicial protection of their rights" (Khan and Rahman 2011, 97–98). In an overview of PIL in South Asia, Sara Hossain, Shahdeen Malik, and Bushra Musa observe that the emergence of PIL in the 1990s can be seen as a part of "post-colonial constitutional regimes and as a collaborative initiative undertaken by members of the legal community and human rights activists" (1997, xiv).

Inspired by the Ministry of Home Affairs' statements about the Tazreen fire, including the suggestion that a case could be made regarding the "unpardonable negligence" of the factory owner (Manik and Yardley 2012; Sarkar 2013), we filed a PIL in the High Court of Bangladesh on April 28,

2013. When the Ministry of Home Affairs' report became available in 2013, we noted that although it did not come to a decisive conclusion about the cause of the fire, it openly stated that casualties would have been fewer had the owner and managers upheld health and safety regulations: "In the history of Bangladesh, no factory fire has surpassed the Tazreen Fashions Ltd fire. It is evident that the owner's *unpardonable negligence* is responsible for these appalling deaths. It is indisputable and evident that this is a *crime of negligence*. The owner of Tazreen Fashions should be convicted under statute 304(A)" (Ministry of Home Affairs 2013; our translation and emphases).

Usually, the High Court does not decide on a matter already under investigation by the lower Court of Magistrates, hence there was a strong possibility that the petition would not be granted. But we wanted to proceed in order to overstep the stalled police investigation of Hossain, and to challenge the culture of impunity that exists in Bangladesh. All three authors of this article were among the signatories of the PIL (Writ Petition No. 4467, Naznin Akter Banu and Others vs. Government of Bangladesh and Others, 2013).

The High Court accepted our petition and ordered Hossain's appearance at the first hearing of the petition. But by the second hearing on May 19, 2013, it became evident that the police administration was utterly uninterested in actually implementing the Ministry of Home Affairs' recommendation that Hossain be tried and convicted for negligence. When the judges asked where he was, the state prosecutor informed the court, "My lord, we don't know the whereabouts of the owner." At that point, the lawyer representing Activist Anthropologist, Barrister Jyotirmoy Barua, informed the court that Hossain was actually sitting quietly inside the courtroom. In annoyance, the judges gave the state prosecutor a warning for making such ill-informed remarks. After much argument, the court ordered a travel ban for the owner.

The first two hearings in early May 2013 focused on the owner's negligence in ensuring worker safety and adhering to government fire regulations. In response to questions regarding workers' safety, the factory owner's lawyer kept repeating, "My lord, my client is a law-abiding citizen; he has given all the dues to the deceased and injured victims of the fire." Our lawyer argued that because the Tazreen fire was an act of negligence on the part of the owner, and thus amounted to something that can be called a "death caused by negligence," Hossain should be punished. But the judges in the case saw things differently and suggested that our approach needed to go beyond a narrow focus on "negligence" and consider compensation for the Tazreen victims too.[6] One judge advised us to take guidance from a case from another bench of the High Court where the issue of compensation was being dealt with. The judge expressed his opinion in the following way: "What's the point in sending the owner to prison, this will eventually hamper his other garment [factories]; much better would be to see if we could arrange some compensation for these poor people."

The judges were of the opinion that we would not gain much from getting the owner imprisoned and that it would hamper the other garment enterprises owned by Hossain. The factory owner's negligence soon became a secondary concern of the petition because the judges gave a *suo moto* ruling to include the issue of compensation as part of the petition. Later in the proceedings, we were asked to provide the court with a list of missing or unidentified victims of the Tazreen fire. In a later hearing—incidentally taking place on the first anniversary of the fire—the judges made an unconventional ruling. They asked us as petitioners to submit a report on global compensation standards, and suggested the need for a specific compensation scheme for Bangladesh. We appreciated the opportunity to have missing workers' compensation claims heard in court as well as the possibility of an amendment in the labor law related to compensation. But we were confused by how the question of justice became conflated with, and restricted to, compensation during the legal proceedings.

In collaboration with a legal team from Syed Ishtiaq Ahmed and Associates, we researched different global standards of workers' compensation practices including ILO Convention 121 and submitted a compensation proposal to the High Court. In this proposal, we argued that in the case of the Tazreen fire, compensation should be calculated by considering the fire not merely an "accident" or "industrial accident," but a tortious liability of the factory management, on the basis that the deaths and injuries were caused by "negligence of the employer" and "inactions or supervisory lapses of the government authorities."[7]

Compensation for the injury or death of workers on the job is a fundamental component of labor rights. ILO Convention 121, which Bangladesh has not ratified, sets a global standard for the benefits workers should receive in the event of injury or death on the job. Instead, compensation for workers in Bangladesh has been ruled by colonial legislation, including the 1855 Fatal Accidents Act (FAA) and the 1923 Workers' Compensation Act (Miller 2012, 51–53). This legislation lags behind in terms of types and amounts of compensation given. In 2005, for example, when the Spectrum sweater factory collapsed, as Doug Miller writes, legal compensation was a paltry sum that had not been updated in many years, causing the need for more cash assistance and aid to workers. In that instance, activists and trade unionists pushed for a private scheme that would tap the resources of foreign buyers (brands and retailers) and thus augment the amounts of compensation to be granted. According to the labor law (2006), the compensation for a deceased worker is BDT 100,000 (US$1,282), and in the case of Tazreen financial assistance of BDT 700,000 was given to the victims' families. This amount included contributions from two brands (C&A and Li & Fung), the Prime Minister's relief and rehabilitation fund, and the BGMEA. We were disheartened that all our efforts to shift judicial attention onto the criminal liability of the owner were sidelined and overshadowed by ever more elaborate discussions of compensation.

A Regime of Compensation

Many scholars and activists have tried to emphasize the complicity of foreign buyers in sweatshop conditions, showing that demand for low prices and shortened lead times creates unsafe factory conditions. Among transnational NGOs and global trade unions involved in the anti-sweatshop movement, there has been a push to "internationalize" industrial disasters, such as the Spectrum sweater factory collapse and the Tazreen Fashions fire, in order to make foreign brands accountable for injuries to workers in their supply chain (Miller 2012, 60). But such calls for accountability of factory owners and global brands are not new. Demands for compensation have been a perennial feature of the Bangladeshi response to garment factory disasters. Shamsul Alam describes a worker protest in response to the 1990 Saraka Garments fire in which "20,000 women garment workers from various factories marched through the streets of Dhaka demanding compensation for their dead and wounded sisters, a government investigation into the accident, and the application of proper safety measures in the factories" (1995, 41 in Zaman 2001, 155). Researching newspaper archives on the Saraka Fire, we came across photographs of protests demanding not just safe workspaces but also democratic ones, in which profits would be shared with the workers (*The Daily Star* 1990).

What distinguishes that period of labor organizing from today, as described by one of the organizers from that time, is that then the labor movement was at least trying to connect with a larger movement for social change. It was not "*issue bhittik* (issue based) like we see today." She further explained, "In contemporary labor organizing, workers' rights are understood as human rights, not as a structural concern. It is also momentary; if a violation happens in one factory, there will be agitation, your demand is met, we lose momentum. We still demand structural change, so no violations could happen again. You ought to fight this hateful labor law that does not respect any rights of the workers. If you are demanding compensation, you ought to fight for a pro-worker legal amendment to the compensation law, not just a reasonable amount of financial assistance to individual victims. Movement is not a thing, it is a process" (August 11, 2014).

The workplace disasters that have periodically galvanized public support for labor rights—such as the Triangle Shirtwaist Factory fire in New York in 1911 or the Saraka Garments fire in 1990—not only generated huge demands for compensation of various kinds, but also spurred a wider movement for structural and legally binding improvements in labor conditions and rights (see Bair et al. this volume). By contrast, what emerged in Bangladesh more recently is a more exclusive discourse of compensation that precludes other pursuits of social justice and that has come to shape labor organizing around a narrow set of technical calculations of monetary compensation. We are using the concept of "regime of compensation" as a tool to investigate this new phenomenon, building on the theorization of Aihwa Ong and Stephen Collier (2005), who employed the term "regime of living" to analyze contemporary practices of life science, social administration, urban planning, and finance. In tracing the emergence of this new regime, we draw upon campaigns, agreements, and conversations with lawyers, labor organizers, and NGO professionals during the process of drafting a compensation scheme for the Tazreen Fashions fire.

We would like to start our tracing of the emerging "compensation regime" by presenting a Facebook post about an Oxfam event in Dhaka that commemorated the first anniversary of the Rana Plaza factory collapse. Responding to criticisms that the organization had not done enough to help victims of Rana Plaza, an Oxfam staff member's post read: "Oxfam has created huge pressure upon Kmart and H&M to *compensate*. And what Oxfam want[s] to do through this event is an advocacy for urban disaster which is emerging in Bangladesh. We can criticize the role of NGOs but do we have real sense of understanding how [the] country [is] operating *disaster risk management and response*. If no, then this kind of one-sided criticism will not produce anything" (April 2014, emphases ours).

In the voice of the Oxfam staffer, the concern for compensation is evident. Many NGOs and labor groups pressed global brands to contribute to the Rana Plaza Donor Trust Fund. Set up by the ILO in the immediate aftermath of the collapse, the fund aimed to collect US$30 million from the global brands that had sourced from Rana Plaza. This fund has been a rallying point for NGOs and trade unions. The Netherlands-based Clean Clothes Campaign (CCC), for example, launched a Pay Up! initiative, which attempted to mobilize Western consumers to press brands to contribute to the fund. In Bangladesh, a campaign was coordinated by Sromik Nirapotta Forum (Workers Safety Forum), a network of NGOs collaborating on worker safety following the 1990 Saraka fire. On February 24, 2014, in a direct action to name and shame brands that had failed to contribute, a local chapter of IndustriALL raised an eye-catching purple banner listing all the names of European brands that sourced from the factories in Rana Plaza: "LPP, Essenza, Carrefour, Mango, Primark, Gueldopfenning, JC Penney . . . how long do we have to wait for our dear parents' compensation?" One message on several placards drew our attention: "Brand's duty, come forward, pay now." Both local NGO and trade union organizers were unable or uninterested to include criminal liability in their demands for making brands accountable. A similar indifference was reflected in the tripartite agreement that was signed between the Ministry of Labor and Employment (MoLE), BGMEA, and IndustriALL. However laudable this agreement was, in its sixteen-page action plan, it did not address the irresponsibility or negligence of management, which has historically been the main cause of industrial catastrophes.[8]

Later, during the process of drafting a compensation scheme, we got an opportunity to exchange views with a representative of IndustriALL in Dhaka. A veteran of the labor movement, having started his work in the 1970s as a labor activist, he was passionate about sharing his experience participating in compensation negotiations with brands in Geneva. Referring to the financial incapacity of the local factory owners, he first of all insisted that we need to focus on achieving a global compensation standard. To make his point about the financial difficulties of a local factory owner, he referred to the owner of Spectrum sweater factory, "At the time of the collapse he had too many bank loans, his ship was sinking, but when he recovered from this financial mess, he came to me and paid the deceased workers' family." This exclusive emphasis on the compensation of victims meant that factory owners' callous indifference toward building safety was being completely ignored.

Second, he pointed out that strengthening state mechanisms is not always possible or desirable when dealing with a global apparel industry, and preferred a turn to global actors and regulations. He strongly felt that we needed to campaign and act as a pressure group in order to make the government adopt ILO 121, the convention related to the employment injury benefit. Clearly, he did not prioritize amending national labor laws. He elaborated, "We from the trade union demanded compensation based on ILO 121. ILO is a globally recognized standard . . . we used this in Spectrum [factory collapse], Smart [factory fire], and now with the Tazreen case the negotiation is on and the latest is Rana Plaza." Many involved in this negotiation process consider the Spectrum collapse as a historically significant moment as campaigners purposely attempted to "internationalize" their efforts in order to hold accountable the global brands that sourced garments from Spectrum (Miller 2012, 60 and chapter 5). In the same vein, a local activist working in a Dhaka-based NGO and a witness to the Spectrum collapse remembered:

> After the Spectrum building collapse we felt that all parties should be involved . . . our work had some elements of corporate social responsibility [CSR] at that time . . . we reviewed the incident from the perspective of CSR . . . we realized that this is a global business. . . . We thought that it was important to think in the new rubrics of global corporate social responsibility . . . global in the sense that all parties will take responsibility [i.e., the state, owners, and brands, etc.] . . . we then decided to sit with all the parties . . . International Textile, Garment and Leather Workers' Federation[9] . . . we involved them in an opinion-sharing session by inviting the concerned parties. (December 24, 2013)

In the wake of the Spectrum collapse, local and global trade unions along with international organizations, like the Clean Clothes Campaign (CCC) and Worker Rights Consortium (WRC), gathered in an extemporary coordination committee, which produced a voluntary scheme involving international brands in the compensation of victims. Later, this scheme became known as the "Spectrum formula."

Since the Spectrum disaster Bangladesh trade unions, with the support of IndustriALL and international labor rights organizations, have developed a formula for calculating compensation based on ILO 121. This formula identifies four stakeholders deemed responsible for the provision of such remedy, due to both their responsibilities and their past failures to take the steps necessary to prevent such violations in the first place. These are (1) the direct owner of the business affected, (2) the industry association, (3) the government, and (4) the international buyers. The formula held buyers (brands and retailers) collectively responsible for contributing 45 percent of the final amount, the owner 28 percent, the industry association (in this case the BGMEA) 18 percent, and the government 9 percent. This formula was used to negotiate compensation payments to victims of several building and fire incidents that occurred after Spectrum, including Hameem (2010), Eurotex (2011), and Smart Export (2013). Negotiations about compensation for the victims of Tazreen also began based on these same principles.[10] However, neither the Spectrum formula nor the ILO convention takes into account the preexisting trade inequalities that privilege the global brands, and neither provides us with any legal instrument with which global retailers like Wal-Mart can be made to pay their contribution.

The development of the Spectrum formula is undoubtedly a landmark achievement of the global labor movement. In the absence of any legal mechanism and given the sheer indifference to the lives of workers, these initiatives provided grieving families with much valued and needed financial support. The point we want to emphasize in tracing these processes, however, is that an exclusive focus on paying compensation allows factory owners and international brands to evade criminal prosecution and to continue with "business as usual." Moreover, discussions of compensation put a price on deceased workers, monetize grief, and disincentivize factory owners from focusing on prevention. Distraught by what we interpreted as a self-congratulatory tone from those involved in high-level negotiations of international compensation schemes, we wondered if worker deaths under such circumstances can be adequately addressed through corporate compensations. Is it ethical and adequate to respond to mass loss of life in purely monetary terms without addressing underlying issues of responsibility, accountability, and future prevention?

The process of developing a historically almost unprecedented scheme was accompanied by the rise of global trade union and labor rights organizations like CCC, WRC, IndustriALL, and Solidarity Center. Mostly located in places often labeled as global capitals of international aid, such as Geneva, Washington, D.C., or Amsterdam, these international bodies implicitly set the terms of first response for local organizers. Local labor organizations that collaborated with these international bodies and adopted their campaigns, namely the Awaj Foundation, the Bangladesh Center for Worker Solidarity (BCWS), and the National Garment Workers Federation (NGWF), in turn gained visibility and became the dominant voices speaking for the victims. We argue that both these global and local voices redirected attention away from questions of structural inequality and responsibility.

Moreover, we need to remember that the Spectrum formula and the Rana Plaza Donor Trust Fund (which like the Spectrum formula distributes compensation to victims and their families in keeping with the principles of ILO 121) are extemporary, voluntary schemes. Both local and global labor organizations work as mediators between victims and brands, and campaign for brands to voluntarily participate and contribute to the compensation fund. Negotiations that focus on collecting and redistributing funds may shy away from challenging the unequal relationships that link global brands to local manufacturers, factory owners, and workers at the tail end of the global chain. Instead, they contribute to the commodification of workers' lives and labor in the global South. By commodification, we do not merely refer to the monetary compensations for loss of life and work, but the ideological assumption that prioritizes compensation negotiations over criminalizing the global and local elites involved in apparel production. This became even more obvious when we saw the owner of Tazreen Fashions Ltd. arrested after being charged with culpable homicide for alleged negligence. And yet the response within the labor movement remained sullen and hesitant. In a rather authoritative voice, the representative of IndustriALL asked us, "What good is there when the owner is behind bars?" This statement points to the question of what actions are defined as "good" for the victims, and to the now widespread agreement among local and international actors that compensation negotiations and rehabilitation projects are the main answer.

Thus, in the aftermath of the Tazreen fire and the collapse of Rana Plaza, we do not see labor organizers mobilizing victims' families to file a class action lawsuit against the Fire Safety Department or the Factory Inspection Department for their failure to ensure worker safety. We do not suggest that pursuing the legal route of criminal liability is the only way forward, but we point to the ways in which an exclusive focus on compensation evades questions of responsibility and criminality, and risks normalizing death by negligence.

A Newly Governed Subject?

Among Marxist circles in Bangladesh, "foreign interventions" to fix the garment industry are seen as a ploy to control the country's "growing economy."

These include new inspection regimes created by global fashion brands in the wake of Rana Plaza such as the Accord on Fire and Building Safety in Bangladesh (the Accord) and the Alliance for Bangladesh Worker Safety (the Alliance).[11] In May 2014, a Marxist activist said in a roundtable discussion on the missing garment workers of Tazreen and Rana Plaza organized by Activist Anthropologist, "There is a thing called governance; with respect to garments' governance, the government of Bangladesh has failed." For this Bangladeshi activist, these new inspection regimes do not offer any solutions, and their legal validity to operate in Bangladesh is being questioned. He held a critical view of the newly emerging health and safety regimes on the basis that they are likely to have a negative impact on the country's national economy because "many factories will be closed off." Another activist with years of experience in the labor movement but presently working in an NGO claimed that the launch of the Accord and the Alliance must be seen in the context of government failure. While personally he did not support these new, foreign-led inspection initiatives, he did admit that they were justified in the light of the government's immense failure to protect labor.

However, as far as "labor rights" are concerned, this view is increasingly a marginal one. As we are trying to argue in this chapter, the global garment industry and its transnational governance have constructed a new kind of trade unionism in Bangladesh, whose heads or bosses travel internationally and are exposed to all the new tools of governance and management. Their movement is also evident in the sudden increase of trade unions in the country. It is recorded that while in the previous two years only two trade unions were registered by the Bangladesh Department of Labor, in 2013, ninety-six trade unions were registered. As of 2014 a total of 222 unions were listed as registered with the Bangladesh Department of Labor (ILO 2014). The new trade unions operate much like NGOs in Bangladesh, and can even be registered as NGOs. Like NGOs, often at their core is a "one wo/man show," with a founder whose profile may seem very "authentic" as his or her background is as a worker in the garment sector. Generally, these organizations are run by foreign donations, they accept any international labor-related campaigns and donor prescriptions uncritically, and they take up the role of local implementers of these campaigns. Apparently, these organizations seem more capable compared to the local labor rights organizations in negotiating international trade. The organizations often receive funding from the CSR offices of international brands.

In Nishchintapur, where the Tazreen factory was located, there were a number of such organizations active in the area. They mobilized the workers from the locality by employing a few workers in their offices; they provided money to the workers to participate in their activities. Especially after the Tazreen fire, we saw that such NGO-based labor organizations mobilized workers by committing to give them a big amount of "compensation" from the buyers. One organization in Nishchintapur distributed relief goods such as blankets and powdered milk to the workers a few days after the fire.

It can be argued, based on observations of their activities, that by organizing the workers, the organizations were upholding their own interests. The key credential of these organizations to receive donor funds is that they can mobilize workers for human chains, day celebrations, and processions. With funds on hand, these organizations are able to organize big processions and meetings, while for local workers' rights organizations this becomes difficult. From the workers' point of view, if they join in the local trade union activity, they return home empty-handed, whereas if they participate in the donor-funded activity, they walk away with cash in hand. As a consequence, we have recently observed how a local workers' rights organization, involved mostly with organizing workers from outside the factory, distributed money to workers to buy special food items to celebrate Eid.

As indicated earlier the new trade unions are usually better equipped economically and technologically than the earlier generation of trade unionists. Their offices may be housed in posh areas of Dhaka with all the facilities expected in a networked office space, unlike traditional left "party offices" in the commercial hubs of the capital city. They usually have paid staff, and they are well networked.

Their presence was also felt during the first anniversary of the Rana Plaza collapse. On the first anniversary a number of workers' rights organizations gathered at Rana Plaza, where a mural had been installed commemorating the lives lost. This gathering involved the left political parties as well as the new workers' rights organizations and NGOs. As members of Activist Anthropologist, we witnessed that the space was dominated by the new workers' rights organizations, and one organizer was very much at the helm of things because important guests from abroad were participating in the event. The emergence of these new workers' rights organizations has increased the number of registered trade unions in Bangladesh, a development that garment factory owners publicly support as long as these organizations are "not only talking about the rights of the workers but also taking up some responsibility" (in the words of one factory owner quoted in a 2014 TV program in Dhaka).

For these new trade union organizations, the principles of their activities are set internationally and often in a top-down manner.

Toward an Economy of Compensation?

In one of our PIL hearings, close to the first anniversary of the Tazreen fire, some of the missing workers' families approached us; they wanted to join the court session in Dhaka. On the day of the hearing, a group of thirty people from Nishchintapur, including a few visibly injured workers, gathered in front of the courtroom. The gathering drew media attention to the case. The following day, an injured worker's father demanded a honorarium from us for his presence at the court premises: "My presence has monetary value." While many from Nishchintapur were offended by his remark, it did not come as a surprise to us. From our various conversations with victims' families and labor organizers, we had already come to notice how "compensation talk" had created expectations and demands among the workers and their families, and how the latter had come to internalize and normalize the right to compensation.

As described above, the history of industrial disasters in Bangladesh has largely been a history of nonresponse. In most incidences, injured workers and victims' families have been left to their own devices to recover from the tragedy. Since such events are commonly treated as "accidents," systematic procedures to attend to the needs of the deceased, injured, or missing workers' families were never established. The Department of Disaster Management in collaboration with the Fire Department and the police administration usually took care of the dead bodies, while funds were released from the Prime Minister's relief and rehabilitation fund to cover the costs of burial. Whatever state or private sector response there was, it was only momentary and on an ad hoc basis. Injured workers from the 2005 Spectrum collapse still suffer from their injuries, and missing workers' families are forced to accept their fate with no closure.

Against this particular historical context, labor organizations began to develop short- and long-term relief and rehabilitation projects, funded by global brands and other international aid organizations, to meet the immediate needs of victims and their families. It is this project-based and ad hoc landscape of activism around material demands that has generated new expectations among workers for compensation. It has also transformed the relationship between workers and labor organizers from camaraderie to a patron-client relationship. On many occasions, the injured workers of Tazreen chose to become members of a labor organization in order to access resources. In the same vein, organizers encourage workers to join rallies by hinting at future compensation possibilities.

Here, we present a detailed survival story of an injured worker of Tazreen to illustrate how this public recognition of suffering and the rights of compensation that it entails remains a largely ad hoc affair and generates a political program for compensation that keeps particular demands for structural change at bay:

Shahnoor Begum and Abidur Rahman had migrated to Dhaka from one of the most poverty-stricken northern districts of Bangladesh.[12] Forty-six of the workers killed at Tazreen Fashions were from the same district of Rangpur. They came to the city to secure a better future for their two daughters. At the time of the fire, Shahnoor was working as a helper at Tazreen and Abidur was a line manager at a nearby sweater factory. They lived in a tin-shed rented room right behind the eight-story Tazreen building. On that fateful night, Abidur was still at his factory, working an evening shift. He cannot remember who told him about the fire. He later told us, "I don't know why, I was not worried about my wife, Shahnoor. But I was proved wrong." Rushing to the site, he found his home on fire, "As if the senseless fire is going to eat us all. We were like walked into the belly of fiery beast or something." He was trying to drag some of his belongings from the burning house. For months, since we have known him, Abidur Rahman never talked to us about the night of the fire. On the deathbed of Sumaya Khatun, another injured worker who succumbed to her injuries months later, he finally opened up to us.

Even though it was fourteen months later, fear was still fresh in his eyes, "As I was trying to drag stuff out, still thinking Shahnoor is fine, she must be somewhere around waiting for the crowd to dissipate. Suddenly, I hear a gut-wrenching scream, it was Amena apa, she jumped through the fifth floor window and dropped on the cemented floor of a room next to us. She too died later. I went to help Amena apa and found Shahnoor calling for help. She was covered in her own blood and ashes from the fire. Her rib cage broke and punctured her lung, her left leg fractured in two places. These were just her major injuries. I cannot even tell how many small stitches and bandages there were on her. Months and days that followed the night are still a blur to me. I remember we were rushing from one hospital to another. It took a few days before any help from BGMEA and the Labor Ministry reached us, by then I was knee deep in debt and sold a small agricultural land we had bought in Rangpur."

Six weeks later, Shahnoor Begum returned home from hospital. Lying on her bed, intermittently blowing on her spirometer, Shahnoor Begum reminisces, "Fatema and Moushumi jumped before me and I hear, they couldn't make it. I wonder, I don't know, if I should consider myself lucky or unfortunate to have survived the fire as an incapacitated person." Shahnoor Begum was categorized as "seriously injured" by the medical representative from BGMEA. Thus, she was eligible for BDT 100,000 (US$1,285) as compensation and her medical bill from the Trauma Center, amounting to BDT 350,000 (US$4,500), was paid by BGMEA. However, her recovery was slow, and she needed help. Abidur Rahman could not return to work either. The family was left stranded without any help for long-term care. There was no system in place from the BGMEA or the government to provide victims with medical care and other assistance needed for long-term recovery.

A Dutch retailer, C&A, developed a rehabilitation project in collaboration with a Christian NGO, Caritas, to provide medical care and financial support for the victims of the Tazreen fire. Awaj Foundation, a labor organization registered as an NGO and largely funded by a German development agency (GiZ) and a German retailer, KIK, provided free medical care and distributed quilts and food supplies. Shahnoor Begum received BDT 47,000 worth of prescription drugs and three months of food supplies from Awaj. From the Caritas project, she received free medical care for nine months including prescription drugs. From the same project, she also received three months' of tailoring training. At the end of the training, she received BDT 30,000 to buy a sewing machine and use the rest of the money to start business as a tailor, but she did not feel physically fit enough to work. Her husband instead invested the money in leasing a small piece of agricultural land in Rangpur. Initially, Shahnoor Begum had problems sitting upright, and a bedside commode chair would have been very helpful for her. It was among the supplies provided by Awaj

Foundation, but she was not there to collect one. In a sullen voice, she complained, "Nobody told us."

In the absence of adequate institutional support, solidarity between affected families is often undermined, as they are competing against each other for limited material resources. "In order to gain better access to relief," Abidur Rahman told us, "I have joined two different labor organizations, paid membership fees." He eventually became a leader of the victim community in Nishchintapur. Families needing help with medical bills would come to him for arranging the "right connection." He assisted journalists' visits to Nishchintapur. He is the one reporting any sudden deterioration in an injured worker's health situation to organizers in Dhaka. He mediated a number of cases of Tazreen victims about the distribution of the compensation money among family members of victim workers. He also received some money from this. Recently, in a neighborhood conflict, he was shamed for not returning to work: "Stop living off your wife's illness, stop milking your handicapped wife now, go back to work like a real man." He was heartbroken and shocked. When speaking to us about the incident, he was surprisingly honest, acknowledging, "Everyone is making a life out of this tragedy, no one is talking about justice, or no one is planning on returning to normal life. Why should we? And why should we forget and return to normalcy?"

What we found unsettling in this narrative is how illness and injury remain the primary means of getting ad hoc access to resources for survivors like Shahnoor. In the absence of a standardized compensation process, medical and other rehabilitation services are made available as charitable donations through a range of projects run by NGOs such as Awaj Foundation or Caritas. Here, the victims of Tazreen fire were recruited as "beneficiaries" of such relief projects. In order to ensure continued support from these projects, a victim has to embody an injured way of being.

In Nishchintapur, in the aftermath of the fire, a number of organizations approached victims' families with various types of compensation packages including food supplies. Caritas Bangladesh, a Catholic international NGO that received funds from the Dutch retailer C&A, developed a rehabilitation project for the victims and survivors of the Tazreen fire. According to one survivor, Caritas Bangladesh made a commitment from the very beginning that they would give affected workers a salary for four years. But, only fourteen months after the fire, the organization stopped giving this salary to the survivors and instead proposed a training program. Of sixty-seven project participants, twenty-five received training on tailoring, fourteen people received training on cow rearing, two received training on mobile repairing, and sixteen received training on raising broiler chickens. After the training, they were given a lump sum of BDT 30,000 and were told that if they were able to earn their own livelihoods from their new enterprises, they would be considered for inclusion in the next project. With respect to people who received tailoring instruction, only three out of the twenty-five now earn money by tailoring.

Field workers attached to Caritas and other labor organizations often discouraged or even ridiculed victims for participating in our campaign for justice for Tazreen workers. Our presence was often challenged on the basis that if we could not provide any financial or other material support to the victims, we had no right to be there. Initially, the predominant nature of communication between the labor organizers and the victims of Tazreen was disturbing for us. They would name big brands to suggest that they were "in touch with brands with big money." When, on International Women's Day in 2014, a local trade union called Garments Workers Unity Forum (GWUF) organized a rally on the site of Rana Plaza, it could not gather workers from Nishchintapur because another labor rights organization had told workers that "they will pay them BDT 500,000 in two weeks from Kmart, if they joined their rally instead."[13] On another occasion, to demand compensation, victims of the Tazreen fire were mobilized to attend a press conference. Their transportation was arranged, lunch was provided, and they received BDT 2,000 for their participation. Labor organizations that continue to work with a more traditional model of unionizing now face new challenges, as they cannot mobilize resources to ensure workers' participation. Political solidarity is replaced with economic transactions between the organizers and ordinary workers, and such project-based activism contributes to this transformation.

Our intention in this chapter was not to call into question people's illnesses or disabilities as somehow inauthentic, but rather to understand the effects of a new form of activism, which, in recognizing suffering and responding to emergency, may unintentionally inflict more pain on already suffering workers competing for compensation. Shahnoor would reluctantly travel two hours from Nishchintapur to Dhaka for her physiotherapy; she did not know whether she was getting better or not, but she had to go. She needed to remain ill to be on the list, to feed her family. In another case, an injured worker, Meher Banu, had to negotiate with the doctors and nurses to remain in the hospital, and had to argue to convince the doctors that she needed ear tube surgery. The survivors of the Tazreen fire continue to bear the psychological trauma, they struggle to recover from their injuries, and they remain ill at the same time. In the aftermath of the Tazreen fire, we observed that the labor movement remained seriously constrained by a material approach to justice focused on negotiations over compensation and limited resources. What remained absent in this post-disaster period was a more sustained call for accountability through legal prosecution and liability.[14]

In Nishchintapur, an economy grew out of this regime of compensation and rehabilitation. Social tension grew with it too. The mobilization of material resources would often create fissures among the members of the grieving community that emerged following the night of the fire. Our ethnographic experience bore the mark of this tension as well. We were included in their community of grief, invited to participate in many community prayers and meals, but we were sometimes resented as well. Despite our repeated iteration that we politically oppose this monetized notion of justice, our legal and other campaigns were nevertheless understood as a possible avenue to more compensation. Some workers wrongly thought that a relationship with us would create a route for compensation, and when we failed to provide any material support, our relationship with injured victims sometimes became strained.[15] Compensation regimes isolate people from one another and efface the possibility of horizontal networking, of class-based solidarity, and of collective demands for recognizing liability and accountability. Elsewhere it has been argued that insurance regimes foster vertical relationships between a company and the victims at the cost of worker solidarity (Defert 1991). We suggest that a similar scene is unfolding in Nishchintapur.

Conclusion

In the course of our campaign, we maintained close contact with some of the families of the Tazreen victims. One day during the court procedures, Matin, the brother of a victim, angrily charged over to the owner of Tazreen Fashions. More than a year and a half later, one of our Activist Anthropologist members met the brother again. His situation had changed. Although his sister's body had not been found, he and his family members had been contacted by the government for compensation. However, after this initial communication from the government, there had been some delay in the compensation payment. When an Activist Anthropologist member told him not to worry, his reaction was: "I am not worried; my greatest satisfaction is that the owner is now behind bars."

In response to our critique of this emerging regime of compensation, we have been told by academics and activists alike that workers want compensation and do not demand punishment. We always nod in agreement. It is true, most workers do not talk about justice. In our conversations with surviving victims and their families, they remain silent on the issue of justice because historically the justice system worked against them. But there are voices like that of Sumaya Khatun, a sixteen-year-old injured worker who survived the fire by jumping through the fourth floor window but ultimately succumbed to death in March 2014 after months of suffering. On her deathbed, when the owner came to see her, she spat on him and refused his money. Our understanding of justice is influenced by Sumaya and Matin. On the day Matin received a check from the Prime Minister—two years after his sister's death—he said, "I have received the money, but haven't abandoned my demand for Delwar [Hossain]'s punishment. The struggle for compensation has ended, but I will continue to fight." Unfortunately, such small calls for justice are lost in the overwhelming discourse of compensation.

Notes

1. Activist Anthropologist is a research and activist collective formed by Saydia Gulrukh, Nazneen Shifa, and Mahmudul Sumon in response to the 2012 Tazreen Fashions factory fire. We began by conducting a survey in Nishchintapur, the location of the Tazreen factory, and since then we have been in close touch with many of the Tazreen workers and their families to document their plight.

2. All names of workers are pseudonyms unless otherwise noted.

3. Interview with staff of Anjuman-E Mufidul Islam, a philanthropic organization that has been burying unclaimed bodies in Dhaka for decades, November 26, 2014.

4. DNA testing is new to Bangladesh. In the absence of any official initiative for missing workers, a few of us activists, researchers, and labor organizers went to Nishchintapur to record missing workers' information and interview people of the area. This research led to a campaign for the recognition of the missing workers and to a Public Interest Litigation (see Activist Anthropologist 2013).

5. Rejecting the official number of casualties declared by the government of Bangladesh, Activist Anthropologist published a list of 119 deceased workers and suggested that the actual death toll is higher.

6. This account is reconstructed from memory. In the court premises, due to the excessive number of people and lawyers it is often difficult to hear the conversation between the lawyer and the judge.

7. On March 2, 2013 a complete proposal was submitted by Activist Anthropologist to the High Court.

8. Following the Tazreen fire, a preexisting forum identified as Tripartite Partners that included representation from MoLE, BGMEA, and IndustriALL agreed to develop the National Tripartite Plan of Action on Fire Safety and Structural Integrity in the Ready-Made Garments Sector in Bangladesh (see Bair et al. this volume). This plan of action was signed on July 25, 2013 by all parties. Many international and local labor organizations welcomed this action plan as it clearly stated that all parties would "review the appropriateness of the level of current legal entitlements to compensation, bearing in mind the concept of loss of earnings and the provisions of ILO Convention No. 121."

9. The International Textile, Garment and Leather Workers' Federation (ITGLWF) was a global union federation for workers in this sector that disbanded to become part of IndustriALL Global Union in 2012.

10. This formula, along with a similar process of negotiation involving labor representatives and international buyers, is now also being used to support compensation claims for victims in both Pakistan and Cambodia.

11. The Accord on Fire and Building Safety in Bangladesh is a 2013 agreement between European fashion brands and organized labor, and the Alliance for Bangladesh Worker Safety is an inspection and certification regime created by North American fashion companies (see Ashraf this volume; Bair et al. this volume).

12. We have reconstructed the story of Shahnoor Begum and Abidur Rahman (both pseudonyms) from a series of conversations we had over a period of eighteen months since the fire.

13. Personal communication with the organizer of GWUF from Nishchintapur, March 8, 2014.

14. Our discussion on the ways injury becomes productive in gaining material resources for survivors of the Tazreen fire is influenced by Miriam Ticktin's (2006) examination of the illness clause in France's immigration law.

15. On one occasion, an injured woman expected us to provide some support for her husband's driver's license. When we explained that we were unable to provide such support, she was clearly disappointed.

Bibliography

Activist Anthropologist. 2013. "Tazreen Fire: DNA Test and the Complexities of Compensation." Activist Anthropologist Blog. Online: http://activistanthropologist .wordpress.com. Accessed: 12 October 2014.

Ain o Shalish Kendra (ASK). 2012. "Garment Factory Fire: Tazreen Fashions Ltd, Nish-chintapur, Savar, Bangladesh, 24 November 2012." Ain o Shalish Kendra Investigation Unit Report. Dhaka: Ain o Shalish Kendra (ASK). Online: http://www.askbd.org/web/wp-content/uploads/2012/11/ASK%20Investigation%20Report%20-%20Garments%20Factory%20Fire%20-%2024%20November%2020121.pdf. Accessed: April 28, 2015.

Alam, S.M. Shamsul. 1995. "Democratic Politics and the Fall of the Military Regime in Bangladesh." *Bulletin of Concerned Asian Scholars* 27(3): 28–42.

Bajaj, Vikas. 2012. "Fatal Fire in Bangladesh Highlights the Dangers Facing Garment Workers." *New York Times.* November 25. Online: http://www.nytimes.com/2012/11/26/world/asia/bangladesh-fire-kills-more-than-100-and-injures-many.html?_r=1. Accessed: April 28, 2015.

The Daily Star. 1990. Photographs of protests after Saraka Garments fire. January 5.

———. 2010. "Major RMG Fires Since '90." *The Daily Star.* Saturday, February 27. Online: http://archive.thedailystar.net/newDesign/news-details.php?nid=128066. Accessed: April 27, 2015.

Defert, Daniel. 1991. "Popular Life and Insurance Technology." Pp. 211–233 in *The Foucault Effect: Studies in Governmentality,* ed. by Colin Gordon, Peter Miller, and Graham Burchell. Chicago: University of Chicago Press.

Hossain, Sara, Shahdeen Malik, and Bushra Musa. 1997. *Public Interest Litigation in South Asia: Rights in Search of Remedies.* Dhaka: University Press.

International Labour Organization (ILO). 2014. "Union Registrations Rise Sharply in Bangladesh Garment Sector: New Labour Laws Pave Way to Improve Conditions, Workers' Rights." Press release, February 20. Online: http://www.ilo.org/dhaka/Informationresources/Publicinformation/Pressreleases/WCMS_236042/lang--en/index.htm. Accessed: June 23, 2015.

Kazmin, Amy. 2013. "Retailers Pressed to Compensate Bangladesh Factory Victims." *Financial Times,* May 2. Online: http://www.ft.com/cms/s/0/f7f4ed58-b330-11e2-95b3-00144feabdc0.html#slide0. Accessed: April 29, 2015.

Khan, Borhan Uddin, and Muhammad Mahbubur Rahman. 2011. "Human and Minority Rights in Bangladesh." Pp. 86–106 in *Minority Rights in South Asia,* ed. by Rainer Hofmann and Ugo Caruso. Frankfurt: Peter Lang.

Manik, Julfikar Ali, and Jim Yardley. 2012. "Bangladesh Finds Gross Negligence in Factory Fire." *New York Times.* December 17. Online: http://www.nytimes.com/2012/12/18/world/asia/bangladesh-factory-fire-caused-by-gross-negligence.html. Accessed: April 28, 2015.

Miller, Doug. 2012. *Last Nightshift in Savar: The Story of the Spectrum Sweater Factory Collapse.* Alnwick: McNidder & Grace.

Ministry of Home Affairs. 2013. *Ashuliar Nischchintapure Abasthita Tazreen Fashion Limitede Shangghatita Marmantik Agnikander Bishaye Sharashtra Mantranaloi Kartik Gathita Committer Tadanta Pratibedan 17 December* [Probe Report on Tazreen

Fashion   fire.]   Online: http://www.askbd.org/ask/wp-content/uploads/2013/11
/Final-Recommendation-of-the-Home-Ministry-Probe-Report-Tazreen-English
.pdf. Accessed: April 27, 2015.

Ong, Aihwa and Stephen J. Collier, eds. 2005. *Global Assemblages: Technology, Politics, and Ethics as Anthropological Problems.* Malden, MA: Blackwell.

Sarkar, Ashutosh. 2013. "Tazreen Garment Tragedy: Negligence Unpardonable." *The Daily Star.* Wednesday, June 12. Online: http://archive.thedailystar.net/beta2/news /negligence-unpardonable/. Accessed: April 28, 2015.

Ticktin, Miriam. 2006. "Where Ethics Meets Politics: The Violence of Humanitarianism in France." *American Ethnologist* 33(1): 33–49.

Zaman, Habiba. 2001. "Paid Work and Socio-Political Consciousness of Garment Workers in Bangladesh." *Journal of Contemporary Asia* 31(2): 145–160.

CHAPTER 6

Garment Sweatshop Regimes, the Laboring Body, and the Externalization of Social Responsibility over Health and Safety Provisions

Alessandra Mezzadri

If we allow the politics of health to do no more than
follow the shifting effects of the structural contradictions
in the labour-reserve system . . . then, indeed, we do no
more than accept the boundaries of suffering.

(O'Laughlin 2013, 194)

Introduction: The Centrality of Labor Regimes
for Health and Safety

Concerns over the health and safety of garment workers have recently taken center stage in discussions on the global garment industry, particularly after the collapse of the Rana Plaza complex in Dhaka, Bangladesh. As global buyers and other international stakeholders willingly or forcibly put in place "emergency" measures and sign "new" international agreements, the systemic features of the industry are instead left largely unchallenged. Focusing on the Indian garment sector, this chapter puts forward three main points. First, it argues that the poor health and safety record of the industry has to be understood in relation to its dominant labor regime. In this sense, the disasters hitting the industry—like the tragic case of Rana Plaza—are hardly "exceptional" events, as they are shaped by the harsh and precarious labor relations that characterize the industry. Furthermore, even in the absence of catastrophic events, the health, safety, and well-being of garment workers are extremely precarious, and rather "unexceptionally" subject to high levels of risk and routine minor calamities.

Second, building on this labor-regime approach to health and safety with evidence from India's National Capital Region (NCR), the chapter discusses the limitations of health and safety provisions in the garment industry and shows the different ways in which they remain ineffective for both factory and nonfactory workers. Here, the analysis places emphasis on different processes of labor circulation operating in the industry. It focuses on both productive and reproductive domains, and illustrates the problems of health provisions in the context of highly informalized, poor housing arrangements.

Third, after introducing the debate on corporate approaches to health and safety standards, the chapter zooms further into the reality of home-based work. Focusing on Bareilly in Uttar Pradesh, a key homeworking center linked to the NCR, the chapter discusses how the overlap between productive and reproductive time undermines attempts at elaborating meaningful health and safety measures. In Bareilly, by subcontracting work outside factory premises, employers effectively "outsource" health and safety concerns to households and homes, eschewing their responsibilities toward workers even during labor time. The chapter concludes that the informalization of labor in the sector is intrinsically linked to multiple processes of externalization of social responsibility over health and safety. In this context, corporate approaches to labor standards are unable to significantly address health and safety issues. Framed as technical rules and regulations, they take into consideration neither the social practices of production, nor the power relations shaping them. In fact, field-based evidence suggests that corporate labor standards may even be reinforcing the push toward self-regulation, particularly in home-based settings. Overall, better health and safety provisions can only result from a systemic approach, challenging the dominant labor relations in the sector. This approach, as the conclusion of this chapter explains, cannot be based on corporate "voluntarism."

The chapter is based on a political economy approach to health and safety outcomes in the industry, centered on the capital-labor relations that characterize it. This approach builds on the work of Bridget O'Laughlin (2010, 2013) on the "production of affliction," while insights into social reproduction are inspired by Silvia Federici's (2004, 2012) work on "the making of bodies" under capitalism. The empirical evidence presented here is based on multiple fieldwork rounds conducted in India between March and April 2010, January and May 2012, and April, May, August, and September 2013. The fieldwork rounds were connected to two different research projects. One was an ESRC-DfID-funded project (ES/I033599/1) on labor standards and the working poor in the garment and construction sectors in China and India, in which I jointly acted as India co-investigator with Ravi Srivastava. The second is a British Academy–funded project (SG100684), "The Global Village? Home-working in the Global Economy," for which I was the principal investigator.[1] The analysis is also informed by earlier extensive fieldwork on the Indian garment sector since 2004, in line with what Michael Burawoy (1998) defined as the "extended case study method."

Health, Safety, and Labor Regimes: The Non-Exceptionality of Risk

In April 2013, the garment industry was hit by what is considered to be one of the worst disasters in the history of manufacturing. Rana Plaza, an eight-story commercial building, collapsed in Savar, a subdistrict in the Greater Dhaka Area, the capital of Bangladesh, claiming the lives of at least 1,134 workers and leaving another 2,515 injured (ILRF 2015). Just a few days before, in New Delhi, I had interviewed the corporate social responsibility (CSR) director of a renowned American brand outsourcing from several countries in South Asia and the Middle East. He stressed that all large buyers wanted to source from Bangladesh, due to very cheap labor costs. He acknowledged the country's "infrastructural problems," but was positive that local suppliers were working hard to "resolve" them. After the disaster, many brands probably wished they had never sourced from Bangladesh in the first place. The Rana Plaza case triggered a huge upsurge in national and international campaigning in favor of Bangladeshi garment workers, and many buyers, pressured by national and international campaigning, "agreed" to pay compensation to the victims and their families (Hoskins 2015). To date, two inspection agreements have been elaborated to prevent another Rana Plaza. The first agreement is the European-led Accord on Fire and Building Safety in Bangladesh (the Accord; 2013). According to some, despite its focus on auditing, and despite becoming legally binding only once voluntarily signed (Prentice 2014), the Accord also "takes a major step towards restoring brands' direct responsibility to workers for their conditions" (Kumar and Mahoney 2014, 203). In fact, it is partially inspired by the jobbers' agreements that delivered important changes in labor-intensive industries in now-developed regions (Bair et al. 2013 and this volume; Appelbaum and Lichtenstein 2014). The second agreement, a weaker U.S.-led version of the Accord, is the Alliance for Bangladesh Worker Safety (the Alliance; 2013), which remains voluntary even once signed (Gunther 2013).

Indeed, the Rana Plaza disaster speaks loudly about the infrastructural problems plaguing the Bangladeshi garment industry. However, it speaks as loudly about the type of labor relations that have characterized the garment industry since its origins. Just over one hundred years ago, in 1911, the United States witnessed the first large-scale disaster known in the history of garment making: the Triangle Shirtwaist factory fire in New York City. The death toll of this disaster—"only" 146 workers—pales in comparison to Rana Plaza's numbers. However, the modalities of this disaster, as well as the social practices that enabled it, are strikingly similar to those of Rana Plaza. In both cases, workers were locked into the premises and could not escape once the fire or collapse began. In both cases, infrastructural failure was made particularly lethal by the social practices enforced on the shop floor and by the disciplinary regimes imposed on labor, entailing long shifts during which it was standard practice to lock garment workers—mostly women—into industrial premises. All these considerations should be kept in mind not only when assessing the Rana Plaza disaster, but also the numerous "minor" forms of sickness and injury affecting garment and other labor-intensive industries as waves of a "low-intensity" epidemic. After all, "in the Pearl River Delta, 40,000 fingers are severed each year in work-related accidents" (Sluiter 2009 in Hoskins 2014, 68).

In this chapter, I argue that health and safety concerns and outcomes in labor-intensive industries cannot be decoupled from their labor regimes, that is, the specific set of social relations of production and reproduction shaping their functioning. Factory fires and collapses, and work-related injuries and illnesses are seen as moments of exceptionality only if one does not consider the type of labor relations dominating the "global garment sweatshop." In fact, while the modalities of local sweatshop regimes vary across time and space (Mezzadri 2014a), there is by now significant evidence that garment jobs are primarily "bad" jobs: "informalized," "feminized," and often defined by harsh working conditions and rhythms and low levels of social security (Esbenshade 2004; Hale and Wills 2005; Howard 1997; Rosen 2002). The fact that some of these "bad jobs" may entail health hazards or safety risks is hardly an exceptional outcome. Rather, poor health and safety provisions are de facto manifestations of what a "bad job" entails. Moreover, in the context of declining welfare state provisions, processes of labor informalization further limit access to health services, particularly for certain categories of workers, like migrants and/or women (Gideon 2007).

Reflecting on what she calls the "production of affliction" in Southern Africa, O'Laughlin (2013, 175) reminds us how poor health outcomes not only reflect denial of access to formal health provisioning, but are also produced by the conditions of labor, including capital's struggle "to externalise responsibility for the reproduction of its workers." O'Laughlin looks at various forms of disease afflicting the laboring poor during colonial and postcolonial times, and relates them to specific moments of capital accumulation, epitomized by the formation and reproduction of specific labor regimes. Her analysis highlights how the spread of tuberculosis in the first decades of the twenty-first century in South Africa lay in the organization of mine labor and its system of labor recruitment. She also reveals how the increasing spread of HIV/AIDS in post-apartheid South Africa should be understood in relation to shifts in the movement of migrant labor and its new flexible residential and living arrangements. In these cases, crucially, health outcomes appear as the systemic result of processes of accumulation and their correspondent labor relations, rather than isolated disastrous events in the history of the region (see also O'Laughlin 2010).

Along similar lines, feminist literature has stressed the impact of capitalist transformations and the labor process on "the body." The first hurdle for capital is to create individuals who are "willing" (read: forced) to work for a wage. This involves transforming the body into the "container of labor power"; in this sense, as provokingly put forward by Federici (2004, 146), "the human body and not the steam engine, and not even the clock, was the first machine developed by capitalism." The alienation from the body is a distinguishing trait of capitalist work-relation, as workers submit their bodies "to an external order" (ibid., 135). The labor process, through its working rhythms, organization, and disciplining mechanisms, cannot but have profound implications for the health and safety of those who participate in it. Capitalism is not necessarily interested in the everyday subsistence of the workers (O'Laughlin 2010), or indeed their health and safety. It may internalize health concerns over the reproduction of the workforce if this helps profitability in various ways. However, insofar as it does not—when, for instance, a large reserve army of labor is available, and/or when the ever-falling price of commodities in the world market is ultimately presented as a "lamentable but inescapable reality" (Prentice 2014)—the pressure to reduce overall costs will also entail processes of externalization of costs related to the reproduction of labor. The most generalized and quoted example of this process of externalization is unpaid, reproductive work, mostly performed by women (Federici 2004, 2012; Gideon 2007; O'Laughlin 2010).

What is argued above has important implications for how we are to understand health and safety practices and outcomes in labor-intensive manufacturing sectors like garment production. On the one hand, an understanding of health and safety outcomes anchored to the labor regime dominating the industry enables us to deconstruct oversimplified representations of disasters like Rana Plaza as single moments of rupture in the otherwise linear, progressive development of industrial relations. It provides a glimpse into the routine hardship and dangers experienced by millions of garment workers worldwide—40 million according to some global estimates (Hale and Wills 2005). By deploying this approach, Rana Plaza appears as the outcome of the harshness and intensity of the labor regime at work in the industry; a characterization of the risks that the sweatshop entails, against simplistic conceptualizations "in praise" of cheap labor as providing jobs in depressed areas of the world economy (e.g., Krugman 2000 in Cawthorne and Kitching 2001; Powell 2014). These conceptualizations are still anchored to understandings of factory labor as a liberating experience, eventually leading to "industrial citizenship" (Standing 2007) and to the development of incremental work entitlements and provisions for all. However, today many workers remain at the margins of this citizenship during their entire industrial experience—"denizens" in fact (Breman 2013; Standing 2011)—until they are simply ejected from the factory.

On the other hand, and quite importantly for the scope of this chapter, this approach provides room for a systemic critique of current regulations aimed at "ensuring" particular health and safety standards in the sector. Rana Plaza has occurred in the context of the ongoing globalization of labor regulation in the sector, aimed at ameliorating working conditions and providing garment workers with minimal levels of security against work-related risk and injury. It would be wrong to simply consider this a case of exceptional failure of regulation. At the very least, this is partly due to the fact that regulations are embedded socioculturally and "travel across uneven capitalist production spaces" (Ruwanpura 2013, 102), leading to their irregular—and perhaps erratic—application. However, what is argued here is that in many geographical settings the labor regime at work in the industry is structured around processes of systematic externalization of the costs of social reproduction of the workforce. These processes vary, and so do the failures of regulation, with different implications for workers' health and safety.

The following sections illustrate how these processes unfold in the Indian garment industry in the National Capital Region (NCR) and one of its satellite embroidery centers, Bareilly, in Uttar Pradesh (UP). Luckily, the Indian industry has not experienced its own Rana Plaza. However, the following analysis illustrates the generalized exposure of garment workers to multiple "unexceptional" but systemic health and safety risks. These are part and parcel of garment workers' oppressive laboring and reproductive experiences, and of the overall labor regime dominating the industry. Moreover, the relentless everyday exposure to unhealthy and unsafe working and living conditions contributes to pushing garment workers out of the industrial labor force once their bodies have been exhausted and depleted.

The Indian Case: Labor "Circulations" and the Externalization of Social Reproduction Costs

The Indian garment industry is complex and extremely varied. It is organized in clusters of small and medium enterprises (SME) (Tewari 2008) and characterized by high degrees of informal and informalized labor. In fact, India as a whole is characterized by a dense web of both industrial and artisanal clusters (Harriss-White 2003). According to both national estimates and cross-country comparisons, India also stands out as the country with the highest rates of informal labor (NCEUS 2007; ILO and WTO 2009).

In the Indian garment industry, manufacturing clusters are characterized by clear patterns of regional product specialization, each entailing a distinct "local sweatshop regime" (Mezzadri 2014b). The National Capital Region (NCR)—the Delhi metropolitan conglomerate—is one of India's main garment export hubs. Engaged in tailoring since Mughal times (Blake 1993), today it is the leading center for ladies wear production. This type of production involves numerous ancillary activities and processes of value addition, which result in a complex product cycle. Larger factories tower over the entire cluster, which is, however, primarily composed of medium and smaller units, and by informal workshops. Different relations of (multiple) ownership, subcontracting, and interdependence link these units together, and also to the myriad of processing units scattered around the main industrial areas. The majority of garment companies are also connected to the universe of home-based production, where key activities take place. Locally, given the specific type of product specialization, one of the most significant non–factory-based production tasks is embroidery, but also some stitching activities—particularly buttonholing, locally known as *kaj*—can take place in home-based or "home-based–like" units. Embroidery is not only decentralized around industrial areas in the NCR, but also across towns and villages in Uttar Pradesh (Mezzadri 2008, 2014a; Unni and Scaria 2009).

The local sweatshop regime is complex as it articulates across factory and nonfactory production realms. Factory-based labor is primarily male and migratory, coming from several northern Indian states, but primarily from UP and Bihar. A number of companies are currently trying to feminize their workforce in large factories, with rather mixed results, as the resilience of a labor regime is not only due to capital strategies, but also to labor dynamics. Male migrants can be of different categories: some stay longer and only go back home for festivals and holidays; others engage in more circulatory forms of migration, going back during the whole of the lean season, only to return for the new business year. However, in both cases, the majority remain in the same industrial premise only for a very limited period of time. Indeed, the majority of the factory workforce is in fact temporary or casualized (Barrientos et al. 2010; Mezzadri 2008, 2012; Singh and Sapra 2007).

A survey of more than 300 workers we conducted in 2012–2013, sampled across around 35 firms, found that 91 percent of workers come from rural areas, with around 70 percent owning some land back home. The majority are Other Backward Castes (OBCs), although also other caste groups are present, and Muslims are overrepresented, particularly in lower industrial circuits. While 43 percent of workers considered land owned back home as a crucial part of their livelihood income, the rest reported that they relied primarily on different forms of wage employment. This means that a good percentage of workers still diversify their strategies for social reproduction across the urban-rural divide, although agricultural activities may have more or less of an impact on their overall livelihoods. In line with this outcome, we also found very high "attrition rates" (annual turnover) across factories, even the largest.[2] Altogether, 60 percent of workers worked in the same unit for less than one year, and another 31 percent for less than five years (Srivastava 2015). This is to say that if migrant labor in the industry may be of a more or less circulatory nature—in fact, 43 percent of workers circulate, but the rest engage in longer spells of migration—labor is predominantly circulatory in relation to the labor process.[3] In short, labor circulation is paralleled by what I call here "industrial circulation," that is, the relentless circulation of workers across industrial units. Notably, the endemic presence of industrial circulation significantly undermines modernizing narratives on factory work that overemphasize what Marx called the "civilizing influence of capital" (Federici 2012, 102).

The presence of multiple processes of circulation in the industry is intimately connected to patterns of recruitment. The industry relies heavily on contract labor arrangements (see Barrientos et al. 2010; Barrientos 2008, 2013; Mezzadri 2008). Field findings reveal that these are multiple and highly differentiated, although in many cases layers of intermediation are apparent, hiding attempts by garment companies to simply eschew their responsibility toward the workers. While a significant share of the workforce works in fact for contractors, another more significant share reports the company itself as its primary recruiter. However, also in the case of direct recruitment, a contractor may be employed later to manage and/or supervise workers, or simply register them under his name, so that they will not appear as directly hired by a specific factory. In this case, contracting is simply deployed to "disguise" the wage relation. Recent legislation allowing contracting in core business functions of the industry is likely to further boost this type of practice. Moreover, findings on take-home wages suggest that workers are paid very similarly across different categories of industrial units (large, medium, small), and across contractual positions (Srivastava 2015). Again, this challenges ideas of large capital as able to provide better wages to the workforce, while it also explains why workers themselves may not have an interest in becoming permanent in particular industrial units.

Strikes and labor unrest do not often happen in the industry (Srivastava 2015), except in sporadic instances generally linked to individual cases of harsh mistreatment. Arguably, this is observed across India, including in other sectors (see Bhattarcharya 2014). Trade unions have a very limited role in the industry. Rates of unionization among garment workers are extremely low, and field findings reveal that workers do not seem to have much faith in institutional labor representatives. Admittedly, also at a more general level, India's trade unions hardly represent the laboring poor. With a few exceptions, such as the Self Employed Women Association (SEWA) and the New Trade Union Initiative (NTUI), they are affiliated with political parties; they

often work as labor "brokers" and primarily focus on sectors already characterized by better working arrangements (Breman 2013). National labor regulation, on the other hand, is often simply circumvented by employers through
state support in processes of pro-capital "reformism by stealth" (Lerche 2007;
Shyam Sunder 2005). Moreover, the current Modi government seems committed to further relaxing labor laws (Bhowmik 2015).

In terms of living arrangements, workers generally live in colonies or
hamlets close to the main industrial areas in a variety of informal arrangements. In almost all cases, groups of more than five workers share tiny rooms
for the whole period they work in the NCR. In the most "infamous" colonies,
like Kapashera in southwest Delhi, close to Gurgaon and the Haryana border,
access to water is an issue and workers share filthy common toilets located
at the entrance of the colony. This is generally "managed" by the many local
housing contractors and landlords who thrive in the slum economy.

Non–factory-based labor, instead, comes in different combinations on
the basis of activities. Focusing on hand embroidery, a characteristic feature
of NCR clothing products, one can subdivide workers into two types: *adda*
workers (who work on intricate patterns through the use of a loom called the
adda) and *moti* workers (who engage in classic sequin or bead work). The
former are Muslim workers and primarily male, although women are increasingly engaging in this work too. Moti work is entirely feminized and generally
a Hindu activity, which can be performed by a great variety of castes. While
male adda workers linked to export are more likely to be circular migrants
and work in either small or even micro units at the very end of the informal spectrum, female adda workers and moti workers are generally settled
in Delhi for a longer time, as they came with their families, and primarily
work in their homes.[4] Machine embroidery and buttonholing is primarily
organized in family units, which in India is classified as "own-account work"
(or self-employment). They may hire a few extra workers only during peak
times. The family in this case is either local or migrated to Delhi years earlier
and managed to buy a house—something that is by now unaffordable for
newcomers (the few workers hired are instead once again male circulatory
migrants). The husband, or the dominant male in the family, is the head of
the unit and organizes production while also working (Mezzadri 2015).

A survey of seventy nonfactory workers placed at the very periph-
ery of the NCR industrial formation provided interesting findings. In relation
to production, it showed that the division between the informal micro-units
and homes is increasingly ambiguous and hard to draw, particularly in

metropolitan settings, where being self-employed and organizing a home-based production unit may be becoming a luxury newcomers cannot afford, given the price of real estate and/or rent. The government of India recently reclassified the unit of analysis defining "homework" to include home-based units, home-based work, but also work in "home-based–like" units (Raju 2013). In fact, our survey revealed that quite tellingly own-account workers individually earn an income similar to that of migrant wage-workers, while only women homeworkers, settled or otherwise, earn less than half (CDPR 2014; Mezzadri 2015). This confirms that self-employment can be reconceptualized as "disguised" wage work, as it is significantly proletarianized. In this case, the self-employed appear as one of the many "classes of labor" (Bernstein 2007) inhabiting the NCR urban conglomerate, although, quite crucially, they may not necessarily perceive themselves as such (Harriss-White 2014).

Nonfactory labor is always recruited by contractors who may be relatives or kinfolk. In nonfactory production, the contractor is more likely to be involved in the actual organization and/or supervision of the work and often comes from the same village or district of the worker, a point amply discussed by Breman (1996, 2013) in relation to debates on labor unfreedom or neo-bondage. In nonfactory settings, one can identify different living arrangements; these range from own-dwelling to informal housing in colonies and/ or slums, or even in the contractor's unit. In no case did we find workers in dormitories, unlike what is reported by studies focusing on garment or other labor-intensive industries elsewhere, particularly in contexts characterized by tight labor markets. In China, for instance (Pun and Smith 2007; Smith and Pun 2006), the deployment of dormitories is a widespread practice, leading to the full commodification of workers' daily social reproduction and the tightening of control over the workforce even beyond the space and time of production (see also Pearson and Kusakabe 2012 on Thailand). In Vietnam, instead, a dual "reproduction system" seems to be at work, with workers either living in dormitories or informal industrial hamlets (Cerimele 2016). In India, at least in the NCR, neither garment employers nor the state bear any cost of workers' daily social reproduction. Here, it is the presence of a huge reserve army of labor from the poor areas of the Hindi belt—hence the very lack of tight labor markets—that ensures control over the workforce. "Living" in the NCR metropolitan area is fully informalized, and it is up to workers to find "suitable" housing arrangements.

Across factories and workshops, the labor regime is very intense. The majority of workers (51 percent) across the more "organized" and visible echelons of the industry work for 10–12 hours per day. However, if one focuses only on workshops, findings indicate that this is the normal working day for 67 percent of workers. In fact, in workshops, one-third of all laborers work for 13–16 hours per day (Srivastava 2015). In peripheral units and homes, instead, intensity varies dramatically as the relevance of un(der)employment also clearly emerges. Circular male migrant workers always work more than twelve hours per day, while female homeworkers at the very end of the informal labor spectrum work significantly less, as they lack access to any regular employment. In terms of occupational health, a third of all workers report back pain and 39 percent reported eyestrain. Another 18 percent also report allergies due to dust and cloth particles, which are also reported by 80 percent of all workers as one of the major health issues they face at work (Ashraf this volume). Focusing on the different layers of production and work, workers in workshops and peripheral workers primarily report eyestrain and/or loss of eyesight, particularly those engaged in detailed embroidery work. Many also report exhaustion, although in this segment it is very hard to grasp the extent to which this is due to harsh working rhythms, or simply to workers' overall harsh living experience in the metropolitan space (Mezzadri and Srivastava 2015).

Exhaustion due to the intensity of working rhythms is instead more clearly reported as one of the main occupational health problems by 41 percent of workers employed in large units. These units may or may not work against high targets or production quotas, but the pace of industrial work on the shop floor is always very intense. The former production manager of the largest garment player in the NCR reported that he left that company as workers continued to faint on the shop floor, dropping like flies, particularly during the hot summer months. He found it a particularly difficult sight to bear. He now works for a medium employer, who although breaching regulation in a number of other ways, does not need such "inhumane" working rhythms. On the other hand, "waves" of fainting in the industry are not unheard of, as brilliantly reported by Julia Wallace (2014) in her *New York Times* article, "Workers of the World, Faint!" At given working rhythms, the process of extraction of labor power from its "container"—the body—is always an unhealthy experience. However, evidence suggests that inside garment factories in South Asia, even health personnel may dismiss workers' symptoms as due to "imaginary illnesses" (see Ruwanpura this volume).

Processes of externalization of costs over health and safety provisions clearly emerged from the questionnaires and interviews with workers. Only around one-fourth of all workers—and mainly only those working in larger units—are provided with any emergency medical facility or go through medical check-ups (Srivastava 2015). However, crucially, this is linked to their employment time in a given unit. As workers stay generally less than one year in the same industrial premise, the internalization of health costs per worker borne by employers is minimal, as is the impact of health services on workers' lives. High levels of industrial circulation greatly undermine the already limited health and safety provisions of the industry. Indeed, "industrial citizenship" (Standing 2007) remains largely an unfulfilled aspiration in the sector. The other key provision of health care is supposed to take place via social security and, in India, through the payment of ESI (employees' state insurance) and EPF (employees' provident fund) contributions, providing members with access to different clinics and facilities. However, only around half of all workers are entitled to ESI and EPF in factory settings, and none in nonfactory settings. Crucially, entitlement does not mean access, as the latter again depends on staying in the same company, while "break in service" is the norm. This explains why 80 percent of workers in factory settings and larger workshops declare that they have no entitlement in relation to injury compensation and retirement benefits. Often, in nonfactory settings, we even had to explain what we meant by work-related social benefits during interviews; none of the workers here are covered under any scheme. Across the whole garment labor spectrum, workers generally pay privately for health care and mainly access local clinics (Mezzadri and Srivastava 2015). On the other hand, when working days are extremely long and social entitlements extremely poor, workers hardly perceive highly congested public health facilities as a viable option (Ruwanpura this volume).

Tellingly, across both the factory and nonfactory realms, very few workers continue to work in the sector past the age of 30, with the only exception made by own-account operators (who may well pass a substantial part of actual labor onto younger family members). As a matter of fact, in our sample in factories and larger workshops, 58 percent of workers were between 21 and 30 years of age, while 12 percent were younger than 20. Only around 22 percent were above the age of 30; a meager 5.9 percent were above 40 years old; and only 1.6 percent were above 50 (Srivastava 2015). In nonfactory settings, the average age was even younger, with only 6 percent of all workers sampled older than 40 (Mezzadri 2015). This means that the industrial experience remains a transitory one for the great majority of workers. By the age of 30, workers' bodies are hugely impacted by the intensity of work. In relation to informal migratory cycles, Breman (2013, 57) already highlighted how older workers eventually go back to their village for good, used up like "sucked oranges." Indeed, the majority of both factory and nonfactory workers we interviewed see their place of origin as their primary residence and the place to which they intend to return. As workers go back at the end of their industrial experience, work-related circulation processes finally come to an end. Arguably, this journey back to the village signals a third, final process of circulation of workers. It signals workers' "life-cycle circulation" from the urban, industrial space back to the peri-urban or rural space where they originated, and which must now act as a safety net (Breman 2013). It is through a combination of these three types of circulation—labor, industrial, and life-cycle circulation—that workers' industrial experience remains so intense and relentlessly health depleting. What happens to these workers once they are finally ejected from the factory is perhaps one of the most compelling questions labor studies must ask today, to deepen our understanding of the long-term impact of informalized factory work on the livelihoods of the working poor.

What is discussed above enables us to stress two points. First, health and safety outcomes should be understood in relation to the overall labor regimes characterizing particular industrial contexts. Where labor regimes are complex, volatile, informalized, and dominated by harsh working conditions and rhythms, exposure to risks and a lack of access to health and safety provisions are the norm. They are the outcome of multiple, systemic processes of externalization of costs related to the social reproduction of the workforce. These processes can only be fully captured by analyzing the labor "experience" across the realms of production and reproduction. In the NCR, it is workers' reproductive sphere that bears the brunt of employers' strategies toward the cost minimization of social contributions. The "home," which for many workers is often far away in peri-urban or rural setting, is the place that is supposed to absorb any work-related vulnerability. In fact, it is there that a significant share of the workforce returns on a yearly basis. Moreover, it also seems to be the place where workers return once their industrial experience, and the different types of circulation that shape it, are over. The factory remains a transient moment in the history of workers' overall reproduction. By focusing on both productive and reproductive domains, it appears clear that the informalization of the workforce and the externalization of costs of social reproduction by employers are inextricably linked in a process of mutual determination.

Second, processes of externalization of the costs of social reproduction, as well as workers' exposure to unhealthy and unsafe working conditions, manifest themselves in different ways in different geographical settings. At times, they materialize in apparently "exceptional," catastrophic events, like the Rana Plaza collapse, laying bare the inequities of the global production and trade system. However, more routinely, they produce "unexceptionally" unhealthy and unsafe working lives for those at the bottom, that is, the workers. As shown in relation to the NCR case, these labor circuits are often shaped in ways that involve the slow but relentless depletion of the health of workers, and their constant exposure to multiple risks, until they come to the end of their industrial experience.

As the responsibility and costs of health and safety provisions in the industry are externalized from factories and workshops to households and homes, it seems increasingly misplaced to narrow the debate to a technical discussion of "occupational hazards." Arguably, many approaches to labor standards involving garment corporations fall into this trap and often conceptualize health and safety as technical issues (Ruwanpura 2013; Ashraf this volume). In fact, such approaches may further institutionalize processes of externalization of health and safety concerns, reconstructing them as a primary responsibility of the "home" and of the workers. The next section explores these issues with particular emphasis on realms of home-based work.

Bringing Health and Safety "Home," and the Limitations of Ethical Initiatives

Given the complexity of the labor regime in the NCR and the "composite sweatshop" it generates (Mezzadri 2014a), several studies have acknowledged the limitations of CSR norms in significantly improving working conditions. CSR norms are often disciplining tools in the hands of global buyers (De Neve 2009). They hardly acknowledge the relevance of local architectures of production (Mezzadri 2012) or historical and sociocultural settings and institutions (Barrientos and Smith 2007; Hewamanne this volume). Barrientos and colleagues (2010) highlight the inability of codes to tackle wages and other more "politically charged" issues, as well as the lack of access to social security. They also emphasize how codes target primarily what they refer to as "visual issues," namely health and safety measures broadly defined as how factories look to an external social auditor in terms of fire exits, uniforms, and safety equipment. In our own survey, we found that only larger units "look good" visually, while workshops are generally overcrowded places with exhausted fans and in many cases only a single exit. At the most informalized end of the spectrum, micro-units are often placed in unsafe basements that were never meant to house commercial or industrial activities. Many employers, moreover, have one "show-piece" factory that they present for buyers' audits, while they run numerous other factories that brand representatives never visit—an issue reported by several scholars in relation to different garment-producing areas across the world (De Neve 2014; Taylor 2011).

This "visual take" on health and safety issues is highly problematic, as it hides the potential failures in addressing the actual health and safety concerns experienced by workers. In nonfactory settings, codes are doomed to be ineffective, as they are specifically designed as factory-based regulations and even there they only scratch the surface. However, an attempt to tackle the poor working conditions of the vast army of homeworkers engaged in the industry has been made in recent years. For instance, through the Ethical Trading Initiative (ETI), a multi-stakeholder ethical platform created in 1998, a number of buyers have tried to elaborate labor standards targeting homeworkers in Bareilly, UP, an important embroidery center connected to the NCR (ETI 2006, 2013).[5] The project ran from 2006 to 2013 and became part of the wider DfID-funded Responsible and Accountable Garment Sector Challenge Fund (RAGS) initiative.[6] It was quite understandably praised in U.K. national newspapers as one of the first initiatives to attempt to systematically target the problem of home-based work. However, notwithstanding the well-meaning efforts of ETI, fieldwork in Bareilly revealed that the project had in fact no impact on wages and access to employment for homeworkers involved in embroidery for export (Mezzadri 2014a). Field findings also indicate that, in line with "older" corporate approaches targeting factories, health and safety concerns were put at the forefront of the project agenda. These are in fact potentially less controversial issues for the vast web of contractors towering over local contracting chains, which are organized in neighborhood-based putting-out systems of production involving tight control over informal home-based workers. However, the approach to health and safety in the context of the project betrays a clear push toward workers' self-regulation.

The project involved the formation of an association of contractors, the Bareilly Homeworkers Group (BHG), later renamed the Handwork Foundation (HF), and it financed the work of a local branch of SEWA. A union aimed at organizing informal women workers since 1972, SEWA has since expanded its reach considerably across India. It has increased its collaboration with external partners and, in the context of export-led industries like garment production, it is now part of internationally funded projects, such as the one sponsored by the ETI. Within the ETI project, the role of the contractors' association is effectively only one of "facilitating" the work of SEWA, that is, in practice, "allowing" SEWA's activists to work with homeworkers employed by the contractors (Mezzadri 2014a). Control over their work is so tight and the divide between public and private spaces so blurred in the peri-urban and rural areas where production takes place that it is hard to even talk with homeworkers without the consent of the local contractors and their subagents. Hence, while in theory the ETI project should entail a sharing of responsibilities over the mainstreaming of ethical trade across homeworking networks, instead all the ethical "content" of the project is delivered by SEWA, an issue I discuss in detail elsewhere (Mezzadri 2014a).

Locally, SEWA, by working through the contractors' association network, is in charge of providing health and safety training to artisans and making sure that the artisans engaged in these networks liaise with the local government to benefit from social security schemes. SEWA also runs a medical camp (SEWA 2009). Artisans should be able to access at least two schemes. One is the Rajiv Gandhi Shilpi Swasthya Bima Yojana, approved within the 11th Five-Year Plan, which guarantees medical insurance for artisans, their wives, and two of their children. The second is the Khadi Karighar Janashree Bima Yojana, aimed at providing life insurance to members of vocational/occupational groups below the poverty line or marginally above it (DC-MSME 2013; Development Commissioner for Handicraft 2013). A semi-quantitative questionnaire distributed to 100 local home-based workers across the town of Bareilly and its surroundings and interviews with local key stakeholders revealed that none of them was in fact part of any scheme. Home-based workers did not have access to any form of social security, very much in line with their counterparts in the NCR. In fact, many of them travel to the NCR during given periods of the year and engage in spells of circular migration to access the higher wages offered in metropolitan settings. Workers do so either to escape debt-traps or to repay the debt already accumulated (Mezzadri 2016).

No local contractor and certainly no NCR exporter—let alone international buyer—offers any health and safety provision to home-based workers. In a context where artisans do not in fact sign up for the available local government schemes, which entail the payment of what are expensive contributions for poor families, the entire project fully relies on SEWA's efforts to provide health and safety training to households and homes, while the contractors' association's role seems primarily one of gatekeeping to access households and workers. This means that once more capital in the industry fully externalizes all costs for workers' well-being and safety, in this case even during the time of employment. Across the entire garment chain, originating in the NCR and stretching all the way to Bareilly, capital does not bear the cost of the social reproduction of the workforce, which is asked to self-manage its own precarious health and safety. Or, as argued by Nandini Gooptu (2013, 8), in India, neoliberalization "depends on the development of self-regulation, self-direction, and self-management of enterprising selves." In this case, this process is at the basis of sectoral accumulation patterns and entails the reproduction of vulnerable subjects.

In Bareilly, it is the very logic of subcontracting outside factories that enables the transmission of risks "upstream" toward households, homes, and workers' families. While it is clear that artisans are tightly incorporated into what is effectively a wage relation—reflecting multiple pathways to proletarianization (Mezzadri 2014a) —this relation does not translate into any social security provisions by employers. Despite SEWA's best efforts, the ethical initiative is fully embedded in the relations of domination permeating the local economy, which offload all health risks on workers. Arguably, it may even further entrench these relations. In fact, the ETI initiative conceives of the realms of the domestic/home as the primary locus where the costs of social reproduction must be absorbed. Workers are made to internalize lessons on well-being and "responsible" work, particularly in relation to posture and use of light when working, as the impact of embroidery work on eyesight is particularly harsh. However, employers make no contribution whatsoever to ensure better posture or the stable provision of electricity and/or lights. Workers are the ones who are put in charge of protecting their own bodies against the harshness of their toil for the benefit of others. Effectively, the initiative reinforces the role of "the home" as the primary domain where health and safety measures should be "learned," measured, and guaranteed; where workers should be "educated" on their own well-being and "self-manage" their laboring bodies.

As already mentioned for metropolitan settings, very few workers work beyond the age of 30 in Bareilly, and virtually none above the age of 40. Women generally become supervisors of their daughters' work. Despite the fact that all artisans, men and women, report that they would want a different future for their offspring, very few families manage to break free from this very taxing work. At best, some family members—generally male—will manage to enter other lines of work, while others—generally girls—will continue the family's traditional occupation. The lack of social security provisions clashes with these aspirations, particularly for women, for whom migration is not an option. Quite unsurprisingly, also in this case women seem to be the main victims of processes of externalization of the costs of social reproduction. They are more likely to be at the receiving end of strategies through which households socialize risks and diversify livelihoods in the absence of social provisions and in a framework of self-regulation. As health emergencies of any type are internalized by the household, they may imply the need to enter informal debt relations with local moneylenders or, more often, with the same contractors providing work. These practices reinforce the subordination of home-based workers to local contractors through a process of "interlocking" labor and credit relations, an issue already widely discussed in relation to agriculture (see Byres 1998; Mezzadri 2016; Srivastava 1989).

Overall, the complex process of informalization of labor in the garment sector in India, shaping a labor regime founded on the intensity of work, on minimal social provisions, and on the systematic externalization of the costs of social reproduction of the workforce, has a profound impact on the health and safety of garment workers. From the largest factories of the NCR to the homes in its metropolitan surrounding or in the peri-urban and rural enclaves and villages of Uttar Pradesh, the health and safety of garment workers remains largely unaddressed by the industry as a whole. Health and safety concerns are consistently absorbed by workers and their families across the spectrum of labor relations.

In factory-based realms, the use of multiple contracting arrangements, which may even increase in the context of changing national regulation and in the light of global commercial dynamics, undermines the factory as an arena of work-related social protection.[7] Moreover, the factory seems to remain a transient moment in the complex history of workers' livelihoods. Larger factories, those that at least "look good" to the eye of the social auditor, may impose inhumane rhythms to meet production targets and quotas, with the resulting intensity of work further straining workers' bodies. High attrition rates guarantee that employers will bear minimal responsibility for workers' well-being. As workers enter and exit factories, circulating endlessly across the entire labor process characterizing the NCR and its surroundings, and diversify their reproduction across the urban-rural divide, one should severely question the impact of technical solutions to health and safety provisions inside industrial premises. In nonfactory settings, where productive and reproductive time and rhythms overlap, corporate approaches to health and safety are primarily conceptualized in terms of workers' self-regulation of their own well-being. In both cases, risks and adversities are entirely socialized by the reproductive sphere. Even in the absence of major disasters, like fires or collapses, garment jobs remain unhealthy and unsafe jobs, and are unable to guarantee the health, safety and broader well-being of a highly informalized workforce.

Conclusions: Highly Unequal Production Systems as Sick Systems

As health and safety concerns are taking center stage in discussions of the global garment industry and a new era of international agreements finally begins, this chapter has argued that we should address these concerns systemically by looking at the labor regimes characterizing the industry. In fact, failures in health and safety provisions in the industry are one of the many manifestations of what having a poorly paid, insecure garment job means. While indeed some geographical settings may be better than others and some employers more "socially responsible" than others, health and safety concerns cannot be addressed through a piecemeal approach, when there is compelling evidence that the whole global garment industry is marred with deep structural problems that expose workers to different crises of reproduction. The same concerns cannot be addressed through technical approaches targeting single production units either, as such technical solutions are undermined by the systemic labor relations and practices dominating the industry.

Discussing the case of the Indian garment industry in the NCR and one of its embroidery satellite centers, Bareilly, this chapter has shown that the industry is characterized by systemic processes of externalization of the costs related to the health and social reproduction of the workforce. These processes manifest in different ways across factory and nonfactory settings, but they share a common logic: that of devolving responsibilities for workers' health, safety and well-being from factories, workshops, and employers to households, homes, and workers. Corporate approaches to labor standards and ethical initiatives that focus on the "built" environment and "visual" aspects of health and safety continue to simply scratch the surface. In fact, they may even reinforce the institutionalization of self-regulation in relation to health and safety, particularly in home-based settings. Under the labor regime characterizing this industry, marked by low wages and poor social security provisions, health and safety outcomes cannot but also be extremely problematic. The age of corporate "voluntarism," framed around the voluntary self-regulation of businesses, has failed its alleged goals. In fact, it has been part of the problem, as it has considerably delayed discussions over the need to reengage in the debate over national and/or international binding regulation. While the Bangladesh Accord (as opposed to the weaker Alliance) can be considered a step in the right direction, it is only a very first step. The agreement is limited, for a number of reasons. First, it only focuses on Bangladesh, while sweatshop scandals, including infrastructural problems, are a far more global reality. Second, infrastructures are only the "box" in which labor relations occur, and the latter may remain harmful even once the box is "fixed." For instance, the Accord does not account for high levels of informality, a point raised by a 2015 Stern Report (Labowitz and Baumann-Pauly 2015). While this may not necessarily compromise the effectiveness of the Accord (Anner and Bair 2016) in relation to its stated scope, it does confirm its narrow reach and mission, and its limited purchase in tackling systemic labor issues. Overall, international agreements like the Accord seem to mainly attempt to establish minimal standards—namely, and quite crudely put, the right of garment workers to "remain alive." However, far stronger efforts are needed to systemically challenge the many inequalities at work in the garment sector globally, and to address the multiple health and safety risks garment workers are routinely exposed to. "Unequal societies are literally sick societies," writes O'Laughlin (2010, 5, paraphrasing from Wilkinson 1996). By the same token, we can conclude that so far, and despite the rise of some promising new international legal instruments, the contemporary highly unequal clothing production system remains a sick, unsafe system for those fighting to make a livelihood at its very bottom.

Notes

1. The data collected for the ESRC-DfID project focuses on the NCR and is now collated into a joint report. This chapter makes reference to the data jointly collected and analyzed in the report (Mezzadri and Srivastava 2015; Mezzadri 2015; Srivastava 2015).

The author also wishes to thank the principal investigator of the project, Jens Lerche. The data collected for the British Academy project focuses on Bareilly, Uttar Pradesh.

2. Even "feminized" factories showed high attrition rates of around 15–20 percent.

3. Workers remaining in the NCR for longer spells may be of different categories; 40 percent go back home only during holidays or special occasions, while 18 percent go back also during periods of unemployment (Srivastava 2015).

4. Moti workers can come from different class (occasionally even low middle-class) backgrounds, although our survey focused specifically on vulnerable groups in poor hamlets, as these are more likely to be systematically incorporated into export-led chains.

5. Mainly funded by the U.K. Department for International Development (DfID), ETI was created to facilitate multi-stakeholder cooperation to improve labor standards. ETI defines itself as an alliance of companies, trade unions, and NGOs promoting workers' rights around the globe.

6. The aim of RAGS was to mainstream responsible and ethical production in the garment sector supplying the United Kingdom.

7. The amendment of the Contract Labour Act in 2014 is likely to imply the institutionalization of contract labor practices in the NCR.

Bibliography

Anner, Mark, and Jennifer Bair. 2016. *The Bulk of the Iceberg: A Critique of the Stern Center's Report on Worker Safety in Bangladesh*. Penn State Center for Global Workers' Rights (CGWR). Online: http://lser.la.psu.edu/gwr/documents/CGWRCritique ofSternReport.pdf/view. Accessed: May 4, 2016.

Anner, Mark, Jennifer Bair, and Jeremy Blasi. 2013. "Towards Joint Liability in Global Supply Chains: Addressing the Root Causes of Labor Violations in International Subcontracting Networks." *Comparative Labor Law & Policy Journal* 35(1): 1–43.

Appelbaum, Rich, and Nelson Lichtenstein. 2014. "An Accident in History." *New Labor Forum* 23(3): 58–65.

Barrientos, Stephanie. 2008. "Contract Labor: The 'Achilles Heel' of Corporate Codes in Commercial Value Chains." *Development and Change* 39(6): 977–90.

———. 2013. "Labor Chains: Analysing the Role of Labor Contractors in Global Production Networks." *Journal of Development Studies* 49(8): 1058–71.

Barrientos, Stephanie, Kanchan Mathur, and Atul Sood. 2010. "Decent Work in Global Production Networks." Pp. 127–45 in *Labor in Global Production Networks in India*, ed. by Anne Posthuma and Dev Nathan. Oxford and Delhi: Oxford University Press.

Barrientos, Stephanie, and Sally Smith. 2007. "Do Workers Benefit from Ethical Trade? Assessing Codes of Labour Practice in Global Production Systems." *Third World Quarterly* 28(4): 713–28.

Bernstein, Henry. 2007. "Capital and Labour from Centre to Margins." Keynote address for conference, *Living on the Margins, Vulnerability, Exclusion and the State in the Informal Economy*. Cape Town, South Africa, March 26–28.

Bhattarcharya, Saumyajit. 2014. "Is Labor Still a Relevant Category for Praxis? Critical Reflections on Some Contemporary Discourses on Work and Labor in Capitalism." *Development and Change* 45(5): 941–62.

Bhowmik, Sharit. 2015. *The Labour Code on Industrial Relations Bill 2015: Tough Times Ahead for Labour in India*. Global Labour Column 207. Online: http://www.global -labour-university.org/fileadmin/GLU_Column/papers/no_207_Bhowmik.pdf. Accessed: June 17, 2016.

Blake, Stephen P. 1993. *Shahjahanabad: The Sovereign City in Mughal India 1639–1739*. Cambridge: Cambridge University Press.

Breman, Jan. 1996. *Footloose Labor: Working in India's Informal Economy*. Cambridge: Cambridge University Press.

———. 2013. *At Work in the Informal Economy of India: A Perspective from the Bottom Up*. New Delhi: Oxford University Press.

Burawoy, Michael. 1998. "The Extended Case Study Method." *Sociology Theory* 16(1): 4–33.

Byres, Terence J. 1998. "Inter-Linked Rural Markets/Modes of Exploitation." Lecture notes, *Agriculture and Economic Development*. London: Department of Economics, SOAS, University of London.

Cawthorne, Pamela, and Gavin Kitching. 2001. "Moral Dilemmas and Factual Claims: Some Comments on Paul Krugman's Defense of Cheap Labor." *Review of Social Economy* 50(4): 455–66.

Centre for Development Policy and Research (CDPR). 2014. *The Oppressive Labor Conditions of the Working Poor in the Peripheral Segments of India's Garment Sector*, CDPR Development Viewpoint 81, 2014. Online: http://www.soas.ac.uk/cdpr /publications/dv/file93820.pdf. Accessed: June 17, 2016.

Cerimele, Michaela. 2016. "Informalising the Formal: Work Regimes and Dual Labour Dormitory Systems in Thang Long Industrial Park (Hanoi, Vietnam)." In *A Place for Work: Small-Scale Mobility in Southeast Asia*, ed. by Matteo Carlo Alcano and Silvia Vignato. Chiang Mai: Silkworm Books.

De Neve, Geert. 2009. "Power, Inequality and Corporate Social Responsibility: The Politics of Ethical Compliance in the South Indian Garment Industry." *Economic and Political Weekly* 44(22): 63–72.

———. 2014. "Fordism, Flexible Specialization and CSR: How Indian Garment Workers Critique Neoliberal Labor Regimes." *Ethnography* 15(2): 184–207.

Development Commissioner for Handicraft. 2013. Rajiv Gandhi Shilpi Swasthya Bima Yojana, GoI website. Online: http://handicrafts.nic.in/welfare/rajivgandhi.htm. Accessed: February 3, 2013.

Development Commissioner, Ministry of Micro, Small and Medium Enterprises (DC-MSME). 2013. Khadi Karighar Janashree Bima Yojana, GoI website. Online: http:// msme.gov.in/msme_ jby.htm. Accessed: February 3, 2013.

Esbenshade, Jill. 2004. *Monitoring Sweatshops: Workers, Consumers, and the Global Apparel Industry*. Philadelphia: Temple University Press.

Ethical Trading Initiative (ETI). 2006. *ETI Homeworker Guidelines: Recommendations for Working with Homeworkers*. Online: http://www.ethicaltrade.org/sites/default /files/resources/ETI%20Homeworker%20guidelines, %20ENG.pdf. Accessed: June 17, 2016.

———. 2013. *Indian National Homeworker Group, 2013*. Online: http://www.ethicaltrade .org/in-action/programmes/the-indian-national-homeworker-group.   Accessed: February 3, 2016.

Federici, Silvia. 2004. *Caliban and the Witch: Women, the Body and Primitive Accumulation*. Brooklyn, NY: Autonomedia.

———. 2012. *Revolution at Point Zero: Housework, Reproduction, and Feminist Struggle*. Oakland, CA: PM Press.

Gideon, Jasmine. 2007. "Excluded from Health?: Information Workers' Access to Health Care in Chile." *Bulletin of Latin American Research* 26(2): 238–55.

Gooptu, Nandini. 2013. "Introduction." Pp. 1–24 in *Enterprise Culture in Neoliberal India: Studies in Youth, Class, Work and Media*, ed. by Nandini Gooptu. London: Routledge.

Gunther, Marc. 2013. "Gap Spearheads New Alliance for Bangladeshi Worker Safety." *The Guardian*. Online: http://www.theguardian.com/sustainable-business/gap -alliance-bangladeshi-worker-safety. Accessed: June 16, 2016.

Hale, Angela, and Jane Wills. 2005. *Threads of Labour: Garment Industry Supply Chains from the Workers' Perspective*. Oxford: Blackwell.

Harriss-White, Barbara. 2003. *India Working Essays on Society and Economics*. Cambridge: Cambridge University Press.

———. 2014. "Labour and Petty Production." *Development and Change* 45(5): 981–1000.

Hoskins, Tansy E. 2014. *Stitched Up: The Anti-Capitalist Book of Fashion*. London: Pluto.

———. 2015. "After Two Years, the Rana Plaza Fund Finally Reaches Its $30m Target." *The Guardian*. Online: http://www.theguardian.com/sustainable-business/2015/jun /10/rana-plaza-fund-reaches-target-compensate-victims. Accessed: August 1, 2016.

Howard, Alan. 1997. "Labor, History, and Sweatshops in the New Global Economy." Pp. 151–72 in *No Sweat: Fashion, Free Trade and the Rights of Garment Workers*, ed. by Andrew Ross. London: Verso.

International Labor Rights Forum (ILRF). 2015. *Our Voices, Our Safety: Bangladeshi Garment Workers Speak Out*. Washington, DC: ILRF.

International Labour Organization (ILO) and World Trade Organization (WTO). 2009. *Globalization and Informal Jobs in Developing Countries*. Geneva: ILO and WTO.

Kumar, Ashok, and Jack Mahoney. 2014. "Stitching Together: How Workers Are Hemming Down Transnational Capital in the Hyper-Global Apparel Industry." *Working USA: The Journal of Labor and Society* 17(2): 187–210.

Labowitz Sarah, and Dorothée Baumann-Pauly. 2015. *Beyond the Tip of the Iceberg: Bangladesh's Forgotten Apparel Workers.* New York University's Stern Center for Business and Human Rights. New York: NYU.

Lerche, Jens. 2007. "A Global Alliance against Forced Labour? Unfree labour, Neoliberal Globalisation and the International Labour Organisation." *Journal of Agrarian Change* 7(4): 425–52.

Mezzadri, Alessandra. 2008. "The Rise of Neoliberal Globalisation and the 'New Old' Social Regulation of Labor: A Case of Delhi Garment Sector." *Indian Journal of Labour Economics* 51(4): 603–18.

———. 2012. "Reflection on Globalisation and Labour Standards in the Indian Garment Industry: Codes of Conduct Versus 'Codes of Practice' Imposed by the Firm." *Global Labor Journal* 3(1): 40–62.

———. 2014a. "Indian Garment Clusters and CSR Norms: Incompatible Agendas at the Bottom of the Garment Commodity Chain." *Oxford Development Studies* 42(2): 217–37.

———. 2014b. "Backshoring, Local Sweatshop Regimes and CSR in India." *Competition and Change* 18(4): 327–44.

———. 2015. "Labor Regimes in the Garment Sector in India: Home-Based Labor, Peripheral Labor." In *Labor Regimes in the Indian Garment Sector: Capital-Labor Relations, Social Reproduction and Labour Standards in the National Capital Region (NCR),* by Alessandra Mezzadri and Ravi Srivastava. London: SOAS, University of London.

———. 2016. "The Informalization of Capital and Interlocking in Labour Contracting Networks." *Progress in Development Studies* 16(2): 124–69.

Mezzadri, Alessandra, and Ravi Srivastava. 2015. *Labor Regimes in the Indian Garment Sector: Capital-Labor Relations, Social Reproduction and Labour Standards in the National Capital Region (NCR).* London: SOAS, University of London.

National Commission for Enterprises in the Unorganised Sector (NCEUS.) 2007. *Report on Conditions of Work and Promotion of Livelihoods in the Unorganised Sector.* New Delhi: Government of India. Online: http://nceus.gov.in/Condition_of_workers_sep_2007.pdf. Accessed: June 20, 2016.

O'Laughlin, Bridget. 2010. "Questions of Health and Inequality in Mozambique." Cadernos IESE (Instituto de Estudos Sociais e Económicos, Maputo) 4. Online: http://www.iese.ac.mz/lib/publication/cad_iese/CadernosIESE_04_Bridget.pdf. Accessed: June 16, 2016.

———. 2013. "Land, Labor and the Production of Affliction in Rural Southern Africa." *Journal of Agrarian Change* 13(1): 175–96.

Pearson, Ruth, and Kyoko Kusakabe. 2012. *Thailand's Hidden Workforce: Burmese Migrant Women Factory Workers.* London: Zed.

Powell, Benjamin. 2014. *Out of Poverty: Sweatshops in the Global Economy.* New York: Cambridge University Press.

Prentice, Rebecca. 2014. "A Year After Rana Plaza, Still Unearthing its Causes." *Open Democracy*, April 24. Online: https://www.opendemocracy.net/opensecurity /rebecca-prentice/year-after-rana-plaza-still-unearthing-its-causes. Accessed: July 21, 2015.

Pun, Ngai, and Smith Chris. 2007. "Putting Transnational Labor Process in Its Place: The Dormitory Labor Regime in Post-Socialist China." *Work, Employment and Society* 21(1): 27–45.

Raju, Saraswati. 2013. "The Material and the Symbolic: Intersectionalities of Home-Based Work in India." *Economic and Political Weekly* 48(1): 60–68.

Rosen, Ellen Israel. 2002. *Making Sweatshops: The Globalization of the U.S. Apparel Industry*. Berkeley: University of California Press.

Ruwanpura, Kanchana. 2013. "Scripted Performances? Local Readings of "Global" Health and Safety Standards (the Apparel Sector in Sri Lanka)." *Global Labor Journal* 4: 88–108.

SEWA Bareilly. 2009. Contribution to SEWA Bharat Annual Report 2008–2009. Bareilly, India: SEWA. Online: http://www.sewabharat.org/sewabareilly.pdf. Accessed: June 16, 2016.

Shyam Sunder, K. R. 2005. "State in Industrial Relations System in India: From Corporatist to Neoliberal?" *Indian Journal of Labour Economics* 48(4): 917–37.

Singh, Navsharan, and M. Sapra. 2007. "Liberalisation in Trade and Finance: India's Garment Sector." Pp. 42–127 in *Trade Liberalisation and India's Informal Economy*, ed. by Barbara Harriss-White and Anshree Sinha. New Delhi: Oxford University Press.

Smith, Chris, and Ngai Pun. 2006. "The Dormitory Labour Regime in China as a Site for Control and Resistance." *International Journal of Human Resource Management* 17(8): 1456–70.

Srivastava, Ravi. 1989. "Interlinked Modes of Exploitation in Indian Agriculture During Transition: A Case Study." *Journal of Peasant Studies* 16(4): 493–522.

———. 2015. "Capital-Labor Relationships in Formal Sector Garment Manufacturing in the Delhi National Capital Region of India." In *Labor Regimes in the Indian Garment Sector: Capital-Labor Relations, Social Reproduction and Labour Standards in the National Capital Region (NCR)*, by Alessandra Mezzadri and Ravi Srivastava. London: SOAS, University of London.

Standing, Guy. 2007. *Work After Globalisation: Building Occupational Citizenship*. Cheltenham, UK: Edward Elgar.

———. 2011. *The Precariat: The New Dangerous Class*. London: Bloomsbury.

Taylor, Marcus. 2011. "Race You to the Bottom . . . and Back Again? The Uneven Development of Labour Codes of Conduct." *New Political Economy* 4: 445–62.

Tewari, Meenu. 2008. "Varieties of Global Integration: Navigating Institutional Legacies and Global Networks in India's Garment Industry." *Competition and Change* 12(1): 49–67.

Unni, Jeemol, and Suma Scaria. 2009. "Governance Structure and Labour Market Out-comes in Garment Embellishment Chains." *Indian Journal of Labour Economics* 52(4): 631–50.

Wallace, Julia. 2014. "Workers of the World, Faint!" *New York Times*, January 17, 2014. Online: http://www.nytimes.com/2014/01/18/opinion/workers-of-the-world-faint .html. Accessed: June 16, 2016.

PART III

======

Rethinking Health as Well-Being
at Work and Home

CHAPTER 7

Limited Leave? Clinical Provisioning and Healthy Bodies in Sri Lanka's Apparel Sector

Kanchana N. Ruwanpura

Lately characterized as a lower middle-income developing country according to World Bank typology (World Bank 2016), Sri Lanka registered an annual gross national income of US$2,923 per capita in 2012 (CBSL 2013). Even though Sri Lanka's entry into the lower middle-income bracket is recent, for a "developing" nation Sri Lanka has held a much vaunted place in the development world for its impressive health indicators and care provisioning (Jayasinghe et al. 1998; Russell and Gilson 2006). These indicators have also signaled the Sri Lankan state's early commitment to socioeconomic development and slow growth (Humphries 1993; Sen 1988). This offers a crucial background against which Sri Lankan apparel industrialists make bold claims about their ability not only to produce "garments without guilt" (see Ruwanpura 2016), but also to make proclamations about the ways in which they extend health care to workers on-site and treat illnesses and injuries on the shop floor (Ruwanpura and Wrigley 2011).

Sri Lankan apparel's transition into higher value-added production from the post–Multi-Fibre Arrangement (MFA) period was facilitated by its prior adoption of state-directed minimum labor standards from the 1980s (Ruwanpura 2016). These ground conditions meant that a decade before ethical code regimes came into being, Sri Lankan apparel was the vanguard for effective code regime policies—including in the realm of health and safety. Consequently, interventions and fears around the Alliance for Bangladesh Worker Safety (the Alliance) and the Accord on Fire and Building Safety in

Bangladesh (the Accord) in the post–Rana Plaza era has bypassed Sri Lankan apparel. The apparel sector is comfortably detached from such global interventions as it considers its health and safety record, in particular with regard to the built landscape, to be indisputable.

Industrialist proclamations about these achievements are not mere posturing because there is a visible foundation from which to boast about the various amenities—including on-site medical clinics—offered to workers.[1] However, how medical facilities are actually accessed and used by workers suggests that management's concern with health is not merely about upholding ethical credentials and caring for workers; it is also about recognizing the centrality of healthy bodies to the production process. In this chapter I argue for the importance of exploring the negotiations, contestations, and resistance that emerge around health and the body on the shop floor. Health constitutes an arena of negotiation and resistance between workers and management. It signals that in a post–Rana Plaza context we need to be attentive to dimensions of health and well-being that go beyond structural and building concerns. Shop floor labor and production regimes may be important precursors for understanding how the supply chain is continuously punctured by extraordinary disasters, such as factory fires or collapses, which never occur in a sociopolitical vacuum. Hence, appreciating everyday struggles over health and laboring bodies may be as critical for our understandings of workers' health within global supply chains as a focus on the structural safety of buildings.

This chapter begins with an overview of my field research in Sri Lanka. Only a limited account is presented here as my recent fieldwork has been recorded in detail elsewhere (Ruwanpura 2013, 2014a). As my fieldwork also involved participant observation, I use narrative ethnography and a number of case studies to build my arguments. These ethnographic vignettes follow the sections after the fieldwork methods and feed into the conclusion.

Researching Factories

Fieldwork, as part of a longer term research project on ethical trading and labor practices, started in December 2008, when I interviewed twenty-five variously ranked managers among suppliers of apparel in Sri Lanka (Ruwanpura and Wrigley 2011). A couple of serendipitous interviews meant that two factories opened up their premises as research sites for long-term fieldwork.

This extended phase began with a research assistant, Wasana, who was based at both factories from April 2009; I joined her in July and August 2009. I spent seven and a half months at these factories, visiting each one on alternate days. Subsequently, I made return fieldtrips every four to six months, spending between two to three months on each visit. These revisits provided an evolving sense of factory-based ethical code regimes over a two-year period.

The two factories where I did fieldwork are located in a semirural area of a district adjacent to the district of Colombo, not part of any free trade zone (FTZ). The factories were large production facilities that employed approximately 800 to 1,500 workers each. Both factories supply apparel to high-, middle-, and low-end global retailers primarily based in the United Kingdom and United States; their clientele includes retailers, such as Levi's, Calvin Klein, Eddie Bauer, Marks & Spencer, Next, Debenhams, Matalan, Tesco, and Lily Pulitzer. These factories present themselves as harbingers of strong global standards of ethical production (Goger 2014; Ruwanpura 2014b, 2016).

Data collection involved multiple methods, including participant observation, in-depth interviews, and worker diaries. By being located at the factories over an extended period of time, I was able to observe everyday shop floor activities and develop a close bond with workers. This connection enabled interviewing ninety workers—sixty workers located at the two factory sites and thirty workers drawn from contacts of the initial interviewees—using the snowballing technique (Ruwanpura 2016). In all cases interviews were conducted with informants who were willing to be interviewed and who had given full consent. All the interviews were conducted at their homes or boardinghouses; and over the two-year period, a selected subgroup of workers kept in touch with us via phone and personal visits on a regular basis (Ruwanpura 2015). This rapport encouraged twenty workers to maintain a weekly journal over a one-year period.

To acquire a grasp of the industry, I made additional visits to other factories within and outside FTZs, and interviewed trade unionists, labor rights organizations, and policy makers with the aim of cross-checking our factory data. During this time, we collected information on media interventions as well as campaign material used by industrialists to get a comprehensive picture of the apparel industry. Throughout the entire research, my particular class position, as a Sri Lankan from an English-speaking upper-middle-class family now living and working overseas, made me aware of the need to steer my fieldwork in a sensitive manner (Ruwanpura 2013, 2014a, 2014b). I use ethnographic evidence to underscore the ways in which negotiations around health and the body surfaced and were expressed on the shop floor.

Health and the Working Body Inflected

Scholars from various disciplines have already documented the health risks and stress involved in assembly line work, and in the clothing sector in particular, across the world (Brown 2009; Root 2008; Strümpell and Ashraf 2011; Vinet et al. 1989). Health concerns include working with hazardous material, the repetitive nature of piece-based and hourly work, sexuality and health, the prevalence and spread of HIV/AIDS, and the manifestation of stress. They have traced the ways in which workers navigate and negotiate their perilous transition from rural to factory life with an invocation of complex inventories that include religious tropes, industrial knowledge, legal framings, and the like (Root 2008). According to Robin Root, worker understandings around their sexual health and related sexually transmitted diseases are always inflected via everyday religious, moral, and legal tropes. In a contribution that focuses on Bangladeshi workers, Christian Strümpell and Hasan Ashraf (2011) draw out the connections between how workers' sense of their health is shaped by how they feel they are (financially) valued. They note how worker predisposition toward their bodily comportment and health are influenced by the imbalances they experience between their work effort and financial rewards. This scholarship thus suggests the need for us to be alert to the ways in which workers negotiate their health, whether on or beyond the shop floor.

For Sri Lanka, Sandya Hewamanne (2008) chronicles the perils associated with working with dangerous chemicals and lacking appropriate safety equipment. She also comments on how the medical profession assists the industrial environment "to monitor and discourage claims on factory production time" (2008, 116). Her perceptive remarks, while not pursued in depth for Sri Lankan apparel, suggest the need to further investigate how workers, health care providers, and management negotiate the terrain of worker health, particularly in a context where industrialists are proud of the on-site clinical facilities they offer.

Concerns around worker health in the Sri Lankan apparel industry have been examined from different angles by Chamila Attanapola (2004) and N. C. Amarasinghe (2007); they report the health issues of musculoskeletal disorders and anemia, respectively. Attanapola's (2004) focus is on the health of women workers in Sri Lanka's largest free trade zone (FTZ). She observes that despite being plagued with musculoskeletal disorders and recurrent headaches, workers normalize illness and poor health at work, which in turn prevents them from seeking the necessary medical treatment.

For Amarasinghe (2007), many of the illnesses that she recorded followed from a nutritional deficit and were due to the lack of a living wage in the apparel sector, which she also links to workers' compulsion to do overtime. Where overtime is recurrent, it encroaches on the time that workers have for resting, preparing evening meals, and other daily domestic work. Recurrent overtime also signals that workers are likely to economize the time spent on cooking because of other financial commitments (see also Ashraf this volume). According to Amarasinghe (2007), taken together, these factors go some way to explaining why garment sector workers are the most affected workers in terms of deficiency anemia and malnourishment.

These studies suggest that medical provisioning within factories alone is unlikely to meet the complex health needs of the working body. More importantly, working bodies may be afflicted by various types of stress associated with "modern" industrial employment that evolve according to how conflicting class interests within the factory play out in everyday working life (Ashraf this volume; Root 2008; Strümpell and Ashraf 2011). The impacts of having health facilities within factories are thus in need of further exploration in order to reveal their entanglement with the contemporary capitalist pressures emanating from global supply chains. Such an exploration will also further our understanding of how worker health is implicated in exploitative labor regimes that Sri Lanka's exemplary health achievements or workplace provisioning of medical facilities alone are unlikely to redress. Put differently, the politics of labor regimes suggest that we need to be attentive to wider structures that make and unmake healthy working bodies. In an attempt to address this issue, the next section of the chapter describes the clinical facilities available at the factories I studied before moving on to a discussion of the negotiations around access to and use of factory clinics and their implications for working bodies.

Navigating Complexities

A number of episodes that occurred early on during my fieldwork made me aware of the need to pay close attention to how factory-based health facilities, which were introduced in the pre–ethical code era and in response to diktats by the Premadasa political regime (circa 1989), were accessed and used by workers. These incidents, as I outline below, suggest that both workers and clinical providers within factories navigate a complex terrain of power and competing interests. Consequently, workers carefully assess when and how to access the clinics, while clinicians constantly gauge what kind of health care to provide, and whether workers' claims are genuine and legitimate (see also Hewamanne 2008). Equally, the available sick room facilities varied in quality and purpose. The ways in which these amenities were used suggested that there is a need to further scrutinize management's claims that providing clinics within production facilities signals their commitment to worker welfare (Ruwanpura and Wrigley 2011); whether this is actually the case or not is unpicked in this chapter. I sketch my initial experiences of health facilities provided at the two factories before detailing the incidents that reveal the different stakes that medical personnel, shop floor managers, and workers hold in ensuring the health of the workforce. Shop floor incidents and negotiations over the use of health facilities and care offer us a glimpse into why workers' good health is not guaranteed by the mere existence of health facilities at work. Workers' ability to access on-site clinics is framed by a number of facets that need to be carefully teased out in order to appreciate how workers try to remain healthy while engaging in garment work. It was evident that as workers often got sick, they constantly had to negotiate what health care they could access while at work. I start with the sick room at the two factories I studied—the first available point of contact for workers when seeking medical attention.

Quiet Sick Rooms?

When we took ill unexpectedly as schoolchildren, our place of recovery was the school sick room. Usually it was a space of quietness and calmness. Perhaps because this was my expectation of what a sick room is like, my unexpected illnesses during two distinct stages of my fieldwork—at the beginning in one factory and toward the latter end of the fieldwork in the other factory—meant that I had to appreciate that there were different ways in which the clinical area was used as a lived space.

When I fell ill at the start of my fieldwork, the sick room I attended did not merely have sick workers trickling in and out; it had also become an extra space for storing new uniforms. This dual—and possibly even multiple—usage meant that it was also a space that was inordinately busy, with new workers coming and going to collect their new uniforms. The nurses at the clinic split their time between tending to ill workers and informing new workers about the type of uniforms they should be picking up, from which box, and so on. A quiet space it was not.

While it may have been possible to demarcate a soundproof room with beds for resting in order to offer workers the peace they needed when ill, this was clearly not a priority. This was also evident when I ended up using the sick room in the other factory toward the latter part of my fieldwork. This sick room was larger and had multiple beds for workers to rest, and yet it too was tremendously noisy because the nurses and attendants did not think it was a priority to maintain a quiet space. Yet, at both clinics, dedicated nurses and attendants were present and a qualified medical doctor, with whom workers could have regular consultations, visited the clinics on a weekly basis. All these provisions were creditable initiatives on the part of the apparel industrialists, at least at first glance.

Accessing Medication

During my initial episode of illness, when my gynecological pains were severe, bed-resting in the sick room was not possible. The steady flow of workers coming in and out, and their carefree chatter, disrupted any possibility of rest; equally, the pain I was in required a strong painkiller. As my health condition was ongoing, I stepped into the nurses' quarter to request ibuprofen. The two nurses seemed nonplussed by my request, which initially made me think that the medicine was not available. I then requested Panadol, a tablet commonly available in the country, and again with equal bewilderment they said that they could not give it to me. Seeing my confused look, the nurses informed me that I needed to get a *chit* (note) from Human Resources (HR) or the HR manager because the medical doctor was not at the clinic. Before I decided to walk to the office area, I pointed out that I was only asking for Panadol—a drug that did not need a prescription at the pharmacy. Yet it seemed that the nurses had strict procedures to follow.

When I went to the HR office to ask the HR manager for a chit, he called the clinic and requested that I be given ibuprofen or Panadol. At that point, I inquired whether workers always had to get a chit before they got medicine; being relatively new to this production site, he seemed somewhat oblivious to the existence of these measures himself. When he called the clinic, he communicated his agitation to the nurses around needing his approval to have painkillers released as he did not seem to see the point of this additional layer of approval.

Because of my own pains, I did not pay attention to what exactly the HR manager said to the nursing staff. However, the existence of a protocol to access medication when sick was evident. Yet it was not until I witnessed an episode of worker illness in the factory that I began to realize that although the provision of an on-site clinic would seem to signal management's interest in protecting health, *accessing* the clinic was not straightforward. Workers had to navigate a complex terrain to access the medical facilities available at the factories, which raises questions about the extent to which worker health was the paramount concern of management.

Faked Maladies?

From the start of my fieldwork, I had taken to the habit of writing detailed field notes during various meal breaks in the canteen. I did so because between meals it was a quiet space, permitting me to write more detailed accounts than what could be put on paper on the shop floor.[2] On one such occasion, I noticed from the corner of my eye a younger worker coming into the eatery accompanied by a couple of workmates. They had a short conversation with the medical staff who were having a late lunch, which was followed by some sudden commotion. It was only when I heard the shouts "*vettanawa, vettanawa . . . alla ganna*" (falling, falling, catch her/hold on) that I shifted my gaze and caught sight of a young worker fainting. Instantly my mind went to Aiwa Ong's (1987) research on spirit possession on the factory floor, which led me to wonder if I should walk toward the group or observe from a distance. Being Sri Lankan myself, workers and staff probably expected me to be curious and come forward, and so my semi-frozen self is likely to have come across as awkward. Although I am Sri Lankan born and bred, twenty years of living in the West had by now well reduced my assumed "natural" instinct to be prying. Consequently, there were many occasions when I was torn between nosiness and non-interference, with this episode being one of them. Because my writing was interrupted and in the end my purpose was to gather an ethnography of labor practices around ethical codes, including health and safety concerns, to remain unmoving would have been odd.

Cautiously I went over to where the worker was lying down on a bench and her accompanying peers were talking to the nurses. The workers' disapproval of the slow response of the nurses was made clear by their chastisement of the nurses in my presence; their annoyance was around the fact that the nurses did not take notice of their fellow worker when she said that she was feeling weak. As they said this, they were expecting me also to reprimand the medical staff. The workers were trying to draw on my distinct class position, but probably also took me for a "Miss" (a member of management) and assumed that I was in a position to wield authority. Instead I queried "What happened?" in an attempt to avoid further awkwardness, and in response, I received another rendering of the episode by the nurses. They insinuated that these incidents were not unusual and that more often than not workers were feigning illness. Their response suggested that they were expecting me to accept their version, hinting at worker irrationality.

These conflicting accounts signaled the complex ways in which workers and medical staff at the factory clinics navigate access to medical care on the shop floor. Ill health at work does not automatically guarantee immediate access to medical attention, and health is clearly a site of contestation in which workers and health carers alike negotiate around conflicting priorities. Hence, I subsequently witnessed the weekly lining up of workers patiently waiting to see the medical doctor and had numerous conversations with workers about health matters, which ranged from common colds to gynecological issues to recurring muscular pains. These observations and interactions suggested the need to examine closely how healthy bodies were of vital interest to both the industrialists and the workers themselves. Using vignettes I explore this point further below.

Ailments, Rest, and Medication

Back to Basics: Ayurvedic Tea

Workers frequently suffered from common colds or flus, and their teary eyes, sore throats, or hoarse voices made it clear to us that they were unwell. Despite having these common illnesses, they sat at their machines sewing or were packing, supervising, or training their peers. While this was evident to us, worker ill health was almost certainly a challenge to production-level managers and supervisors. On a recurrent basis they had to negotiate production pressures and make decisions about which workers to take off a line because of ill health.

The two factories attempted to thwart these recurrent illnesses by implementing what management perceived to be practical, preventive measures. Workers were sometimes forced to wear their face masks; this rule was implemented diligently at certain times, only to fall away a few weeks later. Throughout the swine flu contagion in Sri Lanka toward late 2009, both factories turned off their air conditioning while strictly imposing mask wearing. In a bid to signal the seriousness with which management took their policy at the time, they too wore face masks. Workers, however, had mixed views on wearing face masks: most either did not wear the masks or feigned doing so by pulling the mask below their mouth or around their neck. It was only a minority of workers who wore a mask on a regular basis, although amid swine flu fears almost all workers wore face masks. While most workers recognized that wearing masks was potentially beneficial, at least in preventing fine dust from entering their lungs, their lack of familiarity with the masks and the difficulty in using face masks, rather than recurrent ill health, was the determining factor that stopped them from doing so.

Partly recognizing that trying to get workers to wear face masks was a faltering effort, one factory decided to change tack in the middle of my fieldwork period and introduced *kottamalli* (coriander tea) during tea breaks on a twice weekly basis. *Kottamalli* is seen as an effective ayurvedic treatment against flus, colds, and coughs—it is also considered a preventive medicine. By introducing *kottamalli* during tea breaks, I was told by the HR manager, they were trying to ensure the immune system of workers did not get regularly battered and their health was strong. Since *kottamalli* has a bitter taste, workers sometimes complained about having to take it during their tea break and doubted its beneficial effects in a context of relentless work routines. However, its implementation was consistent and some workers even saw its introduction as a good thing: "Yes, it is bitter, but at least we know that *kottamalli* is a tried and tested antidote against colds, coughs, and flus." Whether regularly taking *kottamalli* has the ability to prevent frequent illness on its own is debatable, but managers were convinced that this was a fitting measure to introduce. What the HR manager left unsaid, however, but what was communicated by production-level managers and section supervisors, was that recurrent illnesses of workers affect the production process, which is an issue management was much preoccupied with. Not only do mid-level managers have to try to meet production targets, at the time of illnesses they also have the additional pressures of having to shift workers around different operations—which always risks both delaying production and causing outright conflicts among workers. Since both illness and conflict affect productivity, it was in management's interest to maintain a healthy workforce at all times, and if *kottamalli* could play a role in this, then it would be used. By adopting preventive measures, there was an attempt at reducing time lost due to ill health and trying to perpetuate uninterrupted work routines. Clearly, the sphere of health forms an arena of continuous contestation between managers and workers.

Beheth Ganna (Take Medicine)

Workers, by contrast, placed their faith much more in access to the on-site factory clinic. Their confidence in the ability of biomedicine to treat most common ailments and injuries became clear during our fieldwork. They would urge Wasana and me to visit a medical doctor when we had poor health, or were horrified to learn that we were more likely to take *kottamalli*, *paspanguwa*, or *venivalgata* (all ayurvedic potions) than allopathic medicine. The fact that Wasana's spouse was a medical doctor and that she too preferred ayurvedic remedies added to their bewilderment. As Jamie Cross and Hayley MacGregor note, "allopathic drugs continue to be invested with social and symbolic meanings which lead to them being highly valued" (2010, 1598). Hence, despite having to maneuver layers of workplace hierarchy to visit the factory clinic and the strategizing this entailed, workers opted for biomedicine offered by the clinic. The clinic was always their initial port of call, despite having to get permission from their immediate supervisors and sometimes even production zone managers before being able to leave the production line. Consequently, it sometimes meant they had to become really ill before getting the medical attention they needed, given that supervisors or production zone managers were often skeptical of workers' initial claims of pains or illness. Within the first two weeks of my fieldwork I saw Dayani, who had started chatting to me from the start, assisting a worker named Mayanthi to walk. She held Mayanthi close to her and caringly took her away from the shop floor. I took notes, waiting to speak with Dayani until she came back from the clinic. She then explained to me how Mayanthi had already been ill for a while: "For a few days, Mayanthi has been suffering from fever—but she kept coming for work because we only have a limited number of sick leave days. Today her fever was soaring and she obviously could not work anymore; I told the supervisor, 'it is not right; she needs to lie down' (*hari na, ayeta elewanna denna*), and it is only then that we were able to take her off the line. Now she probably won't be able to come to work for more days than if she had rested from the start."

Avindra, a line supervisor who was passing by and overheard our conversation, acknowledged that a worker not taking sick leave during the early stages of an illness can become a greater "problem" later on. He then went on to note how there had been an instance in which an operator was so ill they had to "rush her to the local hospital."

The simple presence of on-site clinics did not guarantee that workers could access care or treatment automatically when feeling unwell, nor did it ensure they obtained adequate time off work when needed. An initial visit to the clinic needed supervisors or zone managers to sign them off, and workers needed to convince the relevant members of the shop floor hierarchy that their illness was real and not feigned, and their request legitimate. Where workers sensed that their ability to get the necessary sign-off would require too much effort or convincing, the more usual pattern was that they would work through the early stages of any onsetting illness. This, coupled with their trust in biomedicine, meant the possible neglect of home remedies, ayurvedic treatments, or rest during early symptoms, which might help prevent a subsequent period of prolonged or worsening ailment. Under these circumstances workers strategically decide whether to plead with their team leaders, supervisors, or floor managers, or to suffer in silence until their bodies give up and they are physically unable to continue working. A sniffling worker may be expected to continue working, while a teary-eyed worker with demonstrable fever is likely to be signed off, with a visit to the clinic guaranteed. However, episodes of fainting workers, Dayani having to escort Mayanthi off the shop floor, or the hospitalization of a worker that Avindra alluded to all suggest that for many workers this moment comes too late. Supervisors and managers who do not detect the symptoms of a potentially serious or long-lasting illness early on might lose a worker for several days or weeks. Yet, in the short term they have to carefully assess whether a worker is genuinely sick, or is feigning an ailment because of exhaustion or in order to go home early to deal with domestic matters. What their experiences tell us is that, in a context of limited leave, workers have to carefully balance their health issues. Because their interests are often in opposition to those of management and supervisory staff who need to keep their workers on the line—and yet not too long when there may be serious health issues at stake—workers negotiate a fairly tricky situation in trying to keep their bodies healthy.

Because Mayanthi worked in Dushyantha's zone, I got into a conversation with Dushyantha about how they decide when to allow a worker to visit the clinic. He explained the difficulties associated with signing off workers because workers can feel poorly due to domestic worries, personal difficulties, alcoholic-related spousal and domestic violence issues, or physical illness. He felt that family issues have a bearing on how workers feel at work and can affect their physical well-being. He said he also needs to assess if a worker has caught a virus that may affect the health of others, suggesting that they make a distinction between contagious diseases and family issues, although there was some sympathy for the connection between the two. He said that sometimes distinguishing between the two is difficult, but acknowledged that neglecting or downplaying symptoms of illness can lead to the loss of the all-important work rhythm on a line over an extended time period. So middle management and supervisory efforts at labor control related to workers' health can be heinous for what it may ultimately entail for the production process, production targets, and incentive payments. As much as they did not want to be considered an easy target for getting sign-offs, managers also realized that taking an exacting and unsympathetic stance might work against their long-term interests in maintaining an uninterrupted production schedule. From the perspective of managers, then, the effort to control labor with regard to worker health was a contested process requiring sensitive negotiations without falling out of favor with workers.

It was not only evident that workers were subject to an exacting labor regime, but also that supervisors had to juggle a difficult balancing act between production pressures placed on them and productivity levels becoming affected due to the neglect of workers' health in the early stages of illness. Yet, for workers, initial access to the on-site clinics was crucial for it enabled them to make subsequent visits to have their illness treated. Initially, it seemed to me that workers were signed off by management to meet the doctor; yet, over time it became apparent that this was possible only insofar as the medical doctor or nurses had given a chit to workers approving repeat treatment or visits to the clinic. So even though a worker unexpectedly and visibly being afflicted seemed to guarantee an initial visit to the clinic, when such episodes occurred while the medical doctor was not present, it fell upon the nurses to assess and give a chit for the worker to see the doctor. However, as Hewamanne points out in the context of her research, medical staff and specifically nurses "worked as disciplining agents who controlled unnecessary disruptions to the assembly-line work" (2008, 115). Hence, my witnessing a weak young worker fainting because of nurses failing to appreciate the gravity of her malady. Yet, the upshot of a misjudgment can mean at best an embarrassing situation and at worst a more dangerous result for the worker that requires his or her hospitalization. While Hewamanne (2008) notes that workers avoided the possibility of hospitalization because it meant losing half a day's pay, my fieldwork suggests that this was not always the case. In what follows, I discuss how and why workers accessed hospitals, sometimes on their own volition, in a bid to escape labor controls at their production premises.

Negotiating Leave Entitlements

During the initial phase of my fieldwork, managers constantly pointed out that Sri Lanka has an inordinate number of public, including mercantile, holidays and that as a result Sri Lanka's productivity levels are below those of neighboring countries.[3] What managers left unsaid—and I discovered through the fieldwork—was that despite having at least one monthly mercantile holiday, it was rarely the case that factories upheld these holidays because of their practice of "covering." With covering, workers were expected to work on holidays without getting their eligible overtime payments (see Ruwanpura 2016), and most stipulated mercantile holidays could be subject to covering depending on production needs—the exceptions were state-declared holidays related to significant religious occasions.[4] This slip between claims made by managers about the inordinate number of annual holidays that are registered in the Sri Lankan calendar, and the reality of being expected to "cover" on such days, has a bearing on workers' lack of rest, which impacts both their physical and mental well-being. With the repetition of "covering" and mercantile holidays not being upheld, garment workers had fewer holidays than suggested by managers.

Against this backdrop, the annual number of legally stipulated sick days—fourteen days—is a measly figure. Moreover, state-run outpatient clinic hours do not reflect the cadence of working life (see also Russell 2005; Shaikh and Hatcher 2004), which meant that workers had to come to work late or leave the factory early in order to be able to attend doctor consultations at state hospitals between 9 a.m. and 5 p.m. The limited days of sick leave available to workers also meant they had to assess whether to access the local hospital's outpatient clinic, seek a private consultation after working hours, or try to get a sign-off from a supervisor or floor manager to visit the factory-run clinic. None of these options were choices workers could make without sacrificing their time, pay, effort, and skill. Most workers seemed acutely aware of the labor regimes placed on them by the state or their factory managers, yet what transpired during my fieldwork was that workers also negotiated these regimes in ways that allowed them to address their health needs, despite the knock-on effects on the factory or production process. As I delineate below, workers employ a number of strategies that involve withdrawing from the workplace altogether, while at other times they cover themselves from potential workplace fallout by going to extraordinary lengths to legitimize their absence.

Hence, because of illness, workers sometimes withdraw altogether from working life for a week or two by getting the necessary medical certification—either because they got themselves hospitalized or via a privately consulted medical doctor. In one instance, a worker left the factory for more than two months altogether, with the factory middle managers eventually having to cajole her into returning to work, as she was a highly valued worker. I use a couple of illustrations to elaborate how some workers went about achieving their aims to guard their health and well-being at work.

Madhavi had started talking with me from the inception of my fieldwork, and I continue to keep in touch with her and her mother to this day. During the latter part of my fieldwork, her father unexpectedly passed away and she was given compassionate leave[5] to attend the funeral rituals—including the seven-day *dana* (alms-giving). She had invited me for the seven-day *dana* and at that point she mentioned to me that she was planning to return to work in the coming week. However, when she did not reappear at work by the end of that week, I asked others on her line about her. I was told that she had fallen ill. I then called her one evening to inquire about her health, and she informed me that she had come down with flu and hoped to return to work the week after. When she did not turn up for another week or so and I made inquiries again, I was now told by other workers that she had decided to quit work because she had to deal with lots of family problems that had cropped up after her father's death.

En route to Colombo, where I often returned on Saturdays, I decided to call on her one day. I mostly wanted to ensure that she and her mother were all right and meet her in person to get a better sense of the problems she was struggling with. On meeting them, I was told about a number of family arguments over the division of the *budale* (family wealth, which was

the house they lived in), about her boyfriend demanding that she stop working, and about how her health was affected by all this. She said that once she
recovered, she would return to work (despite her boyfriend's protests). She
had also received a call from HR to inform her that she had already taken
too much time off work, and that her compassionate leave would therefore
be deducted from her entitled annual leave. There had been an argument
over this misunderstanding and in response Madhavi had handed in her
resignation, much against the wishes of her immediate supervisor and zone
manager—both of whom appreciated Madhavi's machinist skills. So a mix-
ture of factors led Madhavi to become sick, but because the HR department
was not aware of her value as a shop floor operator they attempted to control
her lack of labor discipline by usurping her entitled annual leave as a way of
penalizing her errant and prolonged absence. The response from Madhavi in
turn was to withdraw from working for the factory altogether, being upset
that the factory management did not appreciate her personal circumstances.
Staying away from the factory to resolve family issues or as a response to
factory managers' perceived disinterest in her personal circumstances was
the strategy Madhavi adopted. However, she was not alone in adopting this
strategy—I came across other workers who did the same, with some of them
returning to work and others not. While Madhavi stopped working at this
factory for about three months, she went back to work at another factory near
her natal home after about two weeks. Later on, she returned to the original
factory after her immediate supervisory managers visited her at home to coax
her back with a more attractive wage package (i.e., hired her at a higher wage
scale as a skilled and senior worker).

Limited statutory leave allowance also means that ill health at times leads
workers to take more drastic measures, such as hospitalizing themselves
in state-provided clinics, in an attempt to justify their absence from work.
Nimanthi was someone I had gotten to know from my very first day at one of
the factories that I visited regularly. She had talked to me that day because of
what in her view was a wardrobe malfunction with regard to my dress, and
later apologized that she might have caused me to become flustered with her
frankness. After this bemusing episode I would always speak with her on my
regular visits, although she never agreed to be formally interviewed. During
my fieldwork, at one point Nimanthi was noticeably absent for a few days and
inquiries about her from others on the line suggested that she might be ill.
When I eventually saw her back at her machine, I got to talk to her about her
prolonged absence. She said that she was kept in the local hospital because

she had come down with a flu and stomach pain. I continued the conversation, partly because I was perplexed as to why flu and a stomach bug would warrant hospitalization:

KANCHANA: Hospital? Why did you go to hospital for flu and a stomach bug?

NIMANTHI: My stomach was really hurting; I did not know what it was—may be appendicitis, I thought.

KANCHANA: Appendicitis does not come with flu. What did the hospital staff say when you were discharged? What was the diagnosis?

NIMANTHI: Oh, they thought I needed some rest because I was worn out; they were not able to diagnose anything more specific than that. So when my flu abated and my stomach pains were gone, I got discharged. I had all the relevant documents to show HR when I returned to work.

During our conversation Nimanthi placed more emphasis on the medical certificates and discharge papers that she obtained from the hospital than her health itself. It was almost as if her sickness was less of a concern; far more important was the fact that she now had the necessary documents to verify that she had been ill. With those in hand, HR was unlikely to hassle her about her lengthy absence from work; she had the medical backing in her hand—literally. These cases illustrate how workers devise strategies to deal with routine exhaustion from high stress and manually strenuous work. Moreover, given tight entitlements of leave, workers feel compelled to go to extraordinary lengths to ensure that their leave is seen as acceptable and legitimate, and that their employment does not come under threat—particularly where they may already have spent their leave entitlement within a given calendar year.

It seems that limited statutory leave entitlement has a severe impact on the ability of hardworking garment workers to withdraw from work and allow themselves to recover from what are highly taxing and unsustainable labor regimes. Workers are well aware that given the arduousness of manufacturing work, their leave entitlements are miserly, and the practice of covering means that their actual rest periods are much more limited than what may appear on paper. Hence, they are aware that continuing to work at the same factory sometimes requires twisting and bending the system to suit the needs of their working bodies—because healthy bodies are necessary for industrial work. To evade labor pressures on the shop floor, workers would strategize to seek medical treatment through official channels so as to avoid being questioned or challenged by management. Workers who do not have medical certificates or letters from the GP yet have taken time off work because of sickness may find themselves in a predicament similar to Madhavi's. While her defiance and circumstances made her withdraw from the shop floor altogether, other workers may not have the confidence to defy supervisors and managers nor the skills that made Madhavi a highly sought-after employee. Where this is the case, healthy bodies are not prioritized, despite claims of outstanding health and safety standards and on-site medical clinics at Sri Lanka's garment factories.

Conclusion

When Sri Lankan managers proudly speak about the multiple medical facilities and subsidies they offer workers, these initiatives seem impressive and appear to offer the workforce real benefits. While workers undoubtedly gain from these amenities, the mere presence of an on-site clinic does not automatically mean that workers get the appropriate medical attention as and when they need it, nor that the primary cause of much ill health—physical and mental exhaustion caused by relentless labor regimes—is in any way recognized, let alone addressed (see Mezzadri this volume). While in theory medical care is on offer, in practice, accessing on-site health care facilities entails negotiations around social dynamics and production pressures on the line. As Christian Strümpell and Hasan Ashraf (2011) remind us, experiences of stress and modern-day work afflictions are also inflected and experienced via the class position of workers in relation to management, a social dynamic that is never absent from the shop floor.

Workers have to balance their bodily health needs with financial pressures, because taking time off beyond their statutory leave entitlements may mean losing a bonus payment or taking a cut in wages. And as the entitled leave period is limited, their class vulnerabilities (or not) are likely to shape how and when they approach their line supervisors, zone managers, or production managers for accessing the on-site clinics or requesting sick leave. As my evidence shows, workers often suffer ill health in silence until their symptoms become acute, at which point it is unlikely that their seniors will turn down a request to visit the clinic or to take rest at the on-site surgery.

Equally, workers' reliance on biomedical treatments also determines their health-seeking practices; here too, assumptions about the efficacy of biomedicine are rooted in a denigration of ayurvedic treatments as outmoded (Cross and MacGregor 2010).

As Sri Lanka's low-income groups have been absorbed by a burgeoning apparel manufacturing sector, they are confronted with health problems that require rest or attention, and that are not necessarily solved with medication. The depletion of working bodies by the prevalent production regime means that they need more regular opportunities to rest, recover, and reenergize their exhausted bodies. When they fall ill because of a lack of leave or failure to uphold prescribed mercantile holidays, their problems are further compounded by the social structures of the factory that workers have to navigate. The problem is at least in part associated with a public health care system that has not adapted to the cadence of working lives nor to the recurring health problems engendered by these new forms of employment. Their limited entitlement to sick days coupled with long working days means that accessing the state sector becomes prohibitive because of the time they likely will need to spend at outpatient clinics during working days. Within this context, workers' prudence and decision-making are filtered through existing labor laws and socioeconomic structures that are iniquitous and laden with power dynamics. Hence workers may prefer to hospitalize themselves or withdraw from work altogether, albeit for a short period of time. These constitute contested ways in which workers routinely seek to protect their health at work.

Front-line middle and junior management staff too face a tricky balancing act. They have to make judgment calls, which at a professional level they are ill-equipped to do. They have to ensure that they do not overwork ill workers and need to constantly judge whether workers are genuinely ill, feigning ailments, or whether they can carry on despite early signs of a bug. Their decisions have a bearing on the production process and productivity levels, in both the short term and the middle to long term. This may also affect worker-staff dynamics because workers do not always take kindly to being asked to work on another machine because of a worker shortage; at the same time, workers do not appreciate why a supervisor or manager may be unwilling to show sympathy or empathy toward ailing workers.[6]

Creating large-scale factory employment in the apparel sector was the outcome of neoliberal policies introduced in Sri Lanka more than three decades ago. Sri Lanka's commendable human development achievements (Sen 1988) gave apparel industrialists an educated and healthy workforce. Yet, we have seen that manufacturing jobs bring with them recurrent health problems. In seeking medical treatment, workers appear to be driven by a need to negotiate and control everyday working lives affected by frequent ill health; the workspace terrain that middle-to-lower managers have to navigate is no less complex. Providing health care amenities within factory premises is as much about labor regimes as it is about "healthy" bodies needed for production.

Health and safety issues in the Sri Lankan apparel sector cover factors that extend well beyond the visible and the discernible, and we need to be attentive to this because otherwise, the everyday health of workers risks being neglected. So despite the availability of clinics at production sites, as I have shown, access to them is not straightforward—workers always need to carefully negotiate the social and managerial hierarchies of the shop floor. Equally, and perhaps more importantly, the limitations around leave entitlements and the lack of upholding the apparently "large number of holidays" by managers mean that workers end up using a range of strategies to allow their bodies to recover from relentless labor regimes that cause much of the ill health, stress, and sheer exhaustion in the first place. Consequently, ethical codes deployed globally are inadequate because they do not even scratch the surface of problems associated with intensive shop floor labor regimes. In addition, they often intensify antagonisms between workers and managers, who struggle to uphold global codes, meet production targets, and keep working bodies healthy at the same time. The evidence from Sri Lanka, despite its seemingly laudable record on health and safety, suggests that the global interventions of the post–Rana Plaza era, such as the Alliance and Accord, are unlikely to be able to address the root causes of ill health on the global garment production line. While such initiatives are right to make retailers and industrialists responsible and liable for offering labor at least a safe built environment, they leave untouched the everyday health and well-being of workers who toil in arduous manufacturing jobs shaped by global processes and pressures.

Notes

1. In Ruwanpura and Wrigley (2011) we explain how the establishment of medical clinics in factories and other basic standards came through an early initiative introduced by former president Ranasinghe Premadasa in the late 1980s and early 1990s. While unions had limited direct influence on the introduction of these policies, there is little doubt that labor struggles and collective actions of women in the late 1970s and early

1980s in particular are likely to have influenced these state-level policies (see Ruwan-pura 2016).

2. When this was the case, I would invariably be distracted by a worker asking about my welfare, querying what I was writing down, or asking a host of other related questions, or I would be drawn into casual conversations that would detract from my task of writing, although it is important to note that often these passing chats revealed important matters that formal interviews did not capture.

3. While this was often stated, I have not come across any credible study or survey that did research on a comparative basis to justify this point.

4. So *Vesak* (the *poya*—full moon day to commemorate the Buddha's birth, attaining of nirvana, and cessation of life), Christmas, or *Ramazan* are more likely to be observed than are any other monthly full moon holiday.

5. Sri Lankan labor laws do not make explicit allowances for compassionate reasons; this was given in the case of this factory. While initially it was not clear whether this period would be deducted from the annual leave, events afterward suggested that this would be the case as narrated to me by Madhavi.

6. While for this research I did not interview or speak with the nursing staff or medical doctors visiting the clinic, the episodes I experienced, both directly and indirectly (participant observation in action), suggest that they too face a social setting that is contested and complex.

Bibliography

Amarasinghe, N. C. 2007. "Nutritional Status of the Female Garment Factory Workers in the Katunayake Free Trade Zone, Sri Lanka." *Labour Gazette*. Sri Lanka Department of Labour: 67–72.

Attanapola, Chamila. 2004. "Changing Gender Roles and Health Impacts among Female Workers in Export-Processing Industries in Sri Lanka." *Social Science and Medicine* 58(11): 2301–2312.

Brown, Garrett. 2009. "Genuine Worker Participation—An Indispensable Key to Effective Global OHS." *New Solutions* 19(3): 315–333.

Central Bank of Sri Lanka (CBSL). 2013. *Economic and Social Statistics of Sri Lanka, 2013*. Colombo: Sri Lanka. Online: http://www.cbsl.gov.lk/pics_n_docs/10_pub/_docs/statistics/other/econ_&_ss_2013_e.pdf. Accessed: May 19, 2014.

Cross, Jamie, and Hayley Nan MacGregor. 2010. "Knowledge, Legitimacy and Economic Practice in Informal Markets for Medicine: A Critical Review of Research." *Social Science and Medicine* 71(9): 1593–1600.

Goger, Annelies. 2014. "Ethical Branding in Sri Lanka: A Case Study of Garments Without Guilt." Pp. 47–68 in *Workers' Rights and Labor Compliance in Global Supply Chains: Is a Social Label the Answer?*, ed. by Jennifer Bair, Doug Miller, and Marsha Dickson. London: Routledge.

Hewamanne, Sandya. 2008. *Stitching Identities in a Free Trade Zone: Gender and Politics in Sri Lanka*. Philadelphia: University of Pennsylvania Press.

Humphries, Jane. 1993. "Gender Inequality and Economic Development." Pp. 218–33 in *Economics in a Changing World, Volume 3: Public Policy and Economic Organization*, ed. by Dieter Bos. New York: St. Martin's Press.

Jayasinghe, K. S. A., D. De Silva, N. Mendis, and R. K. Lie. 1998. "Ethics of Resource Allocating in Developing Countries: The Case of Sri Lanka." *Social Science and Medicine* 47(10):1619–25.

Ong, Aihwa. 1987. *Spirits of Resistance and Capitalist Discipline: Factory Women in Malaysia*. Albany: State University of New York Press.

Root, Robin. 2008. "'Controlling Ourselves, By Ourselves': Risk Assemblages on Malaysia's Assembly Lines." *Medical Anthropology: Cross Cultural Studies in Health and Illness* 27(4): 405–34.

Russell, Steven. 2005. "Treatment-seeking Behaviour in Urban Sri Lanka: Trusting the State, Trusting Private Providers." *Social Science and Medicine* 61(7): 1396–1407.

Russell, Steven, and Lucy Gilson. 2006. "Are Health Services Protecting the Livelihoods of the Urban Poor in Sri Lanka? Findings from Two Low-Income Areas of Colombo." *Social Science and Medicine* 63: 1732-1744.

Ruwanpura, Kanchana N. 2013. "Scripted Performances? Local Readings of 'Global' Health and Safety Standards (the Apparel Sector in Sri Lanka)." *Global Labour Journal* 4(2): 88–108.

———. 2014a. "Metal Free Factories: Straddling Workers Rights and Consumer Safety." *Geoforum* 51(1): 224–32.

———. 2014b. "Global Governance Initiatives and Garment Sector Workers in Sri Lanka: Tracing Its Gender and Development Politics." Pp. 207–20 in *Routledge Handbook of Gender in South Asia*, ed. by Leela Fernandes. London and New York: Routledge.

———. 2015. "The Weakest Link? Unions, Freedom of Association and Ethical Codes: A Case Study from a Factory Setting in Sri Lanka." *Ethnography* 16(1): 118–41.

———. 2016. "Garments Without Guilt? Uneven Labour Geographies and Ethical Trading—Sri Lankan Labour Perspectives." *Journal of Economic Geography* 16(2): 423-46.

Ruwanpura, Kanchana N., and Neil Wrigley. 2011. "The Costs of Compliance? Views of Sri Lankan Apparel Manufacturers in Times of Global Economic Crisis." *Journal of Economic Geography* 11(6): 1031–49.

Sen, Amartya. 1988. "Sri Lanka's Achievements: How and When?" Pp. 549–56 in *Rural Poverty in South Asia*, ed. by T. Srinivasan and Pranab Bardhan. New York: Columbia University Press.

Shaikh, Babar, and Juanita Hatcher. 2005. "Health Seeking Behaviour and Health Service Utilization in Pakistan: Challenging the Policy Makers." *Public Health and Epidemiology* 27(1): 49–54.

Strümpell, Christian, and Hasan Ashraf. 2011. "Stress and Modern Work: Ethnographic Perspectives from Industries in Bangladesh." *Vietnamese Ethnomedicine Newsletter* 13(2–3): 1–9.

Vinet, Alain, Michel Vezina, Chantal Brisson, and Paul-Marie Barnard. 1989. "Piecework, Repetitive Work and Medicine Use in the Clothing Industry." *Social Science and Medicine* 28(12): 1283–88.

World Bank (2016) "Sri Lanka: Overview." http://www.worldbank.org/en/country /srilanka/overview. Accessed: January 5, 2017.

CHAPTER 8

Toward Meaningful Health and Safety Measures: Stigma and the Devaluation of Garment Work in Sri Lanka's Global Factories

Sandya Hewamanne

This chapter examines the marginalities and vulnerabilities of women working in Sri Lanka's garment industry, which persist despite a nationwide effort to position the country as an "ethical" production site over the past ten years. It argues that health and safety measures that do not take into account labor devaluation and its resulting stigma fail to improve workers' lives in a meaningful manner. Drawing on long-term ethnographic research among global garment workers at Sri Lanka's Katunayake Free Trade Zone (FTZ), the chapter argues that disregarding workers' cultural backgrounds, gender norms, and immediate living environment as factors shaping health and safety results in meaningless rules and regulations that have little impact on the workers once they leave the factory. Additionally, the chapter discusses how by failing to provide workers with a living wage, Sri Lankan garment factories set in motion a chain of consequences that adversely affect workers' overall well-being, health, and safety long after they leave the factories.

The enduring stigmatization of garment workers is an important but neglected dimension of their well-being that has been left out of debates on health and safety. Ethical production regimes and corporate social responsibility policies focus on the auditing of quantifiable processes rather than the social and symbolic violence that is endemic in the industry. I argue that stigma in this particular local context is intimately tied to women's experience of working for a transnational production regime that actively devalues their labor. Throughout the developing world, a discourse of women workers' "disposability" has been nurtured by multinational corporations in order to justify low wages. I explore ethnographically how this devaluation contributes to stigma. Tracing women workers' experiences on their return from FTZs back to their home villages, I show how hard they must work to rid themselves of the lowered social status of having been a "garment girl," and how they attempt to restore their reputation at home. I conclude with a suggestion that paying workers a living wage may go some distance toward alleviating FTZ stigma and increasing women's social power, thereby improving their long-term well-being.

Disposable Workers: Devaluation of Global Assembly Line Work

It is by now widely established that adverse gender assumptions and stereotypes have contributed to highly unfavorable terms of work for women in global factories (Fernandez-Kelly 1983; Hewamanne 2008, 2016; Lynch 2007; Mills 1999; Peña 1997; Pun 2005). Diane Elson and Ruth Pearson (1981, 93) made one of the first documented connections between gendered assumptions about "third world women" and the devaluation of female labor on the global assembly line. According to them, women are considered to have naturally nimble fingers; be more docile; willing to do tedious, repetitive, and monotonous work; and less inclined than men to join trade unions. By showing how household activities, including sewing, from a very young age train such "nimble fingers," Elson and Pearson make a valuable link between how the invisibility of this training results in women's assembly line work in global factories being termed "unskilled," thus making workers easily replaceable.

Melissa Wright's (2006) work further develops the idea of disposability by analyzing how it has grown to mythical proportions. According to Wright global assembly line workers' disposability is scripted, told and retold in many ways, and corporations, managers, and consumers use it as a resource to justify their varied participation in terrible labor practices. Within this disposability myth, young women in developing countries over time become a "form of industrial waste that can be discarded and replaced easily" (ibid., 2). By using this constructed notion to subject women workers to abhorrent working conditions and then getting rid of them after a few years of work, global factories both perpetuate and benefit from the "disposability" myth. Furthering how the myth of "disposability" leads to working women's worthlessness, Wright argues that the story of disposability is one of the reasons the murders of maquiladora workers in Ciudad Juarez do not receive police or public attention (ibid., 168).

Elson and Pearson (1981) also discussed the disposability of global assembly workers by noting that due to the capacity to bear children, women's work is considered secondary and women workers easily disposable. The assumption is that women would naturally be unwilling or unable to continue work once they get married. Women leaving factories when they get married or pregnant were thought to be "natural wastage" (ibid., 93). In many developing countries where young women work in global factories, the understanding is that women only work until they get married, and in South Asian countries, especially in Sri Lanka, until they have earned their dowries. This understanding is, in fact, incorporated into global factory work in Sri Lanka in an official capacity via Board of Investment (BOI)[1] stipulations.

In this economic context where women's labor is actively devalued, Sri Lanka has attempted since the 2000s to be seen as a champion of workers' rights and ethical garment production. In 2006, the government and the national manufacturers' association launched a "Garments Without Guilt" program, which required member companies to pay for an annual third-party audit that would certify their labor standards (Ruwanpura 2011). Export-oriented garment producers throughout the developing world have since the 1990s been subject to increasing demands from foreign buyers (retailers and brands) to show compliance with corporate codes of conduct and other "ethical" initiatives.[2] But, as Annelies Goger (2013) has argued, "Garments Without Guilt" was created both to address local concerns that employment in garment factories was morally compromising young village women, and to help producers maintain their market share after the 2004 phase-out of the international quota system known as the Multi-Fibre Arrangement (MFA). Sri Lanka sought to distinguish itself from lower-wage rivals by promoting its labor standards, professionalism, and quality production.

I have conducted research among Sri Lanka's Katunayake FTZ factory workers for more than fifteen years. Fieldwork in the early 2000s, including a year-long ethnographic study based in a factory and in workers' boardinghouses, focused on how workers negotiated new identities once they became FTZ workers (Hewamanne 2008). While corporate social responsibility (CSR) policies were only talked about in 2000, they were an established part of factory life ten years later. During the summers of 2012, 2013, and 2014, I conducted focused research on the ethical codes that have been a cornerstone of CSR policy. Research included interviews with three Human Resource (HR) managers and three CSR officers from six factories, health officials, the Deputy Director for Industrial Relations, and the Deputy Director for Operations at the BOI. In addition to countless conversations with current and former garment workers in the FTZ and in their home villages, I draw upon a questionnaire administered in July 2013 by a research assistant to sixty workers, in-depth interviews with twenty selected workers, and a focus group discussion with fourteen workers.

My long-term research in Sri Lanka has given me insight into the disjuncture between CSR policies promoting safe and healthy workplaces and the enduring ways in which women workers suffer from a devaluation and denigration of their labor that affects their well-being at the workplace and beyond. I argue in this chapter that "ethical" production regimes in Sri Lanka—"Garments Without Guilt"—define health and safety narrowly, failing to capture, on the one hand, the diffuse, moral, and embodied ways in which women suffer from working in this industry, and on the other hand, the extent to which the stigma of garment work affects their lives outside the workplace and long after their work in garment production has come to an end. Drawing on ethnographic data from workers' boardinghouses, the FTZ area, and their home villages, I show how women intimately experience the ramifications of their FTZ time, with adverse consequences for their long-term well-being.

I explore these links in the next section by discussing how workplace health and safety measures improved in some ways over a twelve-year period within the Katunayake FTZ, and how different actors understood the changes and their effectiveness. However, adverse health outcomes in the FTZ area and in workers' home villages result partly from the stigma attached to FTZ work in Sri Lanka. This stigma is directly related to the above noted gendered assumptions that led to the devaluation of women's labor, bodies, and lives within transnational production networks. However, as long as corporations benefit from the devaluation of female labor, adverse labor regimes might be difficult to change despite the existence of CSR and similar interventions (Cross 2010; De Neve 2009; Goger 2014; Ruwanpura 2013). Nevertheless, I argue in this chapter that paying a living wage could form an important first step toward rectifying this devaluation, enhancing the status of women workers in Sri Lanka's FTZs, and reversing the stigma attached to garment work.

Health Standards

"Chandrika, child, now go back to the line," Hemamali, the head
nurse at the factory medical center, called out in a sugary sweet voice
addressing a woman lying down on a bed at the far corner of the
center. The young woman looked tired and in a barely audible voice
complained of new pains in her abdomen and continued to lie down.
While talking to me about her home and family Hemamali asked the
sick woman to leave the bed twice more before she suddenly stood up
and stomped towards the bed.

  "You have been lying here for more than twenty minutes now.
Either you go back to the line or I am going to take you to the hospital.
What do you want? Would you leave on your own or should I make
you do that?" with hands on her hips and bending down close to the
patient's ear Hemamali shouted. The woman stood up and complained
of more pains while walking towards the door, tears coursing down
her cheeks. This threat to take them to the hospital was almost always
effective as workers feared going to the hospital for two reasons: first, it
meant that they would lose their salary for half a day and, second, most
of the time all they needed was a little rest. (Hewamanne 2008, 115)

This scene is drawn from fieldwork I conducted in a factory in the Katunayake
FTZ in Sri Lanka in 2000. Assembly line work was hard and young women
suffered bodily pains and mental stress because of long working hours and
the pressure to meet targets. Aches, pains, and even professionally recognized
illnesses were considered a nuisance that workers should take care of privately. The medical center of the factory mostly worked as a place for quick
remedies to ensure work was not affected and to diagnose and immediately
evacuate workers who contracted contagious diseases such as measles or
mumps, thereby ensuring the safety of other workers and the meeting of production targets.

My summer fieldwork on health and safety standards at the Katunayake
FTZ worker boardinghouses and factories in 2012, 2013, and 2014 provided a
different picture, at least on the surface. Factories maintained bigger medical
centers with qualified staff, weekly doctor visits, nutrition and wellness information sessions, work position adjustments for pregnant workers, maternity
leave according to the 1985 government maternity benefits ordinance, and
compulsory time allocation for breast-feeding mothers for up to one year.

Changes regarding pregnancy are important given that in 2000 pregnancy invariably resulted in losing one's job. That year alone I knew of four workers who hid their condition in fear of losing their jobs, often leading to birth complications. Two of these women gave birth on the shop floor. All four of them lost their jobs when they did not return to work immediately after giving birth.

Workers I met at boardinghouses between 2012 and 2014 were on the whole satisfied with the medical care they received in the factories, and they described the medical personnel as pleasant and caring. Although almost all of them believed themselves to suffer from long-term work-related ailments, most found it acceptable that the factory health services only took care of acute health problems, because overall health and well-being were thought to be the workers' individual responsibility (see Mezzadri this volume; Ruwanpura this volume).[3]

During interviews with two factory nurses and the chief public health professional of the Medical Office of Health (MOH) in June 2013, they all described health standards changing for the better, emphasizing their own roles in these improvements. The two factory nurses noted that they had been thoroughly briefed by the HR office and especially the CSR officer on how to interact with sick workers. One nurse attended a one-day workshop on patient communication organized by the regional hospital. The chief public health officer of the MOH office had more than twenty-five years of service in the Katunayake and Negambo areas and spoke highly of the improvements that she had seen with regard to the health standards and the overall attitude of health professionals toward FTZ garment factory workers. She had recently attended training sessions organized by the Ministry of Health, Ministry of Women's Affairs, and the Sri Lanka Police[4] about patient relations, sex, and sexuality in changing socioeconomic circumstances. She discussed sexuality (premarital sex, legalization of abortion, homosexuality) in a matter-of-fact and nonjudgmental way.

Although workers spoke positively of the health care provided by employers, they complained that health workers and state agents continued to treat them with disrespect. Many felt that the factory nurses and even doctors looked down on them as "bad" women, making the workers reluctant to talk to health professionals about basic gynecological problems, let alone date rapes and unwanted pregnancies. Workers depicted health professionals as kind and polite when they were in their offices but thought they sneered behind their backs. According to one worker, health professionals even "talked to the newspapers about how bad the FTZ workers are." Workers' ongoing distrust of health professionals reflects their marginality, enduring stigma, and sense of powerlessness over their own representation in public discourse.

Safety on the Line

Over thirty-five years of producing for export, Sri Lanka's garment industry has not suffered from factory fires and collapsing buildings as elsewhere in the region (Ashraf this volume; Miller 2012; Sumon et al. this volume). A lack of catastrophic industrial incidents, however, does not mean that production facilities are safe for workers, nor that their health is adequately protected. In 2000 the main problems, as described by workers, were overcrowding, dust, malfunctioning machines, and locking of doors—all fire hazards. But by 2012, workers and employers reported that doors remained unlocked during work time, and that information regarding fire exits and extinguishers was made known to them. Nonetheless, my interviews revealed a disagreement between employers (represented by three HR managers) and workers about whether there was adequate space between machines on the shop floor, sufficient dust reduction, and proper maintenance of machines so that they would not malfunction.

According to the workers, factories remained overcrowded with workers and equipment, were full of dust, and some areas of the shop floor, such as the fuseling section, exposed them to chemical fumes. Workers did not like the face coverings provided to them and believed that the factories cut costs by providing cheap, uncomfortable masks. They also expressed a desire for higher management to talk with them about all safety concerns before implementing sometimes useless measures to improve safety. Workers and employers agreed that machines were usually well maintained, but workers also described intermittent malfunctioning of machines, a fact that all three HR managers vehemently denied. Mr. H noted, "I don't think there is a single factory in the zone that does not maintain machines well. Even if not for worker safety, the factories have to keep well-maintained machines for their own sake because buyers are very concerned. If accidents happen, then it is most likely the worker's fault." Blame of any accidents, in this narrative, was thus squarely put onto workers.

While in 2000 only an occasional researcher or activist talked about safety concerns, by 2012 the vocabulary of "health and safety" seemed to be part of the everyday. As Kanchana Ruwanpura (2013) has shown, compliance with health and safety codes set by foreign buyers and third-party auditors can be used as a disciplinary tool by management and creates a regime of self-governance that further increases the workplace stress experienced by factory workers (see also De Neve 2009, 2014). Workers' knowledge of the importance of compliance was captured by one of the HR managers, Mr. J, who claimed, "Workers are more concerned about safety standards than us. After all, they don't want the buyers to go elsewhere and thus lose jobs." When I related this remark to a few workers, one of them responded, "He can say that because he doesn't know how the line leaders and supervisors harp that every day like a broken record . . . *Make buyers happy or the factory will close down, and you will lose jobs*"—uttering the last part in a high-pitched voice, mimicking her supervisor.

Despite these conflicting interpretations, it would be hard not to notice the improvements to shop floor organization and other health and safety measures since 2000. These included improved ventilation, more bathroom and water breaks, medical center visits, time allocations for health education, and checks and balances to minimize verbal and physical abuses by line supervisors. Although focused research began in 2012, I started noticing these changes since around 2008.[5] However, it is also important to note that while curative care and health education improved, preventive measures in the form of structural changes to the transnational assembly line production system have not taken place. Women still work under tremendous pressure to produce almost impossible numbers of garments within a set period. There are hourly as well as daily targets to meet, and compulsory overtime is imposed when they make mistakes or when a tight deadline has to be met. Many workers are still not allowed to keep water bottles by their machines or go to the restroom whenever they need to. Unlike in 2000, workers are well cared for if they faint while working. However, no measures have been taken to stop workers from fainting due to work pressures in the first place.

Nor has the stigma abated that sees "garment girls" as independently living women who easily fall for physical relations with bad men and end up with unwanted pregnancies and abortions. They are still considered transgressive women who live away from their families, engage in shameful activities, and know too much, unlike sheltered women who live under the control of their families. While the consequences of such stigma are more visible in workers' lives outside the factories, it is easy to see how managerial attitudes are shaped by their internalized cultural understanding of migrant women workers as "bad" and not deserving of their respect. For example, in June 2012, when workers complained about their lunch packets containing spoiled curries, a manager yelled (mostly to himself but also at me) how women, who came here because they did not even have wild fruits to eat and who go from hotel to hotel with any man who asks, can complain about a lunch packet with five curries and a piece of fish. One HR manager informed me that the reason for company-organized Christmas parties and pleasure trips is to get the "desirous energies" (*gaaya*) of these foolish girls spent. Several others expressed the same attitude in more polite ways.

Work, Life, and Culture

They said she worked in a factory office at Ratmalana, and she had a good dowry. So I agreed to the marriage in the beginning. But then we heard that she is actually a garment girl who worked at the FTZ and danced the devil with all the men there. We also heard rumors that she had boyfriends and that she was not a virgin and I canceled the wedding plans. But my son said he liked her. I said that he will not be my son anymore and that he should consider his parents dead if he marries her. He of course soon gave up the hope of marrying her. (Chithrani on why she objected to her son's marriage to a former FTZ worker)

I am not ashamed to tell you, miss, the reason that I cannot visit my friends the way I want to is that I just can't afford the bus fare. My husband gets a steady income but he drinks and only gives me money for bare necessities. If I try to talk to him he starts insulting me and says that unlike other men he was stupid enough to have gotten burdened with an FTZ worker. (Dinithi on her post-FTZ life)

I tried to talk to him about not getting pregnant for a year or two so we could develop our shop. But he thought I may become permanently infertile if I used contraceptive methods. I knew that is not the case. But I did not try to reason with him and tell him about the benefits and side effects of contraceptive methods. The reason was that he might think I am too worldly. He will then immediately connect this to FTZ bad girl stories and think that I am one of those girls who used contraceptives in the FTZ, and that is how I know of all these things. (Kamali, who had a baby in the tenth month of her marriage)

I am so worried that people will soon insinuate that my immoral life-style while at the FTZ is responsible for my not having children. Once I was watching this TV health program with my in-laws and some neighbors. I was so upset when the doctor started talking about infer-tility caused by abortions. I was almost squirming in my chair. . . . And truly, miss, I hate it when I have to pretend that I am a stupid, ignorant fool during conversations about even simple health discus-sions. I really don't want people to think that I led a fast life at the FTZ. I just hate living like this. (Vasanthi, who had not conceived despite being married for about three years)

I do not want these village people to bring up my FTZ past and to say that I am corrupting the other women. I had two babies right after the other so that people would forget my FTZ time. It is not like they talk about this all the time or anything. But if you give any hint of the fash-ions and knowledge you acquired at the FTZ, then they would only stop after making you into the worst slut ever. That is why I did not agree to speak to the village women about contraceptives when Miss Suramya (village family health officer) asked. (Shanika, who helped the health officer in a voluntary capacity)

Turning from the factory to the workers' villages, these quotations reveal what life is like for garment workers once they leave employment in the FTZ behind and return home. Why do women experience incidents such as the ones described above once they are back in the villages? And how are such experiences connected to health and safety matters within industrial production?

In the wake of large-scale disasters such as the 2013 collapse of the Rana Plaza factory building in Bangladesh, public calls to enhance health and safety standards in global factories focus attention on the everyday working environment of the shop floor. But factory-based health and safety initia-tives do not prevent sexual assault and rapes on Katunayake streets or dis-eases spreading within poorly ventilated, overcrowded boardinghouses, nor do they enable workers to consume a nutritionally balanced diet outside of working hours. They do not prevent the embodied consequences of garment work, including stigma and stress-related illnesses, traveling with workers back to their villages once they leave the factory.

Recent scholarship on corporate social responsibility (Cross 2011; Rajak 2011) shows how CSR initiatives create imaginary jurisdictions in space and time, carving out particular places and constituencies to address. In Sri Lanka's FTZs, ethical codes of conduct and other CSR initiatives have limited their attention to the shop floor and to workers' health and safety in the workplace. Yet, one might question whether this is adequate and whether other spaces and times should be considered by corporate interventions, not in the least because workers' experiences away from the factory and after having left factory work are key to their overall health, well-being, and social status back in their villages. As Alessandra Mezzadri (this volume) reminds us, the private spaces of the home and the formal spaces of employment are always implicated in one another, because industrial production relies upon the social reproduction of the labor force, which is largely taken care of at home. Moreover, transnational production has been envisioned, designed, and executed through the operationalization of a number of generalized assumptions about developing countries, cultures, and gender norms. Yet, participation in transnational production work affects the lives of workers not only in the factories, but also outside the factories and after factory work has ended. It therefore seems appropriate to consider how shop floor conditions and labor regimes not only affect workers' health and safety at work, but also how they impact their long-term social reproduction when women return to their villages, get married, and rejoin family life.

Workers around the world have not been incorporated into global assembly line work from a social vacuum. Existing social and economic hierarchies shaped the organization of transnational production and its "ideal" workforce. Participants in the Washington Consensus made certain assumptions about developing countries when they decided that they would welcome multinational corporations and jobs at the bottom of the global capitalist hierarchy with open arms. They decided that those countries should be happy to receive trickle-down benefits as they were debt-ridden and industrially backward. They also decided that increased foreign investment is the way forward for those countries. They then made sure the assumptions were real by imposing structural adjustment regimes on such countries.

With gendered, class-related, and colonial assumptions embedded in the organization of labor in the global garment industry, women from marginalized communities took up jobs under conditions that reinforced their multivalent marginalities. Although the mobilization of educated and capable masses in developing countries for work through transnational production was noted as the key to activating markets and subsequent local production, planners made several assumptions about labor markets in the developing world. These gendered assumptions included the idea that the women are secondary earners in these "patriarchal countries" and thus do not need a family wage because they are financially supported by their fathers, brothers, or husbands.

Not only multinational corporations but also the Sri Lankan state participated in generating such assumptions about Sri Lankan women. For example, FTZ work was originally structured as an opportunity for poor young women to work until they saved enough money for their dowry. This expectation is actually incorporated into Sri Lankan employment policy. Workers are entitled to Employee Provident Fund (EPF) and Employee Trust Fund (ETF) payments, in addition to the factory gratuity payment, if they provide a marriage certificate within three months of leaving factory employment. By getting married, a worker leaving employment in her mid-twenties will receive EPF and ETF payments, rather than waiting until she turns fifty-five years of age. The state thus plays a role in the official intertwining of an essentialized understanding of women's life cycle choices with global factory needs to replace an "aging" female workforce. This adds to the pressure to get married. It also helps the corporations get rid of more expensive and politically conscious senior workers, by exerting informal pressures to push them out, such as supervisors ridiculing senior workers for continuing working because they could not find anyone to marry them.

Low salaries in the garment sector kept urban, lower-middle classes away from FTZ jobs, leaving those to be filled by the female migrants from downtrodden, rural farming families. These migrant women were considered "survival migrants" whose families live in abject poverty and needed to send their sheltered daughters to work in the city as a last resort. Since these rural-to-urban migrants' salaries were not good enough to pay rent at reasonably comfortable and safe boarding facilities, many women ended up taking residence in hastily built, unsafe, and overcrowded rooms that neighbors put up beside their own houses. Also, since women were considered the ideal workforce for global garment production, the new arrivals were more than 90 percent women. The high visibility of this vast group of new female migrants resulted in the Katunayake area being termed a city of women (*sthri puraya*) that attracted the attention of young men from the area, the military, and transportation and shop workers.[6] Living away from their families for the first time, suffering under draconian work regimes at the factories, and experiencing difficult boardinghouse living, many young women sought solace in boyfriends, leading to further stigmatization of the FTZ area as a "Love Zone" (*prema kalape*) and "Whore Zone" (*wesa kalape*) (Hewamanne 2008; Lynch 2007).

As the stigma deepened with exaggerated stories of women living carefree love lives with rampant premarital sex, unmarried cohabitation, and same-sex relations, more and more men arrived, some with the expressed reason of finding FTZ girlfriends. Stories of date rape, unwanted pregnancies, and infanticide featured prominently in the national media, which condemned FTZ workers as victims not only of unscrupulous men but also of their own unrestrained desires. Furthermore, while the barbed wire–fenced FTZ area had well-maintained roads, flowering bushes, and street lights, the area just outside, where workers lived, had poorly lit streets and lacked adequate public transportation after 8 p.m., especially in the early days of the FTZ. Therefore, when workers leave the huge factory gates, they face many dangers on the streets outside: thefts, sexual assaults, abductions, and rape.[7] CSR policies in bigger factories have led to better company-provided transportation for workers who do night duty or overtime work. The company buses serviced major roads and dropped workers at major junctions near their boardinghouses. They still needed to walk along alleyways to reach their residences. But night work transportation led to a reduction in reported cases of abduction and rape in the area from the early days of the FTZ (1980–2002). However, discrimination against garment workers continues, including sexual harassment and assaults on workers' bodies and possessions. These include theft, being cheated out of money and jewelry, date rapes, and crude forms of abortions conducted at roadside clinics (Hewamanne 2010, 2012).

Sexual crimes against workers cause the FTZ stigma to continue, which in turn results in women carrying the stigma of having worked and lived in the FTZ back to their villages on leaving employment. Cultural expectations of ideal Sinhala Buddhist women, such as serenity, timidity, religiosity, and lack of sexual knowledge, which were constructed in the late nineteenth and early twentieth centuries (De Alwis 1997), create conditions in which women must be vigilant about conforming to norms of female behavior. When former FTZ workers return to their villages, they work hard to rehabilitate their reputation through a range of strategies with which they hope their community members will "forget" their FTZ pasts and allow them to build a respectable future for themselves and their families.

Mobilities, Marginalities, and Low Wages

Although all mobile women are open to criticism as transgressors, whether they work in garment production or not, there are differences with regard to the intensity of criticism and subsequent social retributions for different groups of women. For example, early-career schoolteachers and doctors are placed in far-flung regions considered difficult *(dhushkara)*, but women who take up these posts maintain high prestige despite this mobility, due to the social status of these jobs. These jobs are regarded as highly appropriate for women because they are popularly considered to be extensions of their domestic duties of educating and nurturing. Even though sewing could also be seen as an extension of domestic duties, garment workers' low wages compared to the wages of teachers and health professionals means that high prestige is not extended to FTZ work. Also because the former are normally boarded individually in family homes or government-provided quarters, the chances of being stigmatized are minimized. Young women who migrate to universities and training schools in cities in preparation for professional jobs are also respected, because of the prestige attached to education and their residence in school dormitories under the charge of an elderly woman (usually called a "matron"). Students are generally addressed and treated as older children *(campus yana lamai)*, minimizing scrutiny of their sexuality. Mobility always represents a threat to women's social reputation, but doing so in pursuit of well-paid, high-status professions tends to neutralize criticism.

Migration for FTZ work has neither the status nor the salaries attached to it to receive similar social recognition.[8] It is industrial assembly-line work with jobs of low regard, and workers live in congested, "slum-like" conditions where the only leisure and social activities available to them—such as night musical shows and pleasure trips—put them in danger, at best, of losing their good name and, at worst, of being sexually assaulted (Hewamanne 2008). The temporary nature of their employment makes women insecure about their lives. They know that working in the FTZ and having boyfriends tarnishes their reputation and makes it hard to contract a good marriage. Therefore, many young women will hold on to a boyfriend, giving into demands for sex, domestic service, and financial support, in the hope that they will one day get to marry him. Some of the health consequences of coerced sex include unwanted pregnancies, unsafe abortions, infanticides, and suicides. It is also important to note that Sri Lanka's rural communities highly value virginity at marriage. Thus, most garment workers consider it a moral outrage for a man to abandon a woman after having sex with her. The cultural norms, living conditions, and work-related stress unintentionally collude in these FTZs to produce specific harmful health and safety outcomes.[9]

Cultural and gender norms are part of the structuring of the global garment industry and affect the social conditions of employment. Women are incorporated into global garment factories in ways that reinforce rather than mitigate their marginalities and vulnerabilities. There is a contradiction in the ideal of "ethical production" or "corporate social responsibility" in enhancing workers' lives by delivering strong labor standards and the fact that corporations profit from the low pay and low status of employment in this industry. This clash between the interests of employers and foreign buyers on the one hand and workers on the other can be seen in workers' low pay. As Kanchana Ruwanpura (2011) explains in her study of ethical codes in the Sri Lankan apparel sector, the most frequently violated code within the sector is payment of a living wage. Wages have vastly improved from 2000 when the basic monthly salary was Rs. 2,500 (US$25), and an average take-home salary was around Rs. 5,000 (US$50). Today an average FTZ worker's take-home salary is approximately Rs. 20,000 (US$153).[10] However, massive inflation and the devaluation of currency rates during the intervening years have diminished the buying power of this fourfold increase.

The average FTZ boardinghouse fee was Rs. 900 in 2000 and had climbed to Rs. 3,200 by 2013. As a result, wage increases have not enabled women workers to obtain safer accommodation. Moreover, rock-bottom salaries do not enable them to have much sway in marriage markets, thus contributing to their continued dependence on FTZ boyfriends who later find FTZ workers undesirable as marriage partners.[11] These attitudes will not change without substantially increased wages and changes in workers' living and social conditions that can elevate women's reputation in the eyes of onlookers. But since global garment production was initiated to cut costs by using cheap "third world" female labor, such increases are unlikely to happen. Yet, better wages are a necessary condition for any meaningful improvements in workers' health, safety, and overall well-being.

"As the Cart Follows the Bull, FTZ Stigma Follows Us"

The title of this section refers to a common rural saying,[12] which I often heard from former garment workers as they talked to me back in their villages as prospective brides, new wives, and daughters-in-law. What they implied was that the FTZ stigma was like karma (*karumayak*), with consequences even after they had left the zone. Recalling the earlier quotes from ex-workers trying to rebuild their lives in their home villages, it is not hard to see the logic behind their concerns. The earlier sections evidenced how the basic assumptions underlying global garment production set the ground for the creation of the stigma while low wages helped maintain it. None of these prevent skillful, determined, and hard-working young women from achieving success within the limited social and political spaces of their villages. Notwithstanding the fact that they have to engage in highly nuanced performances of social conformity and strategic cultural displays to negotiate new identities, many workers have used their FTZ experiences and the lump sums they receive at the time of marriage to become successful and locally respected entrepreneurs.

Yet, sometimes former workers have found that no amount of discipline and conformity can overcome deeper concerns about religion, nation, and corrupting FTZ influences. Anusha's experience of having to abandon her home-based business elaborates the precariousness of such achievements and its direct connection to their FTZ pasts.

Anusha had to abandon her successful business of raising pigs for meat when neighbors expressed concerns that she was bringing un-Buddhist activities to "a pure and moral Buddhist village." Anusha married her boyfriend and moved in with his parents in a village off Kegalla. "I did not flaunt my FTZ styles or things I learned there. I wanted to be 'someone' in this village, and flaunting city ways is not the way to get there," she said. She learned while at the FTZ that people raised pigs in their compounds for big companies. After her first baby was born, she started a small pig farm with twenty-five piglets, with the help of her Katunayake contacts. This was enormously successful and she earned Rs. 20,000 net profit with the first batch. By this time, she was becoming aware of community displeasure, yet when the opportunity arose to raise forty piglets for the same company the following year, she gladly took it. This was when the community protests became official, with the village agent and the chief monk raising concerns. Some people spoke directly to her in-laws, saying that "Anusha has been corrupted in the FTZ and now she is bringing all these bad influences to this pure Buddhist village." The mean looks and talk behind their backs were too much for the family, and Anusha soon abandoned the business.

Another villager, a middle-aged man, had been raising pigs for village consumption on a very small scale (two or three at a time) for years, and his jealousy of Anusha's larger business seems to point toward anxieties over changing gender roles and women's empowerment following employment in the country's FTZs. Village protest against Anusha occurred in late 2007 through 2008, when the civil war was raging and nationalist discourses on pure Sinhala Buddhist traditions were at their peak. All this resulted in Anusha losing her painstakingly created position as a good, industrious daughter-in-law, although by 2009 she was progressing toward regaining that position. For example, she contributed much labor to the celebrations surrounding the civil war's end in May 2009 and the Wesak and Poson poya day celebrations at the village temple.[13]

Research in former workers' villages revealed how women performed extreme forms of obedience, such as paying obeisance to the elderly, not sitting when older people or men were present, and so on, to repair damaged reputations. Not doing so risked the potential of physical violence against them, such as when village thugs threw acid at a former garment worker who "dared" to walk around the village in tight-fitting jeans she obtained at the FTZ. According to the villagers, one of the men decided to do this so that she would not corrupt other young women via her FTZ fashions and carefree lifestyle. Although this kind of physical violence is rare, social punishments, such as slander leading to marriage proposal rejections and preventing non-migrant young women from associating with former workers, were frequent.

Although many former workers seemingly overcame the stigma after a few years, they all understood that their FTZ history could be deployed at any time to force them back into social conformity. In the case of Anusha, the protests over her business resurrected her FTZ past. Anusha had young women friends who visited her often to help or chat. After the protests started, some were pressured by their families not to visit Anusha lest they become "corrupted" by her. "It is like, suddenly, they all remembered that I had a FTZ past and that whatever bad deeds I committed were due to that. Some people were saying that I converted to Christianity while at Colombo [Katunayake] and that I drank whisky and moonshine: all sorts of nasty lies," Anusha complained. It can take years for former workers to transcend the stigma of having spent time in a place where premarital sex, abortions, and suicide have occurred. Although there are significant changes in attitudes toward former FTZ workers as potential daughters-in-law, due to their accumulated dowries, the latter have to work hard for many years to rid themselves of stigma. Even then, some might never be able to fully shed the stigma.

Additionally, some women complained of sicknesses and diseases that followed them to villages from the FTZ. For instance, Kumudu put the blame for her chronic back and knee pain squarely on the particular assembly line position she occupied for eight years. She has not conceived after many years of marriage, and while she noted a medically diagnosed gynecological condition, she also blamed the relentless pressure at work, dust, and chemical fumes for her infertility. Several others mentioned dust allergies leading to asthma, and unexplainable fatigue and general aches and pains that women of their age should not be suffering, as health problems that followed them home from the FTZ. When I mentioned to a few former workers at a village gathering how conditions have improved in the FTZ and overt stigmatization seemed to have at least partially lessened, Chathurika smiled sarcastically and said, "FTZ stigma is like caste in Sri Lanka. People may not treat you differently when interacting daily, but FTZ workers will find the stigma still alive and well when their parents try to make arrangements for their marriages."

Obviously, the devaluation of their work represented through low wages, bad work and living conditions, subsequent low esteem accorded to the job, low respect from others, and negative health and safety outcomes are intimately connected to the quality of life back home, long after they leave the factory.

I earlier noted that the workers were happy with their factories' improved health measures, such as doctors' visits, rest breaks, and educational workshops. Workers generally thought chronic issues should be taken care of privately and factories should not be too involved in this regard. They had little comprehension of medical benefits and insurance programs with many assuming that such privileges only came with government employment (i.e., for those in the military or state transportation board). They all noted that increased salaries would help them get better care for conditions such as asthma, rheumatism, diabetes, and ENT diseases, which they thought of as unrelated to factory work.

Almost all female workers felt factory contracted and monitored housing would alleviate the hassles they encountered due to substandard boardinghouse facilities. Only a few said factory-run boardinghouses were good for them. Except for a few new workers (those who had been in the FTZ for ten months or less), all others in the focus group said they did not want the factory to rule their private lives, with some insisting that they needed to live as far away as possible from the factory. Some mentioned that higher salaries would allow them to find residence at better boarding places with more facilities and safety. However, they felt that it would be all right for the factories to contract with private boardinghouse owners and thereby provide better facilities.

Some workers said that the factories had entered into such contracts with large boardinghouse owners to accommodate Tamil women workers recruited from the wartorn areas following the end of Sri Lanka's civil war. When I mentioned, based on fieldwork conducted at three such boardinghouses for Tamil women, how such supervised living made it difficult for workers to enjoy leisure activities and gain experience in overcoming various difficulties (see Hewamanne forthcoming), this led once again to discussions about how higher salaries are the only way better housing could be achieved. Providing better housing through factory CSR measures is bound to be a mixed blessing, depending on how such measures are planned and executed. While better facilities, safety and protection, and factory-provided transportation would no doubt reduce the stigma, such factory-provided facilities could also promote compliance with factory regimes, thereby impeding political consciousness and collective resistance.

I earlier noted that workers wanted management to consult them before implementing safety measures so as to ensure they benefited from the new practices. At one focus group, a particularly cynical worker said that the management would never discuss health and safety measures with assembly line workers "because we will ask for more salary instead of face masks or more educational programs. All those safety measures are to appease the buyers, not us. What we need is more salary to look after our own selves."[14] When I told them that in many factories the management consulted the leaders of the Joint Council of Workers before imposing measures, many workers expressed their dissatisfaction with the joint councils and the prohibitions on unionization within factories. Several also noted that even if unions were allowed, women workers' voices were bound to be marginalized by male workers and technical staff. Some of them thought that a national trade union run by women would be the ideal umbrella organization for female FTZ garment workers.

This may be an apt place for a note on trade unions and other organizations around the Katunayake FTZ. During my earlier fieldwork in 2000–2008, none of the FTZ and subcontracting factories had trade unions. The Joint Council of Workers included management representatives and operated as a stopgap measure. Mr. Anton Marcus, a veteran trade union activist, organized an umbrella organization for the joint councils of workers, but it failed to create trust within the main FTZ worker constituency: female factory workers. In the meantime, several NGOs working in the FTZ area with a mandate to improve workers' working and living conditions used creative methods to organize FTZ workers. For instance, Mithursevene and Janasetha, which are now defunct, conducted dancing, embroidery, and beauty culture classes for workers, thereby providing a place for them to gather and discuss grievances. When workers were unfairly treated or summarily fired, both organizations facilitated legal challenges by filing complaints at the labor tribunal and providing legal aid. Workers I met at these two offices spoke highly of the support they received from the staff. Dabindu and Kalape Api, two other long-standing NGOs in the area, published monthly magazines that allowed workers to express their grievances via creative writing or through investigative reports written by the staff. Some of these writings criticized conventional trade unions for their male-centered leadership and patriarchal attitude toward female assembly line workers (Hewamanne 2002). All four organizations conducted educational workshops on topics ranging from reproductive health and rights to workers' rights and women's empowerment. The workers felt such activities at least partially filled the lacuna left by the prohibition of unionization within the FTZ.

Anton Marcus is now the secretary of the General Services Employees Union. Chamila Thushari, who is one of the chief activists at Dabindu, is also the head of the Commercial and Industrial Workers' Union. This organization comes closest to what factory workers said they felt would be the ideal umbrella organization to represent their interests. Unfortunately, there are tensions between Anton Marcus and some of the other organizations, and according to one source the former denies the importance of gendered injustices at government and international NGO forums and tries to project himself as the sole spokesperson for the global factory worker constituency. Understandably, these tensions do not matter much to workers as they are focused on being paid a salary that enables them to live dignified lives. As young women from poor, marginalized communities, most garment workers seem to consider certain injustices in the workplace part and parcel of life. For instance, a rally organized by the independent trade union collective on June 22, 2016 at the FTZ roundabout (the main site of protest for the FTZ) to oppose low salaries, prohibition of unionization, and sexual harassment attracted only about 3,000 workers (BBC 2016). This is because while the need and desire for higher salaries remain paramount, workers appear unconvinced that the government or the trade unions will be of help. Most acknowledged that without higher salaries leading to better living conditions, the stigma surrounding FTZ work would not diminish. They also noted that a positive media portrayal of their work and living conditions, and changes in the attitude toward romantic relationships and premarital sex, were necessary to further alleviate the stigma surrounding women migrating for industrial assembly line work.

Conclusion

My ethnography evidences the need to expand our understanding of health and safety to include diffuse, everyday aspects of well-being that are threatened by the symbolic violence of stigma, discrimination, and marginalization. It also suggests the need to look at spaces beyond the factory and at post-factory life to grasp the complexity of health and well-being outcomes for women garment workers in Sri Lanka (see also Mezzadri this volume and Ruwanpura this volume).

It is obvious that higher salaries were more important to workers than any shop floor improvements. Although increasing a woman's earnings does not always directly translate into increased empowerment and autonomy, the workers seem to believe strongly that higher salaries would address issues arising from discourses of disposability and stigma. Although exact improvements in health, safety, and reputation issues are difficult to measure, a substantial increase in worker salaries would go some distance toward reducing stigma by raising the status of garment work and enhancing the reputation of garment workers when back home. The space for political organization is directly related to salary increases and expected outcomes. Yet, as things currently stand, the available opportunities for political organization do not seem to inspire much enthusiasm among workers. What is apparent, though, is that truly safeguarding workers' well-being must begin from the recognition that capital profits from a discourse of female expendability that directly contributes to workers' stigma and shame.

Notes

1. The BOI (Board of Investment) is the central agency facilitating foreign investment in Sri Lanka. It was established in 1978 to improve and oversee foreign investments, first in the greater Colombo area and then, since 1992, in the entire country.

2. In addition to the government's ratification of core International Labour Organization (ILO) conventions on child and forced labor, discrimination, and freedom of association, Sri Lankan producers have also embraced a range of private initiatives

to raise labor standards, drawing on codes of conduct and third-party certification (Ruwanpura 2011, 2013). The "Garments Without Guilt" program, for example, was launched by the Sri Lankan government and the national manufacturers' association in 2006 to counter the loss of market share to lower-wage countries by certifying the high labor standards of Sri Lankan producers (Wijayasiri and Dissanayake 2008).

3. This emphasis on individual responsibility for health care is surprising in a country famous until recently for its public health care and social welfare. These famed public services have eroded, and public sector workers are bitterly fighting to save whatever workplace-provided health services they can (Hewamanne forthcoming). Meanwhile, private sector employees are keen on higher salaries that would allow them more choices within the increasingly privatized health care sector. Garment sector employees do not have much power to negotiate better salaries. Their lack of interest in receiving health care for work-related illnesses through the employer seems to stem from the fact that 100 percent of the workers I interviewed were born after 1990 and were therefore entirely brought up in a society saturated with neoliberal discourses.

4. According to her, the Sri Lanka Police organized the workshop but university professors gave lectures on culture and changing societal norms.

5. Major factories such as Mass Holdings and Smarts Shirts have significantly improved industrial safety measures; other companies seem to be taking at least a few steps to meet the code requirements.

6. It is important not to gloss over the cultural norms and expectations that make men think that women who are mobile (i.e., living away from patriarchal control) tend to be promiscuous and thus easy targets for temporary intimate relationships.

7. As temporary residents, the women workers do not have voting rights in the Katunayake area, and thus politicians are not interested in addressing their specific concerns.

8. Women migrating for domestic work in Middle Eastern countries are intensely vilified as mobile and transgressive women. However, there are different variables at work with regard to such migrants, creating different social responses, which have been analyzed previously by several scholars (Gamburd 2000; Hewamanne 2000).

9. Several HR managers and CSR officers described factory-owned dormitories and transition housing for workers as successful CSR outcomes. These dormitories are for a limited time (three months in transitionary facilities and two years maximum) and bring their own set of problems, such as rules that include no visitations from boyfriends, brothers, uncles, or male cousins.

10. The highest salary reported to me was Rs. 23,000.

11. Most workers sought to achieve social mobility through marriages and did not find bus or three-wheeler drivers or day laborers desirable. The boyfriends they sought—military men and factory and office workers—did not see garment workers as good enough for them. While some relationships end up in marriage by 2013, most ended unexpectedly or tragically, just as they did in 2000.

12. This is the Sinhala translation of a Pali verse attributed to Buddha himself.

13. In 2011 she wrote in a letter that things were much better and that she was planning a business of making stuffed toys.

14. Later in the discussion, she said that the higher salaries might be a double-edged sword as they would attract male workers and reduce the one type of job that was always open to women from poor, rural families. This was a fear expressed by several workers during 2014 and 2015. I also noted the higher number of male assembly line workers in the factories, which is mostly due to Tamil men from wartorn areas and the hill tea states migrating to work at FTZ assembly lines.

Bibliography

BBC. 2016. "Nidahas Velanda Kalapayen Anduwata Rathu Eliyak" (FTZ sends a red sign to the government). *BBC*. Online: http://www.bbc.com/sinhala/sri-lanka-36598629. Accessed: June 22, 2016.

Cross, Jamie. 2010. "Occupational Health, Risk and Science in India's Global Factories." *South Asian History and Culture* 1(2): 224–38.

———. 2011. "Detachment as a Corporate Ethic: Materializing CSR in the Diamond Supply Chain." *Focaal: Journal of Global and Historical Anthropology* 60: 34–46.

De Alwis, Malathi. 1997. "The Production and Embodiment of Respectability: Gendered Demeanors in Colonial Ceylon." Pp. 105–44 in *Sri Lanka Collective Identities Revisited*, ed. by Michael Roberts. Colombo: Marga Institute.

De Neve, Geert. 2009. "Power, Inequality and Corporate Social Responsibility: The Politics of Ethical Compliance in the South Indian Garment Industry." *Economic and Political Weekly* 44(22): 63–71.

———. 2014. "Fordism, Flexible Specialization and CSR: How Indian Garment Workers Critique Neoliberal Labour Regimes." *Ethnography* 15(2): 184–207.

Elson, Diane, and Ruth Pearson. 1981. "Nimble Fingers and Cheap Workers: An Analysis of Women's Employment in Third World Export Manufacturing." *Feminist Review* 7(1): 87–107.

Fernandez-Kelly, Patricia. 1983. *For We Are Sold, I and My People: Women and Industry in Mexico's Frontier*. Albany: State University of New York (SUNY) Press.

Gamburd, Michele. 2000. *The Kitchen Spoon's Handle: Transnationalism and Sri Lanka's Migrant Housemaids*. Ithaca, NY: Cornell University Press.

Goger, Annelies. 2013. "From Disposable to Empowered: Rearticulating Labor in Sri Lankan Apparel Factories." *Environment and Planning A* 45(11): 2628–2645.

———. 2014. "Ethical Branding in Sri Lanka: A Case Study of Garments Without Guilt." Pp. 47–68 in *Workers' Rights and Labor Compliance in Global Supply Chains: Is a Social Label the Answer?*, ed. by Jennifer Bair, Doug Miller, and Marsha Dickson. London: Routledge.

Hewamanne, Sandya. 2000. "Making Histories Within: Resistance, Contradictions and Agency Among Sri Lanka's Migrant Housemaids." *Asian Women* 11(1): 109–136.

———. 2002. "Uneasy Alliances: Sri Lankan Factory Workers' Writings on Political Change." *SAGAR* 8: 1–7.

———. 2008. *Stitching Identities in a Free Trade Zone: Gender and Politics in Sri Lanka.* Philadelphia: University of Pennsylvania Press.

———. 2010. "Suicide Narratives and In-Between Identities among Sri Lanka's Global Factory Workers." *Ethnology* 49(1): 1–22.

———. 2012. "Negotiating Sexual Meanings: Global Discourses, Local Practices and Free Trade Zone Workers on City Streets." *Ethnography* 13(3): 352–374.

———. Forthcoming. "Respectable Gentlemen vs. Street-Savvy Men: HIV/AIDS Vulnerability Among Two Working-Class Groups in Sri Lanka." *Medical Anthropology.*

———. 2016. *Sri Lanka's Global Factory Workers: (Un)Disciplined Desires and Sexual Struggles in a Post-Colonial Society.* London: Routledge.

Lynch, Caitrin. 2007. *Juki Girls, Good Girls: Gender and Cultural Politics in Sri Lanka's Global Garment Industry.* Ithaca, NY: Cornell University Press.

Miller, Doug. 2012. *Last Nighshift in Savar: The Story of the Spectrum Sweater Factory Collapse.* Alnwick, UK: McNidder & Grace.

Mills, Mary Beth. 1999. *Thai Women in the Global Labor Force: Consuming Desires, Contested Selves.* New Brunswick, NJ: Rutgers University Press.

Peña, Devon. 1997. *The Terror of the Machine: Technology, Work, Gender and Ecology on the U.S.-Mexico Border.* Austin: University of Texas Press.

Pun, Ngai. 2005. *Made in China: Women Factory Workers in a Global Workplace.* Durham, NC: Duke University Press.

Rajak, Dinah. 2011. *In Good Company: An Anatomy of Corporate Social Responsibility.* Stanford, CA: Stanford University Press.

Ruwanpura, Kanchana. 2011. *Ethical Codes: Reality and Rhetoric: A Study of Sri Lanka's Apparel Sector.* University of Southampton: Report for the Economic and Social Research Council. Southampton, UK: University of Southampton.

———. 2013. "Scripted Performances?: Local Readings of 'Global' Health and Safety Standards (the Apparel Sector in Sri Lanka)." *Global Labour Journal* 4(2): 88–108.

Wijayasiri, Janaka, and Jagath Dissanayake. 2008. "The Ending of the Multi-Fibre Agreement and Innovation in the Sri Lankan Textile and Clothing Industry." *OECD Journal: General Papers* 4: 157–88.

Wright, Melissa. 2006. *Disposable Women and Other Myths of Global Capitalism.* London: Routledge.

CHAPTER 9

Beyond Building Safety: An Ethnographic Account of Health and Well-Being on the Bangladesh Garment Shop Floor

Hasan Ashraf

Recent industrial tragedies such as the collapse of the Rana Plaza building and frequently occurring factory fires have stimulated a rethinking of health and safety in Bangladesh's export-oriented garment sector. The accountability of multinational corporations, factory owners, and national governments has come into question, leading on the one hand to a national action plan and changes to Bangladesh's labor laws,[1] and on the other hand to unprecedented international interventions spearheaded by actors based in the global North. The two multi-stakeholder initiatives receiving the most attention are the Accord on Fire and Building Safety in Bangladesh (2013) (the Accord) and the Alliance for Bangladesh Worker Safety (2013) (the Alliance). Both the Accord and the Alliance are factory inspection programs that assess the safety of buildings in which garments are produced, overseeing remedial action or factory closures. These are large-scale programs encompassing more than 2,000 of Bangladesh's more than 5,000 export-oriented garment factories.

The Accord was created in the weeks after the Rana Plaza collapse by a coalition of global trade unions, nongovernmental associations, and multinational corporations, with the International Labour Organization (ILO) serving in an observer role. The Accord can be understood as a pact between multinational corporations and organized labor, to hold corporations accountable for labor standards in sites where their brand-name clothing is produced. The Alliance is a similar inspection regime, but was created by multinational corporations with little input from trade unions and does not hold brands legally liable for factory conditions. While the Accord has been signed by more than 200 companies based primarily in Europe, the Alliance is smaller with 26 member companies and has found favor with North American companies concerned about liability (Greenhouse 2013).

Both the Accord and the Alliance have been developed by external actors (retailers based in Europe and North America, global trade unions, and transnational NGOs, and the ILO) with little or selective participation from Bangladesh-based institutions, such as the Bangladesh Garment Manufacturers and Exporters Association (BGMEA), Bangladesh Knitwear Manufacturers and Exporters Association (BKMEA), trade union federations, and local labor activist groups.[2] With their focus on the structural improvement of factory buildings and fire prevention, these initiatives have responded to spectacular crisis events, but lack a broader understanding of everyday health and safety issues as manifested on the shop floor. These interventions remove health and safety concerns from the broader political economy of global labor regimes and recast them as a narrowly technical issue that can be addressed through audits, inspections, and building repairs.

I argue in this chapter that a narrow and technocratic focus on buildings and building safety in Bangladesh ignores and conceals the actual processes and relationships that produce shop floor risks, ill health, and the systemic exhaustion of the body, and that routinely undermine the overall well-being of workers in the garment industry. The technocratic regime embodied by the Accord and the Alliance depoliticizes health and safety by removing it from the global dynamics of outsourcing and capitalist labor regimes, which comprise highly uneven relations of power and leverage. This argument about the deficiencies of technocratic approaches is informed by Theodore Roszak's (1969, 8) conceptualization of technocracy as "those who govern justify themselves by appeal to technical experts who, in turn, justify themselves to scientific forms of knowledge" (cf. Riles 2004). Both the Accord and the Alliance appoint trained and certified engineers, engineering firms, and building safety experts to advise on measures and interventions, with the aim of removing bad buildings from the supply chain.

Technocratic approaches not only narrow and depoliticize what are inherently political labor issues, they also produce top-down solutions that are imposed upon Bangladesh. The formulation of these two post–Rana Plaza initiatives lack direct consultation with garment workers to begin with, and local institutions such as the BGMEA have had little choice but to accept conditions set by the Accord. Both the Accord and the Alliance have been enacted in the spirit of development intervention in Bangladesh, mirroring the hierarchical relations of international donors and recipients. The risks and dangers of the industry have been framed as a problem specific to Bangladesh, yet such a representation conceals the fact that Bangladeshi factories are part of global production networks that shape shop floor practices of garment firms across the globe.

This chapter is based on fourteen months of ethnographic fieldwork in Dhaka between 2010 and 2013, and a later period of fieldwork (May–June 2014) devoted to interviewing owners of factory buildings under Accord and Alliance inspections as well as garment workers (including Rana Plaza survivors, family members of workers who remain missing, and workers laid off by inspection-led shutdowns of factories), garment merchandisers, and trade union leaders. My research examines how global value chains generate particular risks, pressures, and dangers that impact the health of garment workers on the shop floor. These health impacts mark workers' bodies and lives on a continuing basis, but escape the gaze of codes, standards, and international agreements. I argue that the technocratic solutions—initially embodied in voluntary codes and standards and more recently found in the Accord and Alliance—reproduce damaging labor processes that undermine the health, well-being, and social reproduction of an ever-growing garment labor force in Bangladesh.

Global Initiatives in the Post–Rana Plaza Context

When the eight-story Rana Plaza commercial building collapsed in April 2013, it became one of the most photographed industrial disasters in the world (Ludden 2013). The event received wide media attention and created discomfort and shock in the minds of consumers worldwide. The heap of rubble evoked the image of a "failed" building, with broken pillars, sandwiched and trapped human bodies, body parts, blood, sandals, lunch boxes, workers' ID cards and timecards, torn clothes, sewing machines, threads, zips, buttons, brand labels, unfinished garments, cardboard cartons, and colorful bolts of fabric scattered among the concrete slabs. Dead, unconscious, and mutilated bodies were carried from the building for three weeks, and human bones were found even after several months. Witnessed by the world media, many workers died slowly, stuck underneath tons of rubble, with the "miracle girl," Reshma Begum, dragged out alive from beneath the ruins seventeen days after the collapse (Al-Mahmood et al. 2013).

It was clearly not just a faulty building that took the lives of 1,134 ready-made garment workers and one rescuer, left more than 2,500 workers injured, and led to 150 workers remaining permanently missing. Mohammad Sohel Rana, the owner of Rana Plaza and a leader in the ruling political party, was quickly blamed for the incident along with the owners of five other garment factories housed inside the building. Rana was reported to be the "most hated Bangladeshi" by the *New York Times* (Yardley 2013), and the media focused on how Rana Plaza was built on swampy land and in breach of Bangladesh's building code (Hossain 2013). Among others, Rana and the factory owners were taken into custody by the police and later charged with murder (BBC 2015).[3]

With public curiosity focused on Rana's dramatic arrest at the Indian border, what evaded scrutiny was the complicity of global fashion brands in the disaster at Rana Plaza. On the day of the collapse, workers had been forced by the factory management and political party thugs to enter an already cracked building.[4] All of the garment factories in Rana Plaza were export-oriented and had shipment deadlines for overseas buyers that could not be renegotiated and carried a financial penalty if missed. Having already lost a day's work when cracks were discovered in the building the day before (which was briefly reported in the evening news), factory owners were eager to resume production. Garment workers were made to turn up for work under threats that salaries would be withheld. Other businesses in the building, such as the BRAC Bank on the ground floor, were kept closed until a full inspection of the building was completed. When a power cut occurred at 8:45 a.m. that morning, diesel generators were switched on, leading to the collapse within minutes.

The idiom of a "house of cards" has been used repeatedly to epitomize the collapse of the building (Figure 9.1; Allchin 2015; Marriott 2013; Mollah and Habib 2013; Opu and Chowdhury 2014; Siegle 2013; The Economist 2013). Although factories in Bangladesh have collapsed before—such as the Spectrum sweater factory building in 2005—the enormity of the Rana Plaza disaster has been compared to the 2001 collapse of the World Trade Center in New York. The affective and symbolic power of the collapse, as seen in its immense media attention, has undoubtedly influenced the international response. The two multi-stakeholder initiatives that emerged from

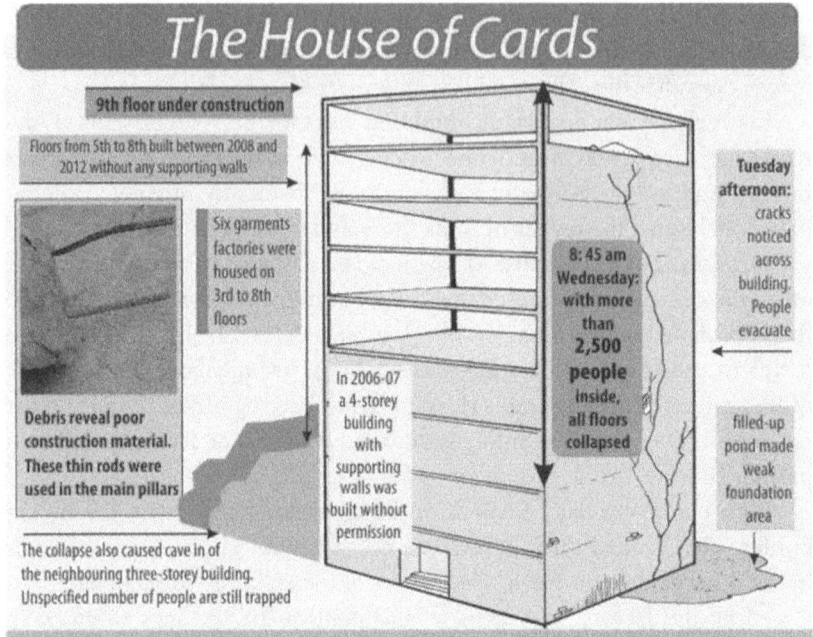

Figure 9.1 "It crumbles like a pack of cards" (Mollah and Habib 2013). © *The Daily Star* (Graphics reproduced with permission of *The Daily Star*.)

the disaster—the Accord and the Alliance—focus on building, fire, and electrical safety, placing the image of the "failed" building at the center of public attention. However, building safety is only one aspect in a much more intricate chain of circumstances that routinely put garment workers' physical and mental health at risk. Factory safety is important, but a narrow focus on buildings precludes a broader analysis of how everyday ill health and unsafe work conditions come about and how they are to be addressed.

The Accord on Fire and Building Safety in Bangladesh

The Accord was the first global initiative to address building safety in Bangladesh in the wake of the Rana Plaza collapse (cf. Bair et al. this volume). Drafted in Europe on May 13, 2013, it was prepared by the Geneva-based UNI Global Union and IndustriALL Global Union in close cooperation with transnational NGOs (including the Clean Clothes Campaign and the Worker

Rights Consortium) and selected Bangladeshi trade union federations. The Accord's aim reads as follows: "The undersigned parties are committed to the goal of a safe and sustainable Bangladeshi Ready-Made Garment ('RMG') industry in which no worker needs to fear fires, building collapses, or other accidents that could be prevented with reasonable health and safety measures. The signatories to this Agreement agree to establish a fire and building safety program in Bangladesh for a period of five years" (Accord on Fire and Building Safety in Bangladesh 2013).

The Accord requires signatory companies to respect the right of workers to refuse work in an unsafe factory without facing discrimination or loss of pay. Garment brands must disclose the identities of their supplier factories; the Accord appoints safety inspectors to identify faulty buildings. Inspection reports are supposed to be public for increased transparency and accountability. If an inspection report concludes that a factory has failed to achieve building, fire, or electrical standards, corrective measures must be taken without delay. A failure of remediation within the first six months after inspection will be treated with punitive action, which means closing the business. The supplier factories are to pay wages for furloughed workers during the maintenance period. Signatory companies are responsible for ensuring sufficient funds are available, but it is a matter of negotiation with the supplier factories to finance the efforts as joint investments, with loans, or through access to donor or government support.

The Accord also promises to initiate safety-training programs for workers and managers and to establish worker complaint processes. The Accord is a legally binding document to be implemented for five years. Two years after the collapse, more than 200 garment brands had signed the Accord and more than 1,600 factories were inspected for building, fire, and electrical safety. Unfortunately, the more pervasive physical and mental health issues caused by the shop floor labor regimes as well as the continuous anxieties and pressures affecting the well-being of garment workers are given scant attention by the Accord and Alliance.

The Alliance for Bangladesh Worker Safety

Global garment brands that did not want to participate in the Accord created a second multi-stakeholder initiative, the Alliance for Bangladesh Worker Safety, which was signed in June 2013. Developed by seventeen brands, mostly from North America, the Alliance was drafted without any legal commitment from brands to ensure decent labor standards in their supplier factories. The Alliance aims to improve the fire and electrical safety and structural integrity of the buildings by implementing an inspection standard based on the factory assessment guidelines developed by the Bangladesh University of Engineering and Technology (BUET). The Alliance has been criticized for not demanding a commitment like the Accord to make all inspection reports public (Oxfam 2013), but it does promise to provide details of technical requirements to the factories in order to ensure building safety.

The Accord and the Alliance have been developed alongside other national and international initiatives. Prior to the Rana Plaza collapse, factory fires were seen as the main safety issue. After a fire at Tazreen Fashions in November 24, 2012 (see Sumon et al. this volume), the Bangladesh Ministry of Labour and Employment (MoLE) and ILO adopted a Joint Statement of Commitment on January 15, 2013 aimed at preventing factory fires (Bangladesh MoLE 2013: 2). Initially it was called National Tripartite Plan of Action on Fire Safety (NAP), and a provision on structural integrity was added after the Rana Plaza collapse. NAP was an attempt to bring policy measures, labor, and industry together to provide an integrated platform for action to prevent further tragedies in the garment sector (see Bair et al. this volume). But like the Accord and Alliance, the NAP does not engage with the complexity of labor rights and workers' health issues, and hence focuses only on a limited set of technical and infrastructural issues.

Nevertheless, the legally binding nature of the Accord marks a significant shift from existing practices of corporate self-regulation through labor codes, and for this reason it has been described as a "paradigm shift."[5] The more than 5,600 BGMEA registered factories employing more than 4.4 million workers have been divided into three categories: (1) the Accord covers approximately 1,600 factories, two million workers, and more than 200 brands; (2) the Alliance covers 652 factories, 1.2 million workers, and twenty-six brands; and (3) factories and workers not covered by either initiative amount to 3,348 factories with more than 1.2 million workers.[6] Of this group, around 1,500 are to be inspected by the NAP. There are, however, numerous sub-subcontract factories that escape these policy processes altogether. Against this landscape of partial inspection coverage and of continued blame shifting, what remains absent is a more grounded understanding of worker health, safety, and well-being that goes beyond a narrow focus on fires and collapses. In what follows I therefore present a detailed ethnography of the multiple and interconnected vulnerabilities, threats, and risks that undermine the safety and well-being of workers on a daily basis.

What a Technocratic Approach Renders Invisible and Irrelevant

The collapse of a building or a sudden factory fire is not the only danger that threatens garment workers' mental and physical health in Bangladesh. During fourteen months of ethnographic research (2010–2013), I was employed for six months as a shop floor worker at Asha Garments.[7] It was a medium-sized knit-wear factory mostly producing T-shirts, tops, sleepwear, and light jackets. In the course of my fieldwork I came across numerous practices and circumstances that seriously compromised workers' health and well-being. The material environment of work inside factories is not separate from the social processes of laboring and from reproduction outside. Workers employed in the garment sector are called *garments sromik* (garment workers) in Bangla, a term that is full of stigma (see also Hewamanne this volume). The workforce is predominantly female and they are called *garments-er meye* (garment girls). Women are mostly employed as machine operators and helpers on the assembly lines, whereas line supervisors and managers are predominantly male. On the shop floor, management draws on patriarchal norms and practices as a technique to control female workers, just as Dina Siddiqi observed in the 1990s (Siddiqi 1996).

Workers consider a job to enhance well-being when they are paid enough to have three meals a day and live a decent life with their husband/wife/in-laws/natal family and children. However, on current factory wages it is not possible to maintain such a life in an urban setting. In 2010, the minimum wage was increased from BDT 1,662.50 (US$21) to BDT 3,000 (US$38) per month, which in 2013 increased again to BDT 5,300 (US$68) per month. These increases followed massive labor protests, but each time the demand for a "living wage" was denied. Wages are not part of the Accord or Alliance. They are considered an internal matter for local factory owners and the Bangladesh government, even though labor costs are precalculated in any work order placed by foreign brands.

In the following section, I first discuss the health issues caused by the material environment of work. Then I detail the health issues caused by the social process of laboring. Finally, I present threats to workers' mental state and well-being as they emanate from the global production regime.

Health Issues Caused by the Material Environment of Work

Daily, after a couple of hours of work when heads, machines, eyelashes, and hands are covered with whitish dust, one can hear jokes such as *it's snowing* or *we all have aged*. The continuous inhaling of fabric dust is said by workers to cause headaches, sinusitis, itching skin, irritated eyes, and tuberculosis. At the end of the working day at Asha Garments, workers attempted to wash their hands, elbows, nostrils, face, neck, and feet, and sprinkled water on their hair to get rid of the dust that covered them. Women workers tried to remove dust by combing their hair behind the supervisors' backs. Wanting to feel fresh by washing off the fabric dust and combing their hair, women workers were often mocked by male co-workers and line supervisors. One male line supervisor commented, "If you think freeing yourself from the fabric dust, tidying up your hair, and then walking on the street hanging a bag from your shoulder would give you an aura of a *versity* girl [university girl], you are wrong. You are a *garments-er chemri* [garment girl] and that is what you will remain. They would not recognize you as a *madam* [respected lady]."

The embodiment of the occupation in workers' stigmatized social identity cannot easily be shrugged off. "It is inscribed on them. You can spot them by looking at them," said the landlady in the labor colony where I rented a room. The distinction that men and supervisors make between women work-ers and "versity" girls in Bangladesh refers to boundaries of class, gender, and social mobility. The increasing enrollment of female students at universities and their public visibility have started to rupture predominantly male pub-lic spaces—but only for the middle classes. One of the dominant and over-used plots in Bangla feature films is that a poor but honest male student falls in love with an affluent female student in college/university. An educated, middle-class woman is a desired identity as it implies a respected and digni-fied position. Comments such as those cited above by male co-workers (even with a similar social background) articulate a concern about women climbing the social hierarchy. With this kind of criticism men attempt to keep women "in their place" by policing and intensifying the social boundaries of expected feminine behavior.

Workers in different sections perceived the hazards of the factory floor differently. In the sewing section, the main health hazards related to fabric dust, smelly smoke generated by care- and size-label cutting machines, heat generated by the electric sewing machines, continuous whirring sounds, use of adhesive stickers, lack of ventilation, and exposure to bright overhead fluorescent strip lights and electric wires. As I was told, "it is very common that working closely to heavy electric wires makes a body weak as it sucks out blood and energy from the body." This was strongly believed by many garment workers in the factories I visited as one of the causes of illness and weakness (see also Siddiqi 2000). Workers link their everyday work experiences with a widely shared notion of a "depreciating body," which is depleted day by day.

Inhaling cleaning chemical sprays, paper carton dust, and the smell of polythene bags and hot vapor from ironing affects workers in the finishing section. Fabric dust is perceived as poisonous, causing headaches and stomach-related problems. Health hazards are well known to the workers and supervisors, but workers make a constant trade-off between earning a living and protecting their health. One male supervisor made a comment shared by many, "If you cut open the stomach you might get a couple of kilograms of fabric dust inside us. It is not just cotton but cotton with harmful chemicals. We will die before our lifetime."

The most common impacts of the constant exposure to these particles are damaged lungs, skin irritations, and bronchitis (Paul-Majumdar 2003). Many of the workers suffer from sneezing, headaches, coughs, and occasional fevers (Steinisch et al. 2013). Wearing face masks was not a common practice in the factories where I conducted fieldwork. Although sometimes encouraged as part of buyers' codes of conduct, masks are not routinely provided. Workers sometimes make their own masks from cut pieces of fabric to prevent inhaling fabric dust, but inhaling chemicals is unavoidable. Those who wear masks are sometimes mocked by co-workers and even by line supervisors, and masks make essential communication on the production line very hard. At the same time, high levels of noise on the factory floor create hearing problems.

(Wo)man Versus Machine

Garment production is based upon intimate interactions between workers and machines, some of which harm their operators. Workers on the shop floor compete to work on the newest and best-functioning machines, sometimes by asserting "this is my machine." Line supervisors, however, tend to relocate working places to prevent workers from developing group solidarities. Workers find that different types of sewing machines require different types of seating positions and bodily techniques, which can cause different types of bodily distress. Some machines demand a stop-start-pause pace; all require the workers' full concentration to avoid mistakes. It is therefore easier for workers to habituate themselves to one type of machine and stick with it.

High levels of concentration are needed to avoid injury from broken needles to fingers or eyes. Overlock sewing machines are considered most dangerous, because they are equipped with a knife to cut the thread joints and edges of the fabric. A small transparent plastic cover called a needle guard is supposed to be attached to prevent eye injury, but it is often missing and not replaced when broken. Yet, injuries caused by machines are usually treated as workers' own fault. Supervisors count the needles and when too many break, a worker will be scolded. Breaking a needle means having to work faster to compensate for time lost, creating a sense of urgency and tension (see also Ruwanpura 2014). When the motor belt gets too warm it becomes loose to work with. It is the individual worker's responsibility to keep the machine in good order, even though a full-time mechanic and his assistant were available to repair the machines when needed.

Working monotonously on a single machine causes different kinds of bodily discomfort, including headaches, neck pain, back pain, shoulder pain, burning eyes, aching joints, and pulled muscles. In the long run these problems may become chronic. For instance, the operation of a plain machine requires hands, legs, and the right knee. Both hands hold the fabric and guide it through the machine. The speed of the machine motor is controlled by both feet, while the right knee is used to raise and lower the needle feet. A lever is attached close to the upper wheel to initiate backstitches. A single task like joining the first shoulder joint of a T-shirt requires continuous concentration. Doing repetitive tasks at one machine for long hours with high-intensity concentration creates body aches, vertigo, stiff muscles, and repetitive strain injury. Moreover, this is often done under huge production pressures exerted by the managers. The daily working hours do not allow workers to have a break apart from the one-hour lunch break, when overtime is declared around 5 p.m., and a snack break around 8 p.m. whenever there is a night shift.

Health Issues Caused by the Social Processes of Laboring

Workers have ambivalent feelings about the factory as a place of opportunity and a place of subordination (Siddiqi 2009). The factory may be perceived as a prison (*jailkhana*) by the workers as they are not allowed to leave their machine, table, line, floor, or building without permission. The feeling of imprisonment (*bondidosha*) is also tied to the regimented assembly line production system used in the garment sector. The main task of the supervisors and managers is to keep the assembly line functioning. The immense power of the managers over workers is reflected in the frequent delays in workers' payment.[8] Most of the workers in Asha Garments had monthly salaries, with a small group of highly skilled piece-rate workers. Production managers in Asha Garments often yelled at workers: "No movement; work in the line!"

Going to the washrooms or drinking water from the tap requires permission from the supervisor. It is also difficult to leave the line because work would quickly accumulate. The numbers of washrooms is not adequate in Asha Garments: only four for more than 400 workers and they are not on the same floor. Speaking about menstruation or other "shameful" topics such as sexuality is taboo but is used to discipline the workers. Some line supervisors humiliate women workers by asking whether "they were spending more time in the toilet to change their sanitary napkin."

The only entrance to the factory is guarded around the clock by professional guards. Apart from senior management personnel, all workers' bodies are patted down (women workers are patted down by women checkers) and checked thoroughly when arriving and especially when leaving the factory building at the end of the day. Body checks and metal nets on the factory windows demonstrate management's distrust of workers. As the security guard of the factory commented, "If you let them go out of the factory they would make the entire factory empty in ten minutes." Shop floor doors are monitored, creating increased risks for workers in the event of a fire. The building was originally constructed for residential purposes, not industrial needs. The regimented production system and lack of mobility creates feelings of suffocation and confinement. Bodily experiences of surveillance and discipline are directly shaped by the labor-intensive production regimes of the garment sector. In this sector the profits of factory owners and brands alike follow from a tight extraction of labor power and a constant attempt to reduce labor costs. Factory fires elsewhere and in the wider neighborhood raised fears among workers about the electric panel board on the shop floor. One of the workers pointed at the electric panel board and said, "We will be turned into pieces of burned coals if it bursts. We will never be able to escape from the floor if fire breaks out and no one will recognize the body remains." But perceived risks are assimilated into the daily life of the factory, and living with fear becomes normalized, disrupted only by occasional reminders of existing dangers by the mechanics present on the shop floor. The sewing section was on the second floor and there was a fire exit, but it was an extension of the staircase and thus often blocked. During the months I worked there, we never had a fire drill.

Unpredictable Working Hours and Shop Floor Discipline

Let me now turn to everyday struggles over overtime (OT) on the shop floor. By 5 p.m., workers were getting ready to go home after an eight-hour shift, but always feared a sudden announcement of overtime work. Mid-level management used this threat of overtime to increase daily productivity toward the end of a workday. As 5 p.m. neared, workers experienced collective anxiety and tension, anticipating whether or not the factory's electronic *chutir ghonta* (bell that declared the end of the workday) would ring and all could go home. On most of the days during my six months in the factory, the bell did not ring on time.

The tensions over the ending of the working day, the need for OT work, and its sudden announcement all had manifold implications on the shop floor. They evoked a range of feelings. "More the OT work, less the family time," said Ritu, a twenty-three-year-old machine operator who needed to go home after 5 p.m. and spend time with her family. As Ritu was newly married and lived with her in-laws, she explained,

> It is a big tension for me whether I can go home on time. I do not need the OT money but I need to go home to cook and take care of my mother-in-law. She is old and sick most of the time. My husband is a bus driver's helper. You know that they are hot tempered. The other day he told me that if I cannot take care of my family then what is the point of marriage. He takes all my money as he doesn't earn much and it is for my family. When they [the factory management] say now I have to do OT, *buk dhorfor* [a mix of throbbing heartbeat with anxiety and annoyance] starts. I cannot work with concentration and tend to make mistakes. When I make mistakes the supervisor screams at me. I cannot even sleep properly for this double *chaap* [pressure]. I am getting *durbol* [weak] day by day. At the end of the work time I always feel tension and *buk dhorfor* starts.

However, many workers relied on overtime work, needing the extra pay on top of their monthly salary in order to make a living in Dhaka. Therefore, the daily changeover moment was filled with both an urge to leave the factory due to exhaustion and a need to keep working to make more money. Overtime work is not illegal in the garment sector according to the 2006 Bangladesh Labour Act, but it is commonly imposed on workers without their consent and often demanded well beyond what is legally allowed.[9] Night shifts were also a common practice, especially in the run-up to delivery deadlines. When work ends after dark, the city streets are not safe for women, and they fear sexual harassment. Not being able to sleep properly as cited in the above quote shows how work experiences have impacts beyond the workplace, and that these are not only physical health impacts, such as exhaustion, but also emotional and mental pressure due to the unpredictability of work routines and the length of the working day. Unpredictable and forced overtime work causes anxiety among workers on the shop floor, while also posing specific risks to women in relation to both their journeys back home and their domestic responsibilities.

Factory staff deploys various disciplining techniques to speed up production on the assembly lines. Extracting more labor by prolonging work hours, increasing the production pace, and lowering payment not only ensures profit for both factory owners and Western brands, but also safeguards the continuing existence of these factories in Bangladesh. Laborers' bodies are thus embedded in the contingencies of global market dynamics. While the collective performance of each assembly line was measured in terms of total output, individual workers were held responsible for the production per machine and monitored on an hourly basis to keep up the production pace. Line supervisors are responsible for the collective production speed and total output. The result is a combination of disciplining individuals and monitoring the line as a whole.

A complex web of relations among workers, staff, factory owners, and Western buyers crystalizes on the shop floor. The factory hierarchy is vertically organized, with factory owners, Western buyers, and buying-house inspectors at the top and with production and quality control horizontally deployed at each machine on each assembly line as well as between different assembly lines on the shop floor. Workers and mid-level staff are divided into two groups: machine operators, line production supervisors, and production managers are on the production side and machine helpers, quality checkers, and floor quality on the quality control side. Meeting daily production targets relies on how well factory management exerts pressures on both sides, which are pitted against each other to produce the maximum output and quality in the shortest possible time.

Sexual Harassment Embedded in Labor Management Practices

As in most other garment factories in Dhaka, while most of the workers were female, almost all of the supervisory staff were male in Asha Garments, creating a highly gendered and male-controlled shop floor environment. Sexual harassment and threats of physical sexual attacks were common. Not all supervisors used sexual harassment as a management tool to speed up and discipline workers, but some male supervisors used abusive words against both female and male workers. One supervisor explained the inherent "logic": "If you cannot be a real bad person, you cannot work in a garment factory to extract highest output from the workers as *malik* (owner) wants. It does not let a human being remain human. You have to be like that."

The managers themselves were subjected to a dehumanization process while carrying out their responsibilities. Different line supervisors managed their lines differently. For instance, one supervisor assumed the role of a father or an elder brother: "I scold them to get the work done but I also care about them most." Another line supervisor used a different technique to control the workers, which was to be violent and threatening. A third line supervisor who approached workers with kindness was considered weak by the other line supervisors. Although he was appreciated by the workers, they also believed he would not remain like that for long. What ultimately mattered was whether daily targets were met.

As in most Bangladeshi garment factories, the number of male workers was considerably lower than female workers in the factory where I carried out my research. Some of the male workers were paid the same or even less than female workers for similar work or job position, depending on job experience and length of employment. This created tensions among men, as they seek to live up to the normative role of family providers. Female workers were vulnerable to male staff and at times encountered sexual harassment from their male co-workers too. As such, we see that workers' everyday health, safety and well-being at work encompasses a range of issues that go well beyond building safety concerns, that are highly gendered, and that can work against the gendered interests of men as well as women, depending on their place in the company and their roles outside of it.

Threats to Workers' Mental Well-Being

Certain terms were used on the shop floor to refer to the time routines and production pressures exerted by management and experienced by workers. Two key terms, *chaap* (pressure) and *bhoy* (fear), are closely related and are produced by the labor process. The material environment of work consists of working in heavy air with high temperatures and with fabric dust, which constantly affect one's health. But more than physical pressures, there is *chaap* and *bhoy* in the mind of workers as they cannot easily leave a job and hence they work with a feeling of confinement.

Management deploys different kinds of *bhoy* ranging from salary cuts, nonpayment of overtime as punishment, and sexual and other kinds of harassment. Since mistakes in sewing, mixing different sizes, or making holes in the fabric can lead to punishment, the work itself generates *mistake-r bhoy* (fear of mistake). Workers also realize that this can lead to being insulted or scolded at any time. The biggest *bhoy* is to lose one's job without warning. Job insecurity works as a disciplinary strategy that embodies other kinds of *bhoy*, such as when the factory owner or higher management visits the shop floor. Factory management stimulates the fear of missing a shipment deadline among the workers in order to speed up production. They blame the buyers for raising production targets, which leads to a different kind of *bhoy* when a buyer visits the shop floor. In a survey I conducted of 320 workers at their residence, they identified two main causes of fear: seeing the factory owner and foreign buyers on the shop floor.

This fearful production regime is accompanied by *chaap* of different kinds. The daily production target is set higher than what is realistically achievable and a plethora of *bhoy* are applied to keep the *chaap* on the workers to get the work done. *Shomoy-er chaap* or time pressure is one of the biggest worries that run through the entire production process, from meeting shipment deadlines to forced overtime, as discussed above. It is not just the general production pressure, but particular *bhoy* also creates particular *chaap*, and vice versa. Workers' bodily states and minds are closely related. The mind (fear in particular) in turn produces certain bodily effects (such as breathing problems, pressure in the head, sleeplessness, sweating, and panic).

The Complexities of Improving Working Conditions

The Accord in Practice: Consequences of Shutting Down Factories

One outcome of the Accord is that factories found to be unsafe must be closed immediately. Although in principle the Accord safeguards workers by ensuring that wages continue to be paid, in practice payment for furloughed workers may not be forthcoming. For instance, after an Accord inspection in 2014, one nine-story factory building that housed three factories with more than 2,500 workers was shut down. According to the management of one of the factories, the Accord closed the factory unnecessarily swiftly and without sufficient time to relocate production. As one of the managers explained, "If they had given us six months we could relocate our business and we could cope. We have been producing in this building for the last eighteen years. The engineer from BUET told us that there is no possibility of crack or collapse. What they have found is that the load of the building is a little higher than the standard but that would not crack even in thirty years. More than 2,500 workers lost their job in one day and now the factory owners are to pay the compensations to the workers and the Accord authority did not care."

The owner of the factory next door hired fifty of the furloughed workers, but commented, "It is just not possible to reemploy all these workers in this factory neighborhood." The sudden closure of factories after Accord-led inspections intensifies already existing fears and anxieties in workers' lives. Moreover, workers are laid off not only when factory buildings are shut down but also because of overcrowding. One merchandiser (intermediary between brands and factories) reported to me, "We had to ask the factories to fire workers to increase the ratio between man and floor space as those factories were identified as overcrowded."

When I arrived in a workers' neighborhood in Dhaka in May 2014, I was immediately surrounded by more than thirty workers who had lost their jobs due to factory closures, some of whom had found temporary night shift employment. They were keen to share their struggles. From one of the three closed factories, the management had reemployed only 700 or 800 workers in one of their other factories to meet a shipment deadline. These workers were taken to the other factory to cover night shifts from 8 p.m. to 8 a.m., while the regular workforce continued to work day shifts. As a result, neither group of workers received overtime payment, on which garment workers usually depend.

The Accord promised that workers of closed factories would be reemployed on a priority basis. This did not happen in this case. A senior skilled operator, Moni, who used to work in one of the closed factories said, "Every day I go to different factory gates. I ask for job and they say there is no job for me. I stand there for hours. My legs get swollen and I come back." Moni became a mother at the age of nineteen, and now depends on the garment incomes of her daughter and sister. They all live in a single room of about nine square meters with a shared kitchen and bathroom. As Moni puts it, "Following the recent increase in minimum wage (which is not a living wage), the house owners raised the room rents by one-third. According to the workers, the foreigners brought this work in Bangladesh and we came here to work and now they are closing the factories without any alternative employment." The sudden shutdown of factories has increased anxiety among workers, as they now fear they might lose their source of livelihood at any time.

Shortcomings of the Technocratic Approach to Improving Safety

Nahidul Hasan Nayan, a labor leader and director of operations at the Awaj Foundation, welcomes the Accord and the Alliance but says that more needs to be done to improve labor standards. The signatory garment brands in the Accord accepted a clause that they would keep their business in Bangladesh for five years, but the Alliance contains no such commitment, and garment brands are known to be constantly searching for alternative production sites. Since the Rana Plaza collapse, at least 118 garment factories have faced cancellations of orders and had to lay off workers. According to Nayan, "We all knew that the business was not safe and we have been trying to improve, and turning their back is not fair." During a discussion in May 2014, one of Bangladesh's most prominent labor leaders, Nazma Akter,[10] asserted, "A collaboration is needed between the workers and the consumers in the West who are deceived by the ready-made garment production system. Increased awareness among the consumers would increase pressure on the brands and increased awareness among the workers will put pressure on the garment factory owners." The industry tends to shed workers when they reach their late thirties and become less productive. Akter felt that a complete lack of a negotiation platform (such as lack of a trade union office at the factory premise) is the main reason for the persistence of bad practices and for the general lack of accountability. Akter emphasized the need for a stable service rule.

During interviews with garment factory owners in May and June 2014, one of the garment industry leaders emphasized the need for a change in buyers' attitude to improve the garment sector in Bangladesh. According to him, "When the buyers place a work order they offer last year's CM [cost of manufacturing] or even lower, and at the same time they want a factory that looks like a five-star hotel. The first thing they say is: if you cannot produce with this price we will go somewhere else." This resonates with what Geert De Neve (2009) observed in the Tiruppur garment manufacturing cluster in Tamil Nadu: the imposition of standards and codes of conduct on supply firms becomes a disciplinary tool, as corporate ethical interventions are "never value-neutral; they aim to promote particular regimes of production, particular values of work, and particular kinds of workers or subjectivities" (De Neve 2014, 186).

The garment brands' threat to source from elsewhere leads factory owners to accept orders at lower prices and tighter deadlines to keep their business going. Emerging destinations of garment production, such as Myanmar and Ethiopia, increase global market competition. This competition is not only between Bangladesh and producers in other countries, but also between factories within Bangladesh. Factory owners, management, and buyers must all contend with ever-rising levels of market competition, risk, and uncertainty.

Conclusion

This chapter has considered initiatives introduced after the Rana Plaza collapse to improve worker health and safety in the Bangladeshi ready-made garment sector. My analysis indicates that the two main international initiatives—the Accord and the Alliance—pursue technocratic approaches to health, safety, and security issues. They extend a tradition of shifting blame by presenting conditions specific to Bangladesh as the root cause of disasters as opposed to the buying practices of brand-name companies that source from low-wage countries. Although the Accord holds foreign brands legally accountable for the fitness of factories in Bangladesh, this is only a limited shift in responsibility. Its predominant focus on technical fixes to infrastructural safety issues also ignores the multiple and routine threats to the health and well-being of an ever-growing labor force.

The collapse of Rana Plaza has made a big dent in the image of *Made in Bangladesh*, which the BGMEA has called an "image crisis" (Ahsan 2013). This image crisis is ultimately also a trade crisis that goes to the heart of the industry's survival in Bangladesh. Commenting on the negative growth in September and October 2014, the BGMEA said, "This is the negative impact of compliance and inspection issues made by the Accord and Alliance during the period" (Ovi 2014). To deal with the crisis, the BGMEA together with the Bangladesh Brands Forum organized the Dhaka Apparel Summit in December 2014 to draw up a sustainable road map for building responsible supply chains in the textile and garment sector and to reach US$50 billion yearly turnover for the sector by 2021, the fiftieth anniversary of Bangladesh.[11]

The "image crisis" in the post–Rana Plaza factory inspection regime prompted BGMEA to deregister factories not compliant with its rules and regulations. These de-registrations had the effect of reducing the official size of the industry from 5,876 factories in 2013 to 4,306 factories in 2015 (BGMEA 2016), bringing the official number of factories more in line with the number actually inspected by the Accord, Alliance, and NAP. As a result, non-member factories have now become invisible to policy and intervention processes. At the same time, the remediation of hazards identified through inspections now appears to have made the industry as a whole safe for workers (Roberts 2014). With 56 percent of identified safety hazards remediated by April 2016, according to one industry leader, "the image crisis has been restored. Bangladesh's export oriented garment industry has raised from the ruins of Rana Plaza."

In this chapter I have tried to show that workers suffer from threats to their mental and physical health beyond the realm of building safety. The transnational system of garment production and trade will not change by a mere focus on dilapidated factory buildings in a single nation state. A top-down technocratic approach to improve infrastructural facilities might ease the conscience of the Western consumer (it may not be a coincidence that brands like H&M launched a "conscious collection" in their fashion lines), but it does not alleviate the *multiple* threats posed to workers' everyday health on the shop floor and to their long-term well-being.

If initiatives by national governments or brands are to address the workers' conditions, the whole system of subcontracting and sourcing arrangements needs to be rethought. Such rethinking will need to be attentive to the needs of two groups who have so far been excluded from the decision-making process: the local factory owners and the workers themselves. Without the establishment of formal and stronger bargaining platforms, such as trade unions at the factory and industry level, however, there still is a long way to go. To date, local trade unions and labor activists who are not affiliated with the global unions have not been included in the policy process. Our knowledge of the global garment value chain needs to be deepened through further research, intervention programs need to be continually evaluated and monitored, and current "corporate social responsibility" ethical governance models need to be subjected to critical review. Only then might the complexity and multiplicity of the health and safety of garment workers be taken more seriously.

Notes

1. Responses by the Bangladesh government included a new Bangladesh Labour (Amendment) Act, 2013, which among other provisions eased the process of trade union and trade union federation formation, but maintained existing strike restrictions and increased surveillance of workers. The number of trade unions has increased but not even 1 percent of Bangladesh's more than four million garment workers are unionized.

2. Bangladesh-based trade unions were not mentioned as signatories in the original Accord (Accord 2013, 7), although eight trade union federations joined later. The Alliance partnered with BGMEA and BKMEA as well as four trade union federations, but in limited scope.

3. This did not include one partner and managing director of a factory in Rana Plaza who was a Spanish citizen and had left the country.

4. The collapse of Rana Plaza happened to occur on the second day of a thirty-six-hour-long *hartal* (strike), which had been called by oppositional political parties to put pressure on the government. Rana would have been expected to prove his loyalty to the ruling party by ensuring workers in his building were not striking, and he deployed a group of thugs (known as "Rana's men") to do so. The use of thugs to threaten and control garment workers, especially during labor protests, is a common practice.

5. The Accord was framed as a "paradigm shift" by the business organization representatives in the Roundtable on Working Conditions in the Garment Industry at the Dutch Parliament on February 10, 2014. See http://www.tweedekamer.nl /nieuws/kamernieuws/newspage2497_rondetafelgesprek_arbeidsomstandigheden _kledingindustrie. Accessed: August 2, 2016.

6. Since 2013, the BGMEA has deregistered a number of factories for not fulfilling their rules and regulations, which reduced the number of member factories to around 4,500; there are, however, factories in operation without BGMEA membership.

7. *Asha* means hope in Bangla. One of my co-workers, Shima Khatun, once suggested that if she ever had a factory of her own she would name it Asha Garments, so I have chosen the name as a pseudonym. I worked at Asha as a machine helper for six weeks and later joined the quality checking team. The fact that I was a researcher was open to all, from workers to factory management. Toward the end of those six months, I gradually extended my fieldwork from the workplace to workers' neighborhoods, conducted a survey of seventy-five factories and a labor colony ethnography, and studied labor protests.

8. Wages are supposed to be paid within seven days after a wage-month ends, but maintaining a gap of two to three weeks is a widespread practice. This reverse indebtedness makes workers stay in one factory and prevents them from switching jobs as the first month's salary would only be paid after six weeks from the starting date.

9. According to the Bangladesh Labour Act (2006), the maximum OT work for any workday is two hours, and twelve hours in total per week or a maximum of sixty working hours per week. The yearly average for a week cannot exceed fifty-six hours. According to clause 109 of the Bangladesh Labour Act (2006) the hours of work for women are restricted. As the clause reads, "Limitation of hours of work for women: No woman shall, without her consent, be allowed to work in an establishment between the hours of 10:00 p.m. and 6:00 a.m."

10. Nazma Akter has been working in the Bangladesh garment sector for more than twenty-seven years and worked for various trade unions. She is now the president of Sommilito Garments Sramik Federation (SGSF), one of the largest trade union federations, affiliated with IndustriALL. She is the founding head of the Awaj Foundation.

11. For details see http://bangladeshrmg2021.com.

Bibliography

Accord on Fire and Building Safety in Bangladesh. 2013. Amsterdam: Bangladesh Accord Foundation. Online: http://bangladeshaccord.org/wp-content/uploads /2013/10/the_accord.pdf. Accessed: April 14, 2014.

Ahsan, Syed Badrul. 2013. "BGMEA and 'Image Crisis.'" *The Daily Star*, April 29. Online: http://archive.thedailystar.net/beta2/news/bgmea-and-image-crisis/. Accessed: June 30, 2015.

Allchin, Joseph. 2015. "A Matter of Class." *Himal South Asian*. Online: http://himalmag .com/matter-class-bangladesh-unions/. Accessed: July 26, 2015.

Alliance for Bangladesh Worker Safety. 2013. Delaware: Bangladesh Worker Safety. Online: http://www.bangladeshworkersafety.org/files/Alliance-Member-Agreement -FINAL.pdf. Accessed: July 26, 2015.

Al-Mahmood, Syed Zain, Saad Hammadi, and Jason Burke. 2013. "Bangladesh Survivor Reshma Begum: I Never Dreamed I'd See Daylight Again." *The Guardian*, May 10. Online: http://www.theguardian.com/world/2013/may/10/bangladesh-survivor-reshma-begum. Accessed: July 1, 2015.

Bangladesh Ministry of Labour and Employment (MoLE). 2013. National Tripartite Plan of Action on Fire Safety and Structural Integrity in the Ready-Made Garment Sector in Bangladesh. Online: http://www.ilo.org/wcmsp5/groups/public/---asia/---ro-bangkok/---ilo-dhaka/documents/genericdocument/wcms_221543.pdf. Accessed: June 30, 2015.

BBC. 2015. "Bangladesh Murder Trial over Rana Plaza Factory Collapse." *BBC News*, June 1. Online: http://www.bbc.co.uk/news/world-asia-32956705. Accessed: July 1, 2015.

BGMEA. 2016. "Trade Information." Online: http://www.bgmea.com.bd/home/pages/TradeInformation. Accessed: July 14, 2016.

De Neve, Geert. 2009. "Power, Inequality and Corporate Social Responsibility: The Politics of Ethical Compliance in the South Indian Garment Industry." *Economic and Political Weekly* 44(22): 63–72.

———. 2014. "Fordism, Flexible Specialization and CSR: How Indian Garment Workers Critique Neoliberal Labour Regimes." *Ethnography* 15(2):184–207.

Greenhouse, Steven. 2013. "U.S. Retailers See Big Risk in Safety Plan for Bangladesh." *New York Times*, May 22. Online: http://www.nytimes.com/ 2013/05/23/business/legal-experts-debate-us-retailers-risks-of-signing-bangladesh-accord.html?_r=0. Accessed: 14 April 2014.

Hossain, Farid. 2013. "Bangladesh: Owners' Many Failings Led to Collapse." *Global News*, May 23. Online: http://globalnews.ca/news/583611/bangladesh-owners-many-failings-led-to-collapse/. Accessed: May 14, 2015.

Economist. 2013. "Disaster in Bangladesh: The New Collapsing Building." *The Economist*, April 25. Online: http://www.economist.com/blogs/banyan/2013/04/disaster-bangladesh. Accessed: July 1, 2015.

Ludden, David. 2013. *Asian Histories of Globalization: Long Distance Mobility and Territorial Power in the Longue Duree*. Dieter Conrad Memorial Lecture, June 27, 2013, South Asia Institute, Heidelberg University.

Marriott, Red. 2013. "The House of Cards: The Savar Building Collapse." *libcom.org*, April 26. Online: https://libcom.org/news/house-cards-savar-building-collapse-26042013 Accessed: May 23, 2015.

Mollah, Shaheen, and Wasim Bin Habib. 2013. "It Crumbles Like a Pack of Cards: National Mourning Today." *The Daily Star*. Online: http://archive.thedailystar.net/beta2/news/like-a-pack-of-cards-it-crumbles. Accessed July 8, 2015.

Opu, Mahmud Hossain, and Syed Tashfin Chowdhury. 2014. "In Pictures: Recounting Horror of Rana Plaza." *Aljazeera*, April 27. Online: http://www.aljazeera.com/indepth/inpictures/2014/04/pictures-bangladesh-remembers-r-201442114058144178.html. Accessed: July 26, 2015.

Ovi, Ibrahim Hossain. 2014. "Makers: Apparel Inspection, Compliance Impact Exposes." *Dhaka Tribune,* November 11. Online: http://www.dhakatribune.com/business /2014/nov/11/makers-apparel-inspection-compliance-impact-exposes. Accessed: July 26, 2015.

Oxfam. 2013. "Understanding the Alliance and the Accord on Bangladesh Worker Safety." *Oxfam Australia Blog,* December 5. Online: https://www.oxfam.org.au/2013 /12/understanding-the-alliance-and-the-accord-on-bangladesh-worker-safety/. Accessed: January 3, 2017.

Paul-Majumder, Pratima. 2003. *Health Status of the Garment Workers in Bangladesh.* Bangladesh Institute of Development Studies (BIDS), Dhaka: Project Report Series No. 01.

Ruwanpura, Kanchana N. 2014. "Metal Free Factories: Straddling Workers' Rights and Consumer Safety." *Geoforum* 51(1): 224–32.

Riles, Annelise. 2004. "Real Time: Unwinding Technocratic and Anthropological Knowledge." *American Ethnologist* 31(3): 392–405.

Roberts, Alan. 2014. "The Bangladesh Accord Factory Audits Finds More Than 80,000 Safety Hazards." *The Guardian,* October 15. Online: http://www.theguardian.com /sustainable-business/2014/oct/15/bangladesh-accord-factory-hazards-protect -worker-safety-fashion. Accessed: May 20, 2016.

Roszak, Theodore. 1969. *The Making of a Counter Culture: Reflections on the Techno- cratic Society and Its Youthful Opposition.* Garden City, NY: Doubleday.

Siddiqi, Dina M. 1996. *Gender and Labor in Bangladeshi Factories.* PhD Dissertation, University of Michigan.

———. 2000. "Miracle Worker or Womanmachine? Tracking (Trans)national Realities in Bangladeshi Factories." *Economic and Political Weekly* 35(21–22): L11–L17.

———. 2009. "Do Bangladeshi Factory Workers Need Saving?: Sisterhood in the Post- Sweatshop Era." *Feminist Review* 91(1): 154–74.

Siegle, Lucy. 2013. "Ethical Shopping: How the High Street Fashion Stores Rate." *The Guardian,* May 17. Online: http://www.theguardian.com/fashion/2013/may/17 /ethical-shopping-high-street-fashion. Accessed: May 14, 2015

Steinisch, Maria, Rita Yusuf, Jian Li, Omar Rahman, Hasan Ashraf, Christian Strüm- pell, Joachim Fischer, and Adrian Loerbroks. 2013. "Work Stress: Its Components and Its Association with Self-Reported Health Outcomes in a Garment Factory in Bangladesh—Findings from a Cross-Sectional Study." *Health Place* 24: 123–30.

Yardley, Jim. 2013. "The Most Hated Bangladeshi, Toppled from a Shady Empire." *New York Times,* April 30. Online: http://www.nytimes.com/2013/05/01/world/asia /bangladesh-garment-industry-reliant-on-flimsy-oversight.html?partner=rss&emc =rss&smid=tw-nytimes&_r=0. Accessed: May 14, 2015.

Afterword: Politics After Rana Plaza

Dina M. Siddiqi

The Rana Plaza Effect

The words "Rana Plaza" carry an excess of meaning; they do not constitute a mere proper noun, the name of a shoddily constructed building in Bangladesh that collapsed and caused the death or disability of those trapped inside. Metaphorically and semantically charged, Rana Plaza has become a cipher, but not just of gendered "third world" labor that cannot speak or act for itself. What lies behind these words is neither fixed nor consistent. For some people, Rana Plaza invokes the dangers of unregulated globalization; for others, the horrors of "third world" sweatshops; conscious citizens may associate it with the lack of accountability of Northern brands and consumers, while many others see it as a twenty-first-century Triangle Shirtwaist Factory disaster.

A globally circulating signifier and above all a spectacle, Rana Plaza appears to be everywhere. A "Rana Plaza effect" effortlessly spilled across national and cultural borders in the wake of the building's collapse. Globally it has engendered a proliferation of discourse and action, ranging from the aesthetic to the prosaic, the sentimental and self-righteous to the academic and the legal. The figure of the Bangladeshi worker (folded into the heart of the meaning of Rana Plaza) rejuvenated transnational activism around the "sweatshop," thereby forging improbable alliances and aspirational solidarities among groups as diverse as Euro-American university students, international fashion models and photographers, Northern consumers, labor rights advocates in the South, and international trade union federations. The 2013 Accord on Fire and Building Safety in Bangladesh (the Accord) and its U.S. counterpart, the Alliance for Bangladesh Worker Safety (the Alliance), are concrete manifestations of such activism.

Rana Plaza has been used at times against Bangladesh's garment industry: American Apparel turned the global gaze on Bangladeshi labor conditions as an occasion to promote its "Made in America" label (for details see Siddiqi 2014). In contrast, an artist somewhere in Europe was so moved by the event that she felt compelled to produce a classical Indian (*Kathak* style) dance drama on the subject. The product of a German-Bangladeshi collaboration, it premiered in Ludwigshafen, Germany in November 2014 (Cultural Correspondent 2015).[1] Finally, as might be expected, seminars, research funds, and donor-driven projects on Bangladesh's ready-made garment sector are in ample supply.

What accounts for this fascination, the affective and symbolic power of the collapse? That is, of course, apart from the billions of dollars in profits generated by the global garment industry, of which Bangladesh was a poster child of sorts? Perhaps the spectacular nature of the incident intensified cracks in the dominant capitalist narratives of female empowerment, narratives that are critical in nurturing neoliberal fantasies of growth without human (or, for that matter, planetary) cost. The horrific event certainly punctured the idea of the brave new borderless world promised by globalization.

Here Rana Plaza recalls but also reconfigures Melissa Wright's analysis of the myth of essentially disposable laboring bodies of women in the global South (Wright 2006). Following Wright, we might say that Bangladeshi workers' bodies are rendered into "waste" in the process of contemporary capital accumulation. Indeed, the ethnographic insights scattered throughout this volume on the various ways workers' bodies waste away bolster this line of thinking. I suggest that in the emergent discourse of ethical production and consumption today, there is no place for *visibly* disposable bodies. Perhaps the widely circulated images of the deaths at Rana Plaza were unacceptable precisely for making visible the violent underbelly of transnational capital and rendering legible the violence that binds consuming bodies in the global North with producing bodies in places like Bangladesh. In other words, the foundational violence of capitalism appeared to be in danger of being unveiled. At the same time, perhaps a politics of pity enfolded individuals living in faraway places who felt compelled to identify with, and so help rectify, matters through a process that Luc Boltanski (1999) characterizes as a media-suffused spectacle of "distant suffering" characteristic of our times.

The response within Bangladesh is easier to contextualize. Progressive activists and artists mobilized actively in the weeks and months after the collapse to register outrage, express solidarity, and demand accountability.

Among the better known initiatives were street theater and plays by Aranyak and Samina Lutfa; an art installation by Dilara Begum Dolly; photo exhibits by DRIK and others; the volume *Chobbishe April* (April 24th), based on a painstaking collaborative effort to identify Rana Plaza's dead and missing, edited by award-winning photographer Taslima Akhter; and a commercial feature film in Bangla (duly banned by the government on the grounds of its potentially inciting unrest). Activist Anthropologist, a group whose work is represented in this volume (see Sumon et al. this volume), emerged as a formidable force in pressing for the criminal liability of factory owners before Rana Plaza ironically became best known internationally after the collapse.

Resisting the Anti-Politics Machine

It should be evident that there are multiple stakes and often contradictory ideological interests in those who claim to speak or act on behalf of the (Bangladeshi) garment worker. The blurring of lines between solidarity and self-interest, between NGO projects and union organizing, between attempts to produce "inclusive" capitalism and protect labor rights, in addition to the appeal of narrowly technocratic solutions that sideline or discredit any interrogation of the systemic asymmetries generated by neoliberal capitalist relations—all effectively depoliticize the terrain. The question arises, how do we avoid reproducing the anti-politics machine (cf. Ferguson 1994) in which so many of the responses to Rana Plaza seem to be embedded? What forms of political solidarity are necessary and viable when humanitarianism itself has become an alibi for the reproduction of hegemonic power—as Didier Fassin (2011), Miriam Ticktin (2014), and others contend?

It is here that this excellent volume makes a significant intervention. Taken together, these chapters echo, unpack, and go beyond the concerns laid out above. They initiate the groundwork for a conversation that is more urgent than ever—of relevance to activists and scholars, labor advocates and policy makers alike, anyone with a stake in the global garment industry, not only in Bangladesh. They take up the "what is to be done" question in a timely and consistent manner.

The volume begins with the practical—a review of past and present in order to help shape future initiatives to protect garment workers' rights.[2] Revisiting the Triangle Shirtwaist Factory fire (and the path-breaking jobbers' agreements that came out of subsequent labor agitation) proves especially useful given the inevitable comparisons between the Rana Plaza collapse and the 1911 fire as critical turning points that led to labor reform. For the authors, a close reading of the conditions that gave rise to the jobbers' agreements can help "inform the fight for workers' rights in one of today's largest centers of export-oriented apparel production" (Bair et al. this volume). They contend that the 2013 Bangladesh Accord, while limited in scope compared to its predecessor, is the fullest instance yet of the jobbers' agreement model in the modern era. One cannot help but applaud such an optimistic outlook. Of course, comparing events a hundred years apart contains pitfalls as well as advantages (see Siddiqi 2015).

The inclusion of Patrick Neveling's chapter on the history of global EPZ (export processing zone) regimes (in relation to worker health and well-being) is also particularly welcome. Studies of labor conditions in the garment industry frequently forget the structuring effect of EPZs. What are the implications of labor organizing and worker resistance when the logic of special economic zones rests on the ability of multinationals to bypass national labor legislation while enjoying tax-exempt status? When labor is devalued and capital represented as a benevolent donor, what are the prospects of justice for workers? As the chapter demonstrates, when capital trumps labor, the results are less than encouraging.

Reflecting the old and the new, this volume brings together the multiple registers and levels of (trans)national activism today—from the admirable advocacy efforts of a woman in the United States to promote ethical sourcing (Lynch and Hagen-Keith this volume) to the determined struggle of a small group of Bangladeshi academics to press criminal charges against a negligent factory owner (Sumon et al. this volume).

The conceptual expansion of worker safety and well-being at the heart of this book enables a move away from neoliberal instrumentality and into the realm of politics. The prism of health broadly conceived becomes a way not only to understand everyday struggles on the shop floor but also a means of tracking the complex web of relations—across intersecting scales—that shape the experience of work within the factory *and beyond*. Prying open the concept of well-being allows authors to ask new questions and revisit enduring concerns.

The volume's thematic stress on the embodied nature of work renders legible connections that otherwise remain invisible in popular and much activist discourse. A number of the richly textured ethnographic chapters underline ties between the spectacular and the quotidian, that is, the connections

between the everyday bodily harms of transnational assembly line production and extraordinary events such as fire and building collapses as mediated
by the specific regime of production in the garment industry—the global
dynamics, the purchasing practices, the pressures of lead times, and so on
(Siddiqi 2009, 2014, and 2015). These connections can be thought of as a set
of tensions or disjunctures that call for further elaboration.

Ideologically driven disjunctures between transnational and national/
local strategies, with different end goals, several authors argue, can end up
undermining worker agency on the ground. Whether it is in relation to the
formation of "core labor standards," the decision to not press charges against
negligent factory owners in the hope that they may eventually recoup enough
to pay workers, or advocating for voluntary codes of conduct that do not take
into consideration power asymmetries within the commodity chain, these
chapters make it clear that decontextualized interventions deliver little to
workers. On the contrary, workers may find other avenues of organizing for
change through collective resistance closed off.

The tension between technocrats and those seeking long-term sustained
changes is another recurring theme in the volume. As we see, it is not always
obvious to "reformists" that deficiencies in labor conditions are a structural
consequence of the current system—not an aberration or corruption of it.
Given that the well-being of laboring bodies is embedded in the contingencies of global dynamics (Ashraf this volume), even the much-debated differences between the Accord and the Alliance recede into insignificance.[3]
Without attending to the broader structures, stand-alone initiatives will have
limited impact.

In contrast, both the Accord and the Alliance see labor conditions—and
so strategies for change—as a consequence of narrow "local" factors. Hasan
Ashraf writes in his chapter, "[T]he risks and dangers of the industry have
been framed as a problem specific to Bangladesh, yet such a representation
conceals the fact that Bangladeshi factories are part of global production networks that shape shop floor practices of garment firms across the globe." The
present volume is structured with such connections in mind: ethnographic
work on Sri Lanka and India, as well as the United States, underlines the
globality of the industry.

Related tensions around sovereignty, accountability, questions of scale,
and individual culpability are not easily resolved. The chapter by Mahmudul
Sumon and colleagues demonstrates the complexities and pitfalls of an
exclusive stress on the complicity of international brands within the current

depoliticized system. The authors argue persuasively that transnational activist demands for compensation overshadowed and undermined "local" efforts to hold the state accountable. In the absence of alternatives, however, compensation becomes the limit or horizon of expectation for survivors and their families. It is not difficult to see how such acts of humanitarianism normalize the "regime of compensation" and enable the emergence of subjectivities for whom justice and compensation appear interchangeable.

If local conditions of labor, including owner negligence, are informed by broader structural constraints and global asymmetries within the current system, as many of the authors seem to imply, then it follows that any effective strategy must incorporate ways to hold both "national" and "international" actors accountable simultaneously. This is a challenge for the future.

Finally, the question of justice is one with which activists and academics alike continue to grapple. Sumon and colleagues problematize the idea of compensation as justice, thereby opening up a different way of envisioning worker well-being. They also raise the thorny issue of ethics in the relationship between ethnographer and interlocutor in such charged circumstances. Their chapter forces the reader to revisit easy notions of justice.

Hope in the Midst of Uncertainty

I finished writing this just as news broke that the Dhaka District and Sessions Judges Court had charged 41 individuals, including Sohel Rana, with the murder of 1,137 workers in the April 24 collapse of the Rana Plaza building (*The Daily Star* 2016). The indictment was a huge victory for activists and workers. Response was relatively muted, perhaps because people were yet to recover from the attacks on the Holey Bakery in Dhaka the week before. Amidst news of the horror, newspapers reported that several foreign brands had reassured the Bangladeshi government that despite the attack, they had no plans to relocate operations elsewhere. These reports are just another reminder of the webs of globality in which the garment industry is immersed "locally."

This exceptional and comprehensive book opens up discussions on what can or must be done, even as it complicates reductive narratives and refuses easy politics. Setting the agenda for research and advocacy, it underlines the necessity of collaboration between labor activists and scholars/anthropologists. It points to the possibilities for collective rather than individual agency and resistance. The chapters do not minimize the difficulties or complexities ahead, but offer a politics of hope, much needed in these times.

Notes

1. The United States has turned out to be an unexpected fieldwork site for me. This, I suggest, is one more effect of the transnational stakes of a problem framed as national, as specific to Bangladesh, and requiring national-level solutions that leave the global structure untouched (see Ashraf this volume). Between 2013 and 2015, I attended and spent time with a leading labor rights activist at a two-day workshop on the future of the garment industry at New York University's Stern School of Business, found myself translating for the current president of an all-women trade union at a Washington, D.C. event organized by the International Labor Rights Forum, interviewed another leading labor leader during a lunch break at a New York conference to which she had been flown in by the South Asia Solidarity Initiative (SASI), and listened to survivors of Rana Plaza promoting the Bangladesh Accord at a Students Against Sweatshops event at New York University.

2. Since this is an afterword, I will not discuss every chapter individually.

3. In April 2014, the Stern Center for Business and Human Rights at NYU issued a report titled, *Business as Usual Is Not an Option: Supply Chains and Sourcing after Rana Plaza*. The Stern report raised a firestorm primarily for minimizing Accord/Alliance differences. Among other things, a coalition of more than 100 U.S.-based academics signed an open letter to the authors of the Stern report demanding clarification (Siddiqi 2014). It is worth asking why a report produced by a U.S. business school should generate this kind of response. What are the circuits through which a report like this travels? What kind of power does this attention index? Inside Bangladesh, few people were aware of the Stern School initiative until it issued a follow-up report, which the Bangladesh Garment Manufacturers and Exporters Association (BGMEA) attacked publicly for the suggestion that subcontracting constituted a large part of the industry. As for the Accord and Alliance, they are generally collapsed into each other and come up only in relation to debates on national sovereignty.

Bibliography

Boltanski, Luc. 1999. *Distant Suffering: Morality, Media and Politics*. Cambridge: Cambridge University Press.

Cultural Correspondent. 2015. "Dance Drama Depicts Woes of Apparel Workers." *New Age*, January 28. Online: http://newagebd.net/89880/dance-drama-depicts-woes-of -apparel-workers/ Accessed: July 26, 2016.

The Daily Star. 2016. "Owner Among 41 Indicted in Rana Plaza Murder Case." *The Daily Star*, July 18. Online: http://www.thedailystar.net/country/rana-plaza-collapse -owner-among-41-indicted-murder-case-1255546 Accessed: July 26, 2016.

Fassin, Didier. 2011. *Humanitarian Reason: A Moral History of the Present.* Berkeley: University of California Press.

Ferguson, James. 1994. *The Anti-Politics Machine: "Development," Depoliticization and Bureaucratic Power in Lesotho.* Minneapolis: University of Minnesota Press.

Siddiqi, Dina M. 2009. "Do Bangladesh Sweatshop Workers Need Saving? Sisterhood in the Post-Sweatshop Era." *Feminist Review* 91(1): 154–74.

———. 2014. "Solidarity, Sexuality and Saving Muslim Women in Neoliberal Times." *Women's Studies Quarterly* 42(3–4): 292–306.

———. 2015. "Starving for Justice: Bangladeshi Garment Workers in a 'Post-Rana Plaza' World." *International Labor and Working Class History* 87: 165–73.

Ticktin, Miriam. 2014. "Transnational Humanitarianism." *Annual Review of Anthropology* 43: 273–89.

Wright, Melissa W. 2006. *Disposable Women and Other Myths of Global Capitalism.* New York: Routledge.

CONTRIBUTORS

Mark Anner is an Associate Professor of Labor and Employment Relations, and Political Science at Penn State University, where he also directs the Center for Global Workers' Rights. His publications include *Solidarity Transformed: Labor Responses to Globalization and Crisis in Latin America* (Cornell University Press, 2011) and "Corporate Social Responsibility and Freedom of Association Rights: The Precarious Quest for Legitimacy and Control in Global Supply Chains" (*Politics & Society*, 2012).

Hasan Ashraf is a PhD candidate in Anthropology at Heidelberg University, Germany whose dissertation explores the relationship between transnational industrialization and physical and mental health among Bangladeshi garment factory workers. He completed a writing fellowship at the University of Amsterdam in 2016, and is currently a member of the Anthropology faculty at Jahangirnagar University in Dhaka.

Jennifer Bair is an Associate Professor of Sociology at the University of Virginia. She is the co-editor of *Free Trade and Uneven Development: The North American Apparel Industry after NAFTA* (Temple University Press, 2002) and *Workers' Rights and Labor Compliance in Global Supply Chains: Is a Social Label the Answer?* (Routledge, 2013), and editor of *Frontiers of Commodity Chains Research* (Stanford University Press, 2009).

Jeremy Blasi is a labor attorney based in Los Angeles and a nonresident research fellow at Pennsylvania State University's Center for Global Workers' Rights. He previously served as director of investigations for the Worker Rights Consortium.

Geert De Neve is a Professor of Social Anthropology and South Asian Studies at the University of Sussex in Brighton, United Kingdom. He is author of

The Everyday Politics of Labour: Working Lives in India's Informal Economy (Social Science Press, 2005), and has published articles on labor practices and ethical governance in India's garment sector in *Economy and Society, Modern Asian Studies,* and *Ethnography,* among other publications. He is also a co-editor of *Hidden Hands in the Market: Ethnographies of Fair Trade, Ethical Consumption, and Corporate Social Responsibility* (Emerald, 2008).

Saydia Gulrukh is a researcher and blogger and also a member of Activist Anthropologist.

Ingrid Hagen-Keith graduated in 2015 with a Mechanical Engineering degree from Olin College of Engineering and currently works in design and development at a global apparel company.

Sandya Hewamanne is the author of *Stitching Identities in a Free Trade Zone: Gender and Politics in Sri Lanka* (University of Pennsylvania Press, 2008) and *Sri Lanka's Global Factory Workers: (Un)Disciplined Desires and Sexual Struggles in a Post Colonial Society* (Routledge, 2016). She teaches Anthropology at the University of Essex, United Kingdom.

Caitrin Lynch is a Professor of Anthropology at Olin College of Engineering. She is the author of two ethnographies about the meanings of factory work in social and economic context: *Retirement on the Line: Age, Work, and Value in an American Factory* (Cornell University Press, 2012) and *Juki Girls, Good Girls: Gender and Cultural Politics in Sri Lanka's Global Garment Industry* (Cornell University Press, 2007), and she is currently working on a book about U.S. textile manufacturing and the "Made in the USA" movement.

Alessandra Mezzadri is a Senior Lecturer in Development Studies at SOAS, University of London. She was co-investigator for the ESRC/DfID project, "Labour Standards and the Working Poor in China and India," and sole investigator for the British Academy project, "The Global Village? Homeworking in the Global Economy." Her research has been published in *Competition and Change, Oxford Development Studies, Progress in Development Studies, Third World Quarterly,* and *Global Labour Journal,* among other publications. She is author of *The Sweatshop Regime: Labouring Bodies, Exploitation and Garments Made in India* (Cambridge University Press, 2016).

Patrick Neveling is a Senior Teaching Fellow in Development Studies at the School of Oriental and African Studies (SOAS), London and Researcher in the Department for Cultural Anthropology, Utrecht University, The Netherlands. He has published widely on the global history and anthropology of capitalism with foci on export processing zones and special economic zones, neoliberalism, colonial and postcolonial transactional orders, the invention of tradition, tourism, and others. He is also a leading editor of www.focaalblog.com.

Florence Palpacuer is a Professor of Management Studies at the University of Montpellier, France. In addition to two co-authored monographs in French, she has published more than 20 international articles and book contributions on global value chains, financialization, employment and work conditions, and the rise of new resistance movements both in global value chains and in multinational corporations in France.

Rebecca Prentice is a Senior Lecturer in Anthropology at the University of Sussex in Brighton, United Kingdom. She is author of *Thiefing a Chance: Factory Work, Illicit Labor, and Neoliberal Subjectivities in Trinidad* (University Press of Colorado, 2015), winner of the Society for the Anthropology of Work (SAW) Book Prize, and has published articles on the politics of labor and health in the global garment industry in *Critique of Anthropology*, *Journal of the Royal Anthropological Institute*, and *Anthropology & Education Quarterly*.

Kanchana N. Ruwanpura is a Reader in Development Geography and a Director of the Centre for South Asian Studies at the University of Edinburgh, United Kingdom. Her research on labor conditions, ethical codes, and the Sri Lankan garment industry has been published widely, including in *Journal of Economic Geography, Ethnography, Geoforum, Progress in Development Studies,* and in other edited volumes.

Nazneen Shifa is a member of Activist Anthropologist. Currently she is an MPhil/PhD student at the Center for Women's Studies, Jawaharlal Nehru University, India.

Dina M. Siddiqi, an anthropologist by training, divides her time between the United States and Bangladesh, where she teaches in the Department of Economics and Social Sciences at BRAC University, Dhaka. Her research on the Bangladesh garment industry, Muslim women, transnational feminism, and human rights discourse has appeared in *Feminist Review, Women's Studies Quarterly*, and *Economic and Political Weekly*, among other publications. She is currently working on a book provisionally titled *Elusive Solidarities: "Muslim" Women and Transnational Feminism at Work.*

Mahmudul H. Sumon is an Associate Professor of Anthropology at Jahangirnagar University and a member of Activist Anthropologist. He holds a PhD in Anthropology from the University of Kent at Canterbury, United Kingdom.

INDEX

accidents, 14, 54, 132, 137, 154, 163, 176, 232

Accord on Fire and Building Safety in Bangladesh, 7, 20–21, 49–51, 78, 160–161, 193, 250–252, 254–257, 266–267, 270; and jobbers' agreements, 30, 52–53, 175–176, 278

accountability, 16, 30, 58, 61, 67, 155–158, 168, 279–280

accumulation, 88, 107, 177, 276

Activist Anthropologist, 15, 147, 277

Alliance for Bangladesh Worker Safety, 20–21, 48, 54, 161, 170, 250–252, 255–257, 267, 279

anti-sweatshop movement, 8, 9, 22, 51, 57–59, 66, 68–69, 111. *See also* Clean Clothes Campaign

Bangladesh Garment Manufacturers and Exporters Association (BGMEA), 45, 152, 157, 165, 170, 251, 269, 271

Bangladesh Labour Act, 46, 47, 263, 270, 271

bodies, 177, 184, 276; dead, 150, 163; depleted, 179, 221; and health, 3, 18, 185, 191, 204, 206, 211, 259; working, 13, 190, 207, 219, 222, 260

capitalism, 9, 62, 131, 177–78, 276, 277

citizenship, 61, 63, 79, 178, 185

Clean Clothes Campaign (CCC), 8–9, 44, 57–59, 80, 157, 158, 254; and corporations, 11, 64–68; and trade unions, 68–73, 76, 77. *See also* anti-sweatshop movement

clinics, 137–138, 185, 204, 208–10, 211, 213–18, 220–22

codes of conduct, 2, 6, 8, 10, 14, 57, 59–67, 74–76, 82, 95, 268; failures of, 17, 19, 43, 103–105, 236, 279

corporate self-regulation. *See* self-regulation

collective bargaining, 61, 64, 79, 98, 127; and jobbers' agreements, 6, 52; as a right, 22, 43, 46, 48; and unions, 39, 69, 71, 72, 76

compensation, 14–16, 147, 162–163, 170, 175, 185; regime of, 148, 155–160, 168–169, 280. *See also* injury

contractors, 30–34, 38–43, 52, 53, 181–183, 188–191

corporate social responsibility, 63, 73, 88, 100, 141, 158, 175, 226, 228–229, 236, 240

court, 15, 39, 74, 77, 78, 147, 152–154, 163, 170, 280

disposability, 19, 227–229, 276

ethical codes. *See* codes of conduct

Ethical Trading Initiative (ETI), 58, 63, 73, 82, 188–189, 190, 194

export processing zone (EPZ), 13–14, 19, 48, 123–124, 127, 133–134, 142. *See also* free trade zone

externalization of costs, 16–17, 177–79, 184, 186, 190–192

face masks, 212, 244, 259

fair trade, 64, 65, 67, 69, 88, 94, 97, 102–103, 111

freedom of association, 43, 46, 48, 62, 64, 69, 77, 98, 104, 246

free trade zone (FTZ), 134, 142, 227, 228–229, 230, 237–238, 240. *See also* export processing zone

garment buyers. *See* retailers

Garments without Guilt (GWG), 18, 97, 228, 247

global production networks (GPNs), 6, 12, 21, 57–64, 74, 76, 79–80

ACKNOWLEDGMENTS

We wish to thank the following individuals who have in big and small ways helped bring this edited volume to fruition: Hasan Ashraf, Jennifer Bair, Michael Blom, Trudy Cadman, Grace Carswell, Jamie Cross, Louis De Neve Aleksandar Dimitrovski, Sandya Hewamanne, Peter Luetchford, Caitrin Lynch, Hayley MacGregor, Matt McMullen, Karen McNamara, Alessandra Mezzadri, Doug Miller, Patrick Neveling, Filippo Osella, Florence Palpacuer, Damani Partridge, Marijn Peepercamp, Kanchana Ruwanpura, Nazneen Shifa, Christian Strümpell, Mahmudul Sumon, Maya Unnithan, and David Walters. We are grateful to the Wenner-Gren Foundation and the University of Sussex for their generous support for the development of this book project. We also thank the anonymous reviewers from the University of Pennsylvania Press whose feedback has been invaluable, as well as Dina Siddiqi for writing a generous Afterword.

www.ingramcontent.com/pod-product-compliance
Lightning Source LLC
Chambersburg PA
CBHW032344280326
41935CB00008B/449